Baedeker

Tokyo

Contents

The Principal Places of Tourist Interest at a Glance

Preface

This guide is one of the new generation of Baedeker guides.

Illustrated throughout in colour, they are designed to meet the needs of the modern traveller. They are quick and easy to consult, with the principal places of interest described in alphabetical order, and the information is presented in a format that is both attractive and easy to follow.

The subject of this guide is principally the Japanese capital city of Tokyo, but also includes excursions to important places of interest.

The guide is in three parts. The first part gives a general account of Tokyo, its population, language, religion, culture and art, theatre and music, state and economy, famous people and history. A selection of quotations provides a transition into the second part, in which the places and features of tourist interest are described. The third part contains a variety of practical information. Both the sights and the practical information are listed in alphabetical order.

The new Baedeker guides are noted for their concentration on essentials and their convenience of use. They contain numerous specially drawn plans and colour illustrations; and at the end of the book is a large map making it easy to locate the various places described in the "A to Z" section of the guide with the help of the co-ordinates given at the head of each entry.

How to use this book

Following the tradition established by Karl Baedeker in 1844, sights of particular interest, outstanding buildings, works of art, etc., as well as good hotels and restaurants are distinguished by either one ★ or two ★★ stars.

To make it easier to locate the various sights listed in the "A to Z" section of the Guide, their co-ordinates on the large city map are shown in red at the head of each entry.

Only a selection of hotels, restaurants and shops can be given: no reflection is implied, therefore, on establishments not included.

The symbol ⓘ on a town plan indicates the local tourist office from which further information can be obtained. The post-horn symbol indicates a post office.

In a time of rapid change it is difficult to ensure that all the information given is entirely accurate and up to date, and the possibility of error can never be completely eliminated. Although the publishers can accept no responsibility for inaccuracies and omissions, they are always grateful for corrections and suggestions for improvement.

Facts and Figures

Arms of the
Japanese capital

General

Tokyo is the capital city of the parliamentary democratic monarchy of
Japan (Nippon = "Land of the Rising Sun"), the Imperial Residence
with the Emperor's Palace, and the seat of Government and of Parliament. The city's latitude is 35°N, its longitude 140°E, and it is situated
on the central east coast of the island of Honshu, the largest of the four
main islands of which the country is comprised. The city area, which is
often shaken by earthquakes, lies on the rivers Sumida, Arakawa and
Tama; these flow into the Bay of Tokyo which opens into the Pacific
Ocean. Together with the two towns of Kawasaki and Yokohama to the
south, Tokyo forms the conurbation of Keihin.

Geographical
situation

Tokyo's climate is determined by its situation off the eastern coast of
the continent of Asia on the one hand and on the shores of the Pacific
Ocean on the other. The regular seasonal changes mean that the
region is dominated in winter by the cold air masses coming from the
north and west, and in summer by the maritime and tropical air masses
from the south (East Asian monsoon climate). Thus, the summers are
cooler and the winters warmer than might be expected at this latitude
(the same as Crete). During the winter and summer months weather
conditions are quite constant, whereas they fluctuate during spring
and autumn.

Climate

From late August to mid-September typhoons frequently occur in the
north-west Pacific, and their effects are also felt in Tokyo.

Japan in
East Asia

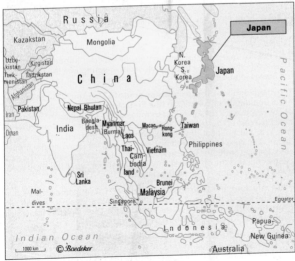

◀ Traditional and contemporary in Shinjuku

7

Japan

Nippon

Nihon

Seasons	Two events linked to the seasons are of especial importance to the Japanese – the cherry and plum blossom in spring and the colours of the leaves in autumn.
Area and population	The megalopolis of Tokyo covers an area of 577sq.km/223sq.miles and has a population of 8.4 million (the Prefecture, or metropolitan district of Tokyo, covers 2154sq.km/831sq.miles with 11.9 million inhabitants), making it one of the world's largest cities after Mexico City and Shanghai. It is the political, industrial, commercial and cultural centre of Japan. The core of the city comprises the area surrounding the Emperor's Palace; industry is largely concentrated on the coast. The city centre contains the office and shopping quarters, while the residential areas lie more and more on the periphery.
Administration	The Prefecture, the metropolitan district of Tokyo, comprises 23 districts (or ku), 26 towns, 7 urban districts and 8 villages. Two urban districts and 7 villages lie on the islands of Izu and Ogasawara, which come under Tokyo for administrative purposes.
City districts	The names of the districts are: Chiyoda, Bunkyo, Meguro, Taito, Adachi, Nerima, Ota, Itabashi, Chuo, Toshima, Sumida, Katushika, Nakano, Shinagawa, Kita, Koto, Edogawa, Suginami, Arakawa, Shibuya, Setagaya, Minato and Shinjuku.

Tokyo is governed by a city council with 126 members and a mayor or governor who is elected for four years.

City government

Population

As early as 1758 Tokyo was the largest city in the world with its population of 1.4 million. However, for centuries it was in no way a cosmopolitan metropolis, because Japan remained an island kingdom cut off from the rest of the world.

Structure

99% of the inhabitants are Japanese, the remainder being made up of small, chiefly Asian minorities. Of the 160,000 or so foreigners most are Koreans born here who are unable to obtain Japanese nationality. Foreigners (*gaijin*) are few and far between; most of them are businessmen or journalists who are only temporary residents.

The *Burakumin* (meaning "people of the hamlets") form a special stratum of society. They are the descendants of tanners, fishermen, dyers, henchmen and executioners who in many cases were involved in the killing of both animals and people and therefore are contemptible in the eyes of all Buddhists. Discrimination against this minority (at present numbering about 3 million) means that they are still treated as social outcasts, even though by law they have been placed on an equal footing with other Japanese for more than a century. They live in slum ghettos, mainly in the Asakusa area. It is said that many of the large Japanese companies still keep a register (red book) containing the names of Burakumin, and that discrimination has excluded them from pursuing professional careers and even prevented them from marrying into other classes of the establishment. In recent years those so affected have joined together to demand their rights.

Social strata

Panorama with the sacred mountain Fuji-san

9

People in Tokyo

Tokyo attracts Japanese from all parts of the country who are hoping to find better working and living conditions. As a result there are now only a few *Edokkos*, natives of Tokyo who have been resident in the city for more than three generations.

Living
conditions

As a result of the continuing influx of outsiders space in the city is at a premium. Almost a third of all dwellings have a floor area of less than 30sq.m/320sq.ft. Cramped living conditions mean that people tend to dissociate and distance themselves from each other. Because of the way the city has grown an inhabitant will never call himself a "Tokyoite" but is always known by the name of the area of the city in which he lives. Rents for apartments have risen astronomically in recent years.

Although since 1947 men and women have been regarded as equals in the eyes of the law, the traditionally rooted ideas of a women being linked to home and family still remain. In the main, women only go out to work after their children have grown up and even then, in the absence of a qualified education, they can take only very poorly paid jobs. While the wife devotes herself to household tasks the husband immerses himself in his profession, which can even intrude into his leisure time. True partnerships in marriage, now often the norm in Europe, are very much the exception in Japan.

Marriage and family

Language

Many regional dialects are spoken in Japan, but the language spoken in Tokyo has established itself as the standard language of social and commercial intercourse.

Japanese

The origins of the Japanese language are still not fully known. However, it has been established that – in spite of the similarity of the characters – it has nothing in common with Chinese. Most experts now link it with the Ural-Altaic family of Finno-Ugric, Turkic, Mongolian and other tongues. Other indications, however, especially in the articulation, suggest links with South Sea languages. Japanese is one of the agglutinative languages, in which simple words are combined without change of form to express compound ideas. Phonetically, the language is distinguished by a rich, basically bi-syllabic vocabulary. This aspect shows itself especially when transliterated into the Roman alphabet; accoustically it is less clear, because the melody of speech which results from individual syllables being stressed in the way they are in European languages, is apparent in Japanese only to a very small degree indeed. The Japanese language possesses a wide range of modes of expression. As well as local dialects there are levels of speech and forms of expression which depend on social status or sex and are also determined by the relationship between the speaker and the person being addressed and by the demands of courtesy and modesty.

The first Japanese script was derived c. A.D. 400 from the Chinese script, which has only ideograms for its mainly monosyllabic words and no abstract characters for sounds and syllables. Since, etymologically and grammatically speaking, Japanese has nothing in common with Chinese, the Chinese system of symbols could not be applied analogously to Japanese. Therefore the original ideograms – regardless of their meaning – were used to represent those syllables of the polysyllabic Japanese language which sounded the same as or similar to the Chinese. This often meant that several of the complex Chinese characters had to be employed to write a single Japanese word. As a result, increasing use was made of certain distinctive individual characters as independent syllabic symbols. Further simplifications were introduced so that by the 12th c. a syllabary system had developed which covered all Japanese phonetic sounds.

Script

This system is known as *hiragana* and is still in use today. Japanese script is now a mixture of some 50 phonetic characters and about 10,000 ideograms (*kanji*) (see below).

Hiragana

In addition to hiragana, a second syllabary system is used, which developed a little later: *katakana*. It was derived in a similar fashion from the Chinese. In contrast to the rounded forms used in hiragana, in katakana the strokes are more angular and employ different symbols. Therefore it is used as we might use italics, for emphasis or for foreign words and borrowings.

Katakana

Basically, *kanji* differs from the two syllabary forms of script. It involves symbols, the meanings of which correspond to the Chinese ideograms

Kanji

from which they are derived. They are used to write nouns, verbs and adjectives, but give no hint of the pronunciation of those words. As Chinese knows no inflexion, declension particles and information about sounds are added in hiragana.

When these ideograms were adopted they caused a problem which still plays an important part in modern Japanese. In the monosyllabic Chinese language there are a large number of words which sound exactly the same when spoken and so require differences of pitch and intonation to indicate their meaning; when written, however, they are clearly different and their meaning can readily be identified. Accoustically conveying meaning in this way is foreign to the Japanese, so in their language a large number of homophones have developed, the meaning of which can be seen only from the written character or the context. Moreover, words that sound different can have a similar meaning, so that a certain kanji symbol can be read in different ways (Chinese = on-reading, Japanese = kun-reading). For example, the symbol for "mountain" can be read as either *san* (on-reading) or as *yama* (kun-reading).

Triple writing system

Modern Japanese script is a mixture of kanji, hiragana and katakana, each used in the manner described above. A combination of kanji and hiragana (to convey meaning and intonation respectively) is standard practice; katakana is used for foreign words (Japanese has borrowed many words from English, German, French, Portuguese and Dutch) and for emphasis. Telegrams are written almost exclusively in katakana.

This complex system of writing requires a far greater number of individual symbols than does a phonetic language such as those used in the Western world. The school curriculum requires children to learn 881 kanji symbols; an averagely-educated adult will master some 2500, while about 4000 are employed in scientific and literary publications. In total, there are some 10,000 kanji.

The number of intonation and syllabary symbols is much smaller; the "fifty-sounds table" uses 46 symbols (in hiragana and katakana) and 25 standardised combinations.

Numbers are mostly written in Arabic script.

Direction of writing

Traditional writing runs in vertical files from right to left. In addition, there has existed for some time now a system of horizontal writing from left to right, based on the Western method. Both forms can be used together, and this can be seen in the daily newspapers, for example.

Transliteration

The phonetic structure of the Japanese language makes transliteration into the Roman alphabet somewhat difficult; this is normally done by means of the "fifty-sounds table". The latter is based on the Hebonshiki romaji system, named after the American missionary and philologist C. Hepburn and produced by a scientific committee in 1895. There is also the Kunreishiki romaji, recommended for official use in Japan.

Use of the language

See Practical Information section, Language for information on pronunciation and the use of foreign expressions in Japan. This section also includes a list of elementary expressions and phrases that can be used in emergencies.

Religion

Denominations

The two dominant religions are Shintoism, an animistic nature religion, and Buddhism, which has its own particular form in Japan. The two religions are syncretic; the curious result of this is that a survey revealed that 112 million Japanese claim to be Shintoists and 89 million Buddhist, although the total population is only 121 million. Furthermore, most weddings are Christian and burials Buddhist. Christians of various denominations account for barely one percent of the population.

Buddhist temples are distinguished by swastikas, an ancient symbol; unlike the "clockwise" swastika of the Nazis, the Japanese swastika, the *manji*, is formed anti-clockwise. Shinto shrines can be recognised by the gates (*torii*) which are usually made of baulks of timber.

Shintoism is a purely Japanese religion. Until 1945 it was the state religion. It is practised only in this country, and only Japanese can be Shintoists. Until the 6th c. it was the sole Japanese religion, and accordingly it did not initially have any particular name. It was only with the introduction of Buddhism that it became known as Shintoism, a name derived from the Chinese and meaning roughly "the divine way". Shintoism is an animistic religion, a nature religion the basis of which is the belief that nature is peopled by spirits and quasi-divine beings. According to early sources, there are 800,000 gods or quasi-divine beings.

Shintoism

Among these divinities – it is important not to give the term its western connations – are mountains (which means that Fuji is a sacred mountain to Shintoists) and trees, the sun and the moon, and animals such as snakes, foxes and cranes. These natural forces are *kami* (higher beings), benign and kindly. Ancestors also become kami. Thus it was that the Yasukuni Shrine in the heart of Tokyo received the souls of all the soldiers who fell in war, as well as those of war criminals.

Above all these kami stood (until 1945) the Emperor (*Tenno*), who was considered to be the direct descendant of the sun-goddess Amaterasu-Omikami. For this reason, too, the Shinto priests were subservient to the throne. In accord with its origins as a nature religion, the Shinto religion requires no fixed faith. It emerged without written rules and regulations, moral precepts or a fixed moral code. It is only in the last two centuries that it has gradually developed a broad system of ethics.

The most important kami are revered in shrines, most of which are surrounded by well-tended gardens, themselves another expression of the relationship between this religion and nature. The faithful may also revere their kami in their own home and celebrate them once a year with a great festival (*matsuri*); the latter can either stress mutual harmony or else help to re-create it. Because cleanliness is extremely important to Shintoism – even contact with the dead is avoided – the faithful wash their hands and symbolically purify their mouths before entering the sacred precinct of the shrine.

Even nowadays Shintoism plays a significant role in Japan, and the aid of the kami is regularly invoked at seed time and harvest, for example, when they are honoured throughout Japan in festivities and celebrations.

Buddhism, coming by way of Korea, reached the kingdom of Japan in A.D. 538. At the time it was violently opposed by the Shinto priests because the Japanese religion which accepted life in all its fullness could not tolerate Buddhism as a religion foreign to nature. It was, however, taken up by the upper classes, especially by Prince Shotoku (574–621), and soon became fashionable at court. Buddhism came to be highly regarded as the expression of a superior, spiritualised culture.

Buddhism

In the course of time Buddhist doctrine took on a Japanese tincture as sects formed, Shintoism interpreted the Buddhist divinities as *kamis*

Japanese Pantheon

Aizen Myoo	God of Passion	**Gongen**	Earthly manifestation of the Buddha
Amaterasu-omikani	Sun Goddess; mythological progenitrix of the Imperial House	**Hachiman**	God of War; kinship god of the Minamoto
Amida	Buddha of Light; ruler of the "Western Paradise"	**Hotei**	God of Good Fortune
Bato	Kannon (Kwannon) with the head of a horse	**Inari**	Rice Goddess
		Izanagi and Izanami	Age-old; creators of Japan
Benten, Benzaiten	Goddess of Love and Good Fortune	**Jizo-basatu**	Tutelary god of travellers, pregnant women and children
Binzuru	One of the 16 Buddha disciples; helper during illness	**Jurojin**	God of Good Fortune
Bishamon	One of the four Kings of Heaven; God of Wealth and Good Fortune	**Kannon (Kwannon)**	The Bodhisattva of Mercy and Compassion; mainly in female form
Bodhisattva	Bosatsu; one who has reached Enlightenment and can enter Nirvana, but remains on earth to aid others	**Kappa**	Water-nymphs
		Kompira	Mountain god revered by seamen and travellers
Bonten	Japanese name for god Brahma; temple guardian (dewa)	**Koshin**	God of the Ape Trinity
		Miroku-bosatsu	Bodhisattva, a future Buddha
Bosatsu	Bodhisattva; an Enlightened One before entry into Nirvana	**Ninigi-no-mikoto**	Descendant of Amaterasu-omikami; legendary founder of the kingdom
Buddha	"The Enlightened One"; honorary title given to Shakyamuni, the founder of Buddhism	**Nio**	Gods of Heaven; guardian figures (Indra and Brahma)
Butsu	Japanese name for the Buddha	**Nyorai**	"Enlightened One", title applied to the Buddha
Daibutsu	Great Buddha	**Oni**	Demons of the Underworld
Daikoku	God of Rice-growing and Wealth	**Rakan**	Disciples of the Buddha
Dainichi	Buddha of Light	**Sengen**	Goddess of Mount Fuji
Dainichi Nyorai	Buddha of Light; in fine art, usually a part of a trinity	**Shaka-nyorai**	The Buddha's earthly existence
		Shakyamuni	The Buddha
Dewa	The two gods guarding temples	**Shichi-fukushin**	Seven Gods of Good Fortune
		Shiki	Demon of Black Magic
Ebisu	God of Good Fortune; patron of workers and fishermen	**Shitenno**	Four Gods of Heaven
		Shoden	God of Wisdom
Emma-O	Ruler of the Underworld	**Susanoo**	God of the Moon, Sea and Storms
Fudo	God of Light		
Fugen	Buddhist assistant figure	**Taishakuten**	Guardian at temple gates
Fukurokuju	God of Good Fortune and Wisdom	**Tenjin**	God of Learning
		Ujigami	God of Kinship
Gakko-bosatsu	Moon Goddess	**Yakushi-nyorai**	The Healing Buddha; ruler of the "Eastern Paradise"
Gochi Nyorai	Five Buddhas of Wisdom and Contemplation		

and the Buddha statues as visible links in artistic form between man and *kami*. Moreover, as Shintoism concerns itself more with this world while Buddhism tends towards the transcendental, Buddhism was eventually accepted as complementary to Shintoism.

As early as the 12th c. the first Japanese form of Buddhism emerged with the development of Amida Buddhism. By the grace of Amida, one of the many incarnations of the Buddha, man could be confident of being born again after death and entering the "Land of Purity" *Jodo*.

This form of Buddhism met its keenest antagonist in the priest Nichiren (1222–82), the founder of a sect that took his name. He linked Buddhism with excessive patriotism, demanded the banning of all other sects and required missionary zeal from his disciples.

A third offshoot of Japanese Buddhism is the Zen doctrine. Its rigorous ordering of the practice of meditation and the fundamental disciplines of life in the sect was in harmony with the code of honour and life style of the Samurai, the Japanese warrior aristocracy. They used the severe meditation exercises as a means to self-discipline, in order to learn to disregard every selfish thought and to cease to fear death, which was the highest stage in self-disregard.   Zen

The central feature of Zen is *zazen* (meditation while seated). It is reputed to lead to *satori* (enlightenment), a sudden realisation by the faithful of the unity of all-being.

The disciples have to provide their masters with reports on what they have experienced during meditation. The masters often try to correct (if necessary by means of corporal punishment) the errors their disciples have made. They also test their disciples understanding by means of *koan*, an exchange of question and answer.

These Zen sayings, which have the character of aphorisms but incorporate challenging and paradoxical ideas, are intended, in accord with the nature of Zen Buddhism, to be the crystallisation of one basic notion. Some are famous in the West.

A similar poetry is also expressed in Zen art and architecture. In painting it is concentration on essentials, with just a few brush strokes, that comes across most clearly. Zen architecture is immediately recognised by its undecorated, simple forms. The famous tea ceremony, too, has its origins in Zen Buddhism.

Soka Gakkai is a sect which was founded in 1930 and revived in 1946. It, too, harks back to the priest Nichiren, and it is very nationalistically orientated.   Soka Gakkai

Soka Gakkai is based on the idea put forward by Nichiren that religious spirituality and political power must be deeply interpenetrated. Accordingly, the sect founded the *Komeito* (Party of Clean Politics) in 1964. It soon grew to become one of the strongest opposition parties in the two Houses of Parliament, but meantime it has severed its links, at least nominally, with the religious movement. It has some 10 million members; they are pledged to unconditional obedience and have to pay large financial contributions. Having become a member it is virtually impossible to leave the party, and control is exerted by means of physical threats by the strictly organised hierarchy of officials.

An estimated 7 million Japanese belong to the Soka Gakkai itself. The sect would like to make its form of Buddhism the state religion and preaches worldwide disarmament and the nationalisation of key industries, all in the pursuit of a new form of Japanese nationalism. The astonishing popular support enjoyed by Soka Gakkai is explained primarily by its identification with certain sectors of society. It organises cultural and educational evenings which provide that feeling of togetherness which is so important to the Japanese.

Christianity was brought to Japan in the 16th c., first by the Portuguese and Spanish, later by the Dutch. It struck a chord in the minds of the   Christianity oppressed peasantry, who saw in it much that corresponded with their own suffering. But as early as 1597 there was persecution of Christians, with over 30,000 losing their lives, some after frightful torture. In 1640 Japan was virtually banned to foreigners. It was 1859 before freedom of religion was promulgated, which probably explains why today barely one percent of the population are Christians. Christian influence on the social and intellectual life of Japan is, however, considerable, not least because of the founding of schools which Christians and non-Christians alike can attend.

Tokyo is the see of a Roman Catholic archbishop.

Culture

Tokyo is not just the scientific and cultural centre of Japan in a purely quantitative sense – it also sets the tone for the whole country.

The city is the seat of the Japanese Academy, the Japanese Council of Science and a great number of learned societies. There are more than 200 state, municipal and private universities, polytechnics, colleges and high schools. Among the libraries the National Library is outstanding. The National Theatre is the most important of the theatres, and the National Museum the most famous of the museums. This music-loving city has seven orchestras; the NHK (Radio Symphony Orchestra) and the Japan Philharmonic Orchestra have the widest international reputations. Support for traditional and modern art is, for the most part, in private hands; large stores, galleries and a number of institutions are particularly concerned with the fine arts.

Tokyo is the place where all the important newspapers are published, and NHk (Nippon Hoso Kyokai), a public radio station, and most commercial TV companies have their headquarters here.

School system

Japan's modern education systems were initially modelled on European patterns, but after the Second World War the US system tended to take over. All children must attend school for nine years – six years in a primary/elementary school followed by three in a secondary school. This can be followed, if desired, by three years in a high school, leading on to college or university.

Universities and colleges

If all the state, municipal and private universities and colleges are taken into account, the total amounts to over 200. Several of them, however, would not be considered of university standard in Europe.

In Japan future career prospects tend to be predetermined by attendance at the "right" university. Selection is on the basis of an examination system which begins at school and which, by European standards, seems to produce an inordinate amount of psychological stress. However, students who have passed the examinations in the university of their choice are usually

Tokyo University

assured of a post in the profession they elect to follow.

The most respected state university is Tokyo University. Many of its alumni enter the civil service.

Private universities are extremely expensive, and virtually no students from abroad attend them. Those most worthy of mention here are Keio and Waseda Universities. Included in the private universities is the United Nations University, founded in 1972. It is hoped that one day it will be a focal point of international research and teaching, but at present the enterprise is not progressing very satisfactorily because Japanese students prefer the established institutions, with the help of which they can expect to progress in their careers.

Colleges in Tokyo are well regarded. They include the Colleges of Fine Arts and Music and the Tokyo University of Arts and Seiha Onga-kuin in Shinjuku.

Tokyo being the educational centre of Japan, it is naturally here that are found the Japanese Academy, the Japanese Scientific Council and numerous other learned societies which do not, however, open their doors to foreigners. Contacts with other countries are nevertheless sought and nurtured, and accordingly there are a large number of foreign learned societies and institutes in Tokyo.

Among the Japanese institutes which have gained a world-wide reputation are Tokyo's Nuclear Research Institute and the University of Tokyo's Institute of Aviation and Space Travel.

Learned societies
and institutes

Art

Most Europeans, when talking of Japanese art, think of 17th and 18th c. objects and often regard them as simply a variation on Chinese art. While it is true that China's influence did play an important part, Indian culture also made a considerable contribution – an example of the far-reaching power of the Far Eastern religions which are so closely bound up with art, and which in Japan have been responsible for the evolvement of a number of unique artistic styles.

Art Epoques

The Ancient Period lasted until the Kingdom of Japan was founded in the first century A.D. Jomon pottery, made without a potter's wheel, and later Yayoi pottery, are evidence of the advanced level of craft skills possessed at that time. Because of its geographical isolation it was the third century B.C. before knowledge of how to make bronze reached Japan.

Ancient Period
(until the
3rd c. B.C.)

Increasing social differences become apparent. Giant, keyhole-shaped burial-mounds point to an increasing Korean influence, from where come new techniques (iron casting, weaving techniques, hard-baked ceramics, etc.).

Kofun Culture
(c. A.D. 300)

Buddhism co-exists with Shintoist worship of nature. Japanese masters take elements of Greek, Persian and Indian culture from China and develop them to a high degree. Temple architecture becomes independent in style and a large number of religious symbols appear. A new craft process is the technique of dry-lacquer painting on a wooden base.

Asuka Period
(552–645)

The Hakuho Period is also influenced by Chinese Buddhism. For the first time works of art are produced in remote parts of the country.

Hakuho Period
(end of 7th/early
8th c.)

Portrait painting develops. Gigaku masks, probably used for scenic purposes, show caricatured exaggeration of facial characteristics.

Nara Period
(710–794)

The culture and art of the early Heian Period are characterised mainly by two new expanding sects of esoteric Buddhism, namely, *Tendai* and *Shingon*. Religious mystification is followed by new forms of the fine arts which break away from the realism of previous epochs and push towards a form of artistic creativity against a background of symbolic symbols. The transfer of the imperial court to the newly-built capital

Heian Period
(794–1184)

city of Heiankyo (Kyoto) and the breach with China at the end of the 9th c. lead to a period of national awareness which brings to the fore artistic skills which are specifically Japanese, followed by a period of cultural ascendancy. At the imperial court important literary works are produced in the newly introduced *kana* script. Sculpture using rich gold leaf and detailed forms of painting find their counterpart in *yamato-e*, a native style of secular painting quite different from that practised in China and highlighted in the *emaki*, narrative scroll paintings of a religious and, above all, historical nature.

Kamakura Period (1192–1333)

The Kamakura period, a prominent political feature of which is the strengthening of the army in the provinces, shows in its simple but powerful form of expression a leaning towards the art of the Nara Period and takes sculpture to heights never again attained. The gradual resumption of relations with China is followed by the arrival of Zen Buddhism in Japan, which is largely sympathetic to the spirit of the Kamakura Period. It refuses all outside help in finding salvation and preaches deliverance by looking inwards into the soul. In art, this change leads to a drastic restriction on forms of expression, which on the one hand results in a degree of stagnation but on the other hand brings calligraphy and water-colour painting to a high standard of perfection. Applied arts and crafts become highly developed. Damascene work of extremely high quality is produced; the tradition of lacquer-work and textile art is continued.

Muromachi Period (14th to mid-16th c.)

In the Muromachi Period the rediscovered court elegance of the Heian Period merges with the influences of Zen Buddhism. Zen has less effect on forms of expression and ousts the colour-loving *yamato-e* in favour of monochrome ink-sketches in lime and wash, in which simple lines and faint suggestions are preferred to detailed portrayal. The objective is now not to paint the actual subject matter but rather its quintessence as it appears spontaneously to the artist.

The Late Muromachi Period ushers in a reaction to Zen-dominated forms of art, and detailed decoration is back in vogue.

Momoyama Period (1573–1603)

In the second half of the 16th c. peace is brought to the country by the Shoguns Nobunaga, Hideyoshi and Ieyasu, and the political revival is followed by a reorientation of culture, which during the Momoyama Period loses its courtly and sophisticated image and turns its attention to the ordinary people. Arts and crafts develop to an increasing degree; rooms are adorned with metal and lacquer-work and become a status symbol among the emerging bourgeoisie.

Namban art signals the arrival of Europeans in Japan.

Edo Period (1603–1868)

Bourgeois culture continues apace during the Edo period. Cut off from all contact with the outside world and constrained on all sides by strict social class divisions, the middle-classes turn to the enjoyment of art and an expensively-elegant life-style. All yardsticks of a religious, ideological or courtly nature lose importance; the impoverishment of the Samurai class reflects the breaking away from the medieval ethic. The versatility and varied natures of the artists stimulate the Japanese art world as much as the growing influences of China and Europe.

At the start of the 17th c. the *bunjinga* art form develops; scholars and calligraphers produce literary illustrations in great numbers, reflecting a genius which has no links with any artistic traditions. Wood-carvers, too, formerly restricted to producing woodcuts for book illustrations, expand their repertoire and the *ukiyo-e* is developed and quickly widens in scope and – following the introduction of colour printing with the use of multiple printing plates (from 1765) – evolves into *nishiki-e*.

In ceramics, glazed ware painted with vitrifiable pigments come to the fore. The discovery of kaolin deposits *c.* 1600 leads to a rapid growth in the production of porcelain.

The Meiji Period represents Japan's first great step forward in modern times. The rapid growth in relations with the West is also reflected in art. Painting separates into two trends – *nipponga* represents traditional japanese painting, while *yoga* artists use Western techniques and means of expression (e.g Impressionism), especially in oil-painting.

Modern Era
(post-1868)

Architecture

The main basic elements of Japanese architecture are simplicity, functionality and harmony with nature. This results in building proportions being geared to their intended function, something which is not found in the West until the end of the last century.

Apart from ultra-modern city architecture, one-storey buildings predominate, often with a clear division into individual living areas. Room sizes can be varied by means of removable and sliding walls, and the open form of construction produces a degree of compatability between the exterior and the interior that is inconceivable in large-scale building techniques. As the country is blessed with large expanses of forest, the favourite building material has always been timber, the structure of which has an important influence on the overall aesthetic impression. Practical considerations also weigh heavily in favour of the use of wood, because in a country subject to earthquakes the elasticity of a wooden building can present a considerably higher safety factor than a rigid stone building.

Methods of
construction

As in the fine arts, a Chinese influence is clearly seen in Japanese architecture too, starting with forms introduced in the 7th and 8th c. and followed by new impulses in the 13th c. These were later fully assimilated and led subsequently to the development of original and individual forms of construction.

Influences

Traditional Crafts

Japanese porcelain (*yaki, toki*), as found today in numerous small workshops which open their doors to visitors and in antique shops, can in the main trace its origins back to the work of Korean specialists who settled in Japan following the Korean campaigns (1592–98) of Toyotomi Hideyoshi.

Ceramics

   The characteristic features of this porcelain are its unobtrusive beauty and unpretentious simplicity, together with the absence of any artificial effects. The variations and irregularities resulting from the free use of colour and form create works of art which are restful to the eye down to the last detail and at the same time can be appreciated by the art collector, lover of porcelain and souvenir-hunter alike.

   Many of the kilns built over the centuries, using different firing techniques, each producing its own favourite shapes and characteristic colourings, are still in use today, thus continuing centuries-old traditions. A number are open to visitors and provide an insight into their production processes, put on exhibitions and have potteries where hobbyists can try out their skills.

The art of working in metal has over two thousand years of tradition behind it and many fine and unique works of art have been produced over the centuries. Bronze is cast, hammered, worked, chiselled, inlaid with gold and silver, punched or pierced. Iron is formed into everyday objects by means of the wax-melting process (*rogata*), gold and silver into consumer objects, jewellery and decorative items of all kinds.

Metallic art

   As in other cultures, the making and decorating of swords and other weapons enjoyed considerable importance in Japan. They were manufactured by the damascene process, in which several layers of metal are welded one on top of the other, folded or overlapped, and hammered. Together with a number of historical museums, the Sword Museum in Tokyo has the best collection of its kind.

The opening up of Japan to foreigners after the Meiji Period (post-1867) brought industrial metalworking into the country; this sounded the death-knell for the art of metalworking in a traditional sense. The government has made certain arrangements aimed at preserving some of this traditional knowledge for future generations. The most outstanding among those masters of traditional metalworking who are still alive are given the honorary title of "bearer of important and sacrosanct cultural works of art", and work and teach in colleges and art studios.

Textile art

In very early times a large number of advanced weaving techniques could be found in Japan, all of which had come from China and Korea. As well as silk, weaving was done using hemp, a form of untreated cotton, and raffia. Later developments led to the use of twill, damask, simple brocades and gauze, followed later still – after the 13th c. – by silver and gold brocade and satin. Treated cotton was not used until the 15th c.

In addition to weaving, dyeing has always been of great importance. As the cut of traditional costume varied little for centuries, developments in fashion and style were restricted largely to colour and decoration. As early as the 8th c. the three basic dyeing processes which are still used today were known and advanced. These are batik, the dyeing of folded materials with the help of stencils, and tie-dyeing, by means of which beautifully pleasing patterns can be produced by allowing the dye only to penetrate in places. Since the 13th c. superb effects have been achieved by means of a combination of various dyeing techniques and by embroidering with gold and silver threads or applying gold-leaf.

Since the introduction of industrial weaving and textile-printing processes the old techniques still have their place in the sphere of arts and crafts and in addition are used in making expensive materials for the coveted silk kimonos which ladies even today enjoy wearing on festive occasions.

The art of tattooing

For many Japanese a male torso is not handsome until it has been tattooed; tattooing is also evidence of belonging to a certain group in society. The parts of the body most frequently tattooed are the back, upper arms, chest, thighs and buttocks. In contrast to the individual designs which are popular in other countries (anchors, lighthouses, girls, butterflies, etc.), in Japan an overall composition covering the largest possible area is preferred. This preference can be traced back to the works of famous woodcarvers and painters of the 18th and 19th c. (scenes from well-known heroic epics); tattoos can also be influenced by water-colour paintings and the decorative ornamentation on *kimonos* or on the backs of the sleeveless jackets worn by the Samurai warriors (dragons, demons, etc.). In the traditional tattooing technique the artist uses needles dipped in dye and fixed either singly or in groups on the end of a pencil-sized stick and pressed into the skin; modern equipment makes this painful and highly stressful procedure more bearable. As the person, both male and female, seeking to undergo this torture can usually not stand more than one to two hours at a time, a large and expensive tattooed picture can take months to complete. Classical base colours include black (which appears blue under the skin), vermilion and brown; more recently, yellow, orange and green have been added.

Lacquer-work

In its simplest form lacquer-work, which originated on the mainland of Asia, spread to Japan back in prehistoric times. The sap of the sumach tree (*rhus verniciflua*), which when dried is resistant to acids, heat and moisture, was used to protect ordinary utensils and it was soon realised that, by adding natural colour pigments, a form of simple decoration could be achieved.

Japanese lacquer-work is carried out by means of three different processing methods, each itself subject to variation – these are known as the flat process, inlaid lacquering and carved lacquering. The *makie* gold-lacquering techniques (*maki* = straw-picture), which form part of the "flat" method of working, are the major processes which have been developed solely in Japan; this particular skill had reached a highly advanced and artistic stage as early as the Heian Period (8th–12th c.) Lacquer-painting, also a "flat" process, was widely used in the 7th c. in particular, but became less so in the 8th c. *Negoro-nuri* is a flat process in which a red top layer is applied and then removed as necessary to reveal a black pattern underneath. It has been used since the Muroma Period and is still popular today.

In the Nara period (8th c.) inlaid lacquering is known to have been used for the first time. In Japan it is often combined with *makie* tchniques. Mother-of-pearl inlay was initially preferred, followed later by gold and silver-leaf, coral, ivory and various semi-precious stones.

Carved lacquer-work (*tshuishu*) was first produced from the 15th c. in imitation of Chinese items, from which it was hard to differentiate. It was the 17th c. before a uniquely-Japanese style of carved lacquering was developed. As well as the very expensive genuine carved lacquer-work, in which the decoration is carved from a thick layer of lacquer, it was not long before the simpler *kamakura-bori* method evolved, in which carved wood is coated with lacquer.

All lacquer-work obtains its shine by having the top surface polished – a painstaking and time-consuming process. Because of the tedious and very careful work involved lacquer-work has always been expensive and has often been prized even more than porcelain.

Today the art of lacquering is practised in the old production centres of Tokyo, Kyoto and Kanazawa; other traditional workshops can be found in Takamatsu and Nagoya. Simpler goods for domestic use are made mainly in the districts of Fukishima, Ishikawa, Toyama and Wakayama.

Netsuke ("ne" = root-wood and "tsuke" = a peg or hanger) first appeared in the 15th c. and became extremely popular from the 17th c. They are artistically carved button-like ornaments in the shape of human figures, animals, plants and various inanimate objects, used to fasten toolbags and other bags in which people carried all kinds of everyday objects about with them, such as writing materials, money, medicines or tobacco. The knobs have one or two holes drilled in them through which were passed the strings of the bag and thus, with the knobs securely tucked under the belt (*obi*), prevented the bag being lost or stolen. The shape of a good *netsuke* had to meet this requirement while also being the right shape to grip comfortably, without any points or sharp edges. Originally these little sculptures were carved from tree-roots, but later increasing use was made of ivory, horn, bamboo, nutshells, lacquer, porcelain, semi-precious stones and metal. There was a completely free choice of designs, so these covered practically all aspects of life, myth, religion, legend and poetry or were the fruit of the artist's own imagination.

Netsuke (knobs)

Paper and its various manufacturing techniques probably first came to Japan from China by way of Korea in the 7th c. A.D. It was produced in many forms and was used for all sorts of different purposes, ranging from delicate paper dolls to brightly-coloured boxes, printed wallets, paper dividing-walls and sliding doors, artistic calligraphy and origami, the art of paper-folding. Originally reserved only for court circles,

Paper

it has also been widely used by the middle-classes since the Edo period (from the mid-17th c.).

Japanese paper is a firm, long-fibred paper made from the inner bark of the paper mulberry tree (*broussonetia papyrifera*). Rice-paper, a very delicate yet surprisingly strong and durable material, is made from the white pith of the rice-paper plant (*tetrapanax papyrifera*). The fine mitsumata paper comes from the bark of the thymelæaceæ (*edgeworthia chrysantha*).

The Paper Museum in Tokyo is well worth a visit and shows not only the various types of paper and printing but also the tools and equipment used to make them.

Packaging
(tsutsumi)

Another form of Japanese craft that must be mentioned is the richly traditional art of harmonious packaging (*tsutsumi*). The idea is based on the assumption that "pure" things should always be suitably wrapped before being passed to the recipient. Originally it was just foodstuffs that were packaged before being transported or stored. This purely practical aspect soon led to an aesthetic desire to make everything as beautiful as possible, and in the course of time this developed into a complete art form which continues today especially in the form of "gift-wrapping". Natural materials such as rice-straw, bamboo and cedar-wood have been popularly used as wrapping materials for centuries.

The art of
gardening

Japanese gardens, with their peaceful atmosphere, harmony and – even though most of them are very small – complexity, exercise a special charm on all who see them. In contrast to Western parks and gardens, the hand of the gardener lies concealed; the garden's perfection and completeness lie more in its apparent spontaneity, in its originality, in the way it reflects a oneness with nature. The garden architecture adds to the artistic nature of the garden by its symbolic nature and the highly aesthetic elements which combine to produce a work of art demanding the observer's attention. Gardens have also always been very closely linked with religion.

The earliest Japanese landscape gardens were modelled on the Chinese. In China the first gardens were thought to have been constructed in the Han Period as imitations of the legendary "Islands of the Immortal". Later, under the influence of Buddhism, they symbolised the "Western Paradise" of Amida. The spread of Taoist ideals led to a deepening quest for unspoilt natural forms; as Taoist scholars often sought refuge in mountain hermitages people liked to construct their gardens with a mountain backcloth or built artificial rock-gardens.

Zen Buddhism, which exercised a strong influence on life in general during the Kamakura Period (12th–14th c.), soon affected garden layouts, and courtly elegance found itself replaced by severity and simplicity. Whereas until then gardens had been places in which to stroll, play and study, they now became purely symbolic, places to be observed from a veranda, not for walking in. Their formal layouts were based mainly on the monochrome landscape paintings of the Chinese Sung Period. The chief objective of the Zen gardener is to create an impression of infinite distance within a limited space.

While in landscape gardens reality and abstract forms mingle to an almost confusing degree, stone-gardens (*kare sansui*) aim at pure abstraction. There are dry gardens made of sand and stones, without any water or plants at all. Nevertheless, they cleverly contrive within the smallest of spaces to imitate expansive landscapes, with sand skilfully raked to imitate rivers or seas, with stones representing islands. In their barren simplicity they accurately reflect Zen teachings.

The classical simplicity of the stone-gardens is perpetuated in the tea-gardens (*roji*) of the Momoyama Period (16th c.), but these have contrived to dispense with the earlier severity of form and reflect nature in an unspoilt form, even though compressed into the smallest of spaces. The tea-houses in the roji express such naturalness in another way.

The Edo Period, commencing in the early 17th c., brought few new styles with it. On the one hand, the increased size of gardens meant they were more pleasant to walk in, but on the other hand it led to the gradual disappearance of this typically Japanese art form.

The art of flower-arranging is a form of aesthetic expression which is firmly rooted in Japanese cultural life. Originally introduced from China as floral decorations to be placed before statues of the Buddha, flower-arranging subsequently broke away from being used solely for religious purposes and developed into an art form in its own right.

Ikebana (Flower-arranging)

The shape of the arrangements, symbolising the trinity of Heaven, Mankind and Earth, was early evidence of the move towards naturalism, as shown in the natural way in which twigs and flowers were used. Today there are various schools which strive to safeguard old traditions while creating new ones.

Ikebana, an obligatory programme of training for young girls but still the domain of male teachers, is becoming increasingly popular abroad as well.

The art of bonsai, the "tree in the bowl", now well-known and prized throughout the world, is of Chinese origin but has been practised in Japan since the 11th c. Zen Budhism did much to promote it. Grown from seed or cuttings, suitable plants such as juniper (*juniperus*), fir (*pinus*), Japanese cedar (*cryptomeria japonica*), several species of maple (*acer*), and others have their shoots and roots trimmed, their branches trained by means of wire, are fed very small, carefully measured doses of plant food and are grown in very little, well-firmed soil; as a result, they become miniature trees only 20–60cm/8–24in. tall. Any cuts must be made so that they heal over completely and are invisible. Wires are removed after a year in order to prevent their cutting into the bark. Under the watchful eye of its grower the bonsai will become a work of art in a bowl, on a piece of bark or on a stone base, and in complete harmony with its surroundings. Over the years shapes have been developed to look like trees bent in the wind, gnarled and grown together, small groves or delicate miniature shrubs bearing flowers and fruit and changing with the seasons like the larger ones on which they are modelled.

Bonsai (Miniature trees)

Bonsai can be several hundreds of years old. They are grown by almost all Japanese families and are passed on to their heirs. The main centres of cultivation include Omiya (near Tokyo), Kurume, Nagoya and Takamatsu (Kinashi). Bonsai are treated like antiques, in that not only the age but also the general appearance is reflected in the price.

Theatre

The traditional theatrical forms which are still alive today can trace their roots back to the ritual dances performed in prehistoric times and which were closely linked to man's life and his needs. Incantations seeking success while hunting, the paying of homage to the sun-god Amaterasu who gave light and life, the sacrifice and glorification of the stag (as the victim of the hunt or the emissary of the gods) and thanksgiving for rich harvests of fish all formed part of the content and unique character of many local dances performed by priests and shamans. Parts of these old traditional dances still exist in a number of folk-dances, in courtly dance and in the classical theatre.

Noh plays have their roots in *sangaku* ("music as a diversion"), from which *sarugaku* ("monkey music") was derived during the Heian Period. Little has changed during the 600 years it has been in existence,

Noh (or No) theatre

Traditional Noh Theatre

and it still enjoys considerable popularity today. This folksy form of traditional entertainment was a kind of farcical prank with artistic tricks and dances in which Buddhist or Shinto spirits were derided, often in burlesque or even obscene ways. *Dengaku* ("field music"), which had evolved from rural harvest festival dances, also made its influence felt. In the 13th c. these rather crude forms of popular entertainment became more serious in content and strictly dramatic in form, and were now performed by professional actors. The resultant spectacles were called *sarugaku-no-no* ("artistic sarugaku") or *dengaku-no-no*. Noh theatre was similar in function to the European "mystery plays" of the time, but in essence was closer to popular theatre.

Noh first became a profound and aristocratic art form under the Ashikaga shogun Yoshimizu, whose favourite Zeami gave it its final poetic form. With the continued support of Yoshimitsu and influenced by Zen aesthetics whom the shogun gathered around him, Zeami produced plays which have never been bettered. The present-day Noh theatre is run by five schools – Kanze (the largest), Komparu, Hosho, Kongo and Kita – the family traditions of which can be traced back to the 14th c. (except Kita, which was not founded until the 17th c.).

In imitation of the original open-air performances, the 5·4m/18ft square covered stage simply made in cypress wood is moved sidewards into the open auditorium. The backcloth is always a painting of pine-trees, in front of which are positioned the musicians (led by a flautist, together with three drummers) who accompany the recitations of the choir seated in two rows on the right of the stage. The footbridge leading from the left rear part of the stage and lined by three pine-trees forms the entrance for the main character (*Shite*), his companion (*TSure*) and the supporting character (*Waki*), all played by male actors. While the supporting cast, some wearing masks and some without, explain what is going on, the action is performed by Shite in his stylised mask, who moves to the front of the stage (*kagami-no-ma*) in his meditative roles as deity, spirit of a dead knight or even as a beautiful woman.

The introductory explanations provided by Waki are followed by the entrance of Shite, always elegantly and sumptuously dressed (even when his part demands something less); his performance technique with its symbolic movements is almost abstract and based on the fundamental ideas conceived by Zeami – blossom (*hana*), elegant beauty (*yugen*) and the attractions of the moment (*mezurashi*). The basic aesthetic principle is in no way violated by dramatic events nor is it supplanted by any kind of realism.

The classical programme, consisting of five Noh plays performed one after the other, is nowadays generally reduced to two, interspersed by clowned farces known as *kyogen* plays (see below). Five groups make up the thematic classification, namely, *kamimono* (also known as *waki-no*), happy stories about gods; *shura-mono* (also *otoko-mono*), tragic heroic epics; *katsura-mono* (also *on-na-mono*), stories of beautiful women; *kyoran-mono*, tales of the mentally confused; and finally *oni-mono*, stories about supernatural beings, the latter bringing a Noh programme to its close.

Kyogen plays are humorous interludes to Noh dramas. Using the vernacular of the 16th c., they parody society and its weaknesses, often touching on the tragicomical. Differences between it and Noh include a dialogue between two people or groups, the extremely rare use of masks and the very realistic method of presentation.

Kyogen

The middle-class *Kabuki* theatre ("ka" = song, "bu" = dance, "ki" = performing art) originated in the Edo Period (17th–19th c.). It combines several elements from different theatrical forms to produce a unique art form which reached its heyday in the more recent past. Consisting

Kabuki theatre

Kabuki-za Theatre in the Ginza

25

of drama, dancing and music and restricted to male actors, Kabuki is extremely dynamic and varied in its portrayals and as a result it appeals to a wider public than the classically formal Noh theatre.

Kabuki is a ribald, often burlesque form of theatre which is worth watching even if one does not understand a single word. The largest Kabuki theatre is the Kabukiza on the Ginza. Performances there are more like a huge family gathering. Many of the audience bring food with them, even though there are restaurants around the hall. Performances last for hours, but people stay only as long as they like; it is not considered impolite to arrive and leave at will.

The actors perform in front of magnificent scenery and in fine, expensive costumes and with an uninhibited intensity and passion that appears in surprising contrast to the normally calm and reserved Japanese temperament. The audience joins in enthusiastically, shouts and laughs, applauds its heroes and does not hesitate to heckle. In days gone by the Kabuki theatre took the place of newspapers and gossip columns for the man in the street. Scandals and murders were epically portrayed here, with the actors ad-libbing to such an extent that at times the story-line became completely lost.

The Kabuki theatre has nothing in common with the more educational form of theatre found in Europe.

Bunraku
puppet theatre

The Japanese *Bunraku* puppet plays hark back to Chinese traditions. They were in their heyday during the 17th and 18th c. and were more popular than the Kabuki. Bunraku was stronger than Noh in reflecting the times, which were bound by the strict moral code of Confucianism, and mirroring the conflict between human emotions and an intransigent state philosophy. The subjects covered concentrated on historical patterns and current events.

Bunraku puppets are very large marionettes (120cm/4ft), controlled by strings or by hand and moved by two or three players, usually dressed in black. It is advisable, if possible, to obtain a seat near the front in order to get a good view of the wonderfully made figures.

Music

Japanese
music

The traditional music of Japan is devoid of any European influences and is completely different from contrapuntal Western music with its set written notation. Therefore it is almost impossible to pick it up spontaneously; the completely different quality of the melody and the strangeness of the sound pattern together with what appears to be a monotonous use of few instruments all combine to present considerable barriers to the European's ability to appreciate the music. The scales either possess no semitones or else they are positioned at unusual places on the scale. Some compositions ignore measured pitch or disguise intervals, others acknowledge only one or two set intervals (core sounds) in a sound spectrum filled by quarter-tonal and microtonal glides and embellishments. As a rule, notes are not "hit" but are "sung to". All this sounds "wrong" to Western ears, even though it follows equally strict and logical rules. The sparse use of resources is peculiar to all Japanese branches of art; as a result, the music is lacking in loud notes and overall volume. Variations in the tonal characteristics of similar instruments are subtle and can be fully appreciated only by connoisseurs. Once an instrument has been made or played differently it constitutes a new genre. Within narrow limits a large range of musical elements, rich in nuances, can be distinguished. The lack of harmony and counterpoint necessitates a completely new approach, both musically and aesthetically; pauses are "silent notes", dissonances have the quality of tone colours. Thus, the abundance of melodic and rhythmic patterns is greater than in Western music and is fully exploited by virtuosos.

Since the Meiji government, for political reasons, introduced Western music into schools and barracks about 1880, generations of Japanese musicologists and teachers have made European classical music so much the norm in Japan that the time of mere imitation is long past. The Japanese are very fond of such European composers as Beethoven and Mozart, and concert audiences are very well-informed and enthusiastic. Tokyo boasts no fewer than seven symphony orchestras of international standing – the NHK Symphony Orchestra, the Japan Philharmonic Orchestra, the Tokyo Symphony Orchestra, the Shin Nihon Philharmony Yomiuri Symphony Orchestra, the Nihon Philharmony, the City Symphony Orchestra and the Tokyo Philharmony. There are also many choral societies and two opera companies, though they perform only rarely. There is virtually no state support for musical groups in Japan. Some are under the auspices of firms, but manage to exist solely as a result of making public appearances.

European music

Customs

Regarded superficially, the tea ceremony (*chanoyu*) is simply the traditionally handed-down method of preparing and serving the crushed green tea (*matcha*). However, something which is thus often viewed rather narrowly as just a part of the education of marriageable young Japanese girls is in fact deeply rooted in aesthetics and in the religious feelings of the Japanese. In order to begin to understand the way the tea ceremony is performed and its deeper significance it is necessary to study the country's cultural history and religious background.

Tea ceremony

Against a background of numerous formalities, beginning with the modest clothes worn by those taking part, followed by the tea-bowls and other items required for use in the ceremony, and not forgetting

Japanese Tea Ceremony

the meticulous and detailed movements made by the hostess and the restricted nature of the conversation permitted during the ceremony lasting many hours, the real aim of the meeting and purification of the participants in this social gathering goes far beyond the bounds of time and place in an atmosphere of modesty, simplicity and peace wherein all the interrelated formalities and actions finally come together completely down to the very last detail.

It is not great flights of fancy which lead to the attainment of the all-embracing awareness which is so keenly sought; true communion with nature and even the universe itself can be reached only through meditative concentration on topics which may appear trivial to the European mind. This shows the tea ceremony to be an art form strongly influenced by Zen Buddhism and orientated to the Buddhist understanding of peace, harmony and simplicity, defined in Japanese by the word *wabi* (aestheticism).

Important criteria of the tea ceremony include the maintanance of inner and outer purity (*sei*), respect for all life (*kei*), harmony (*wa*; contained in the word *wabi*) and peace (*jaku*). These requirements are laid down in strict rules which, depending on the particular school, may differ in detail but are quintessentially similar.

In the ceremony, a silent group of people form a circle. The tea is ground to a fine powder and frothed up with a hand brush. Each gesture plays an important part – the manner in which the water is poured, the tea stirred, the bowl held, studied and finally raised to the mouth.

In many temples visitors can watch the ritual and (for a small fee) take part. As with ikebana (flower-arranging), there are various schools where the tea ceremony is taught by recognised masters of the art. In the main, this skill is reserved for women.

Geisha

Some consider the Japanese geisha girl to be a high-class prostitute, others think of her as an artistic solo hostess and entertainer who plays string instruments, sings and provides witty conversation. The truth lies somewhere in between.

Translated, geisha means "person of the arts". She is an artist who is educated for years in the skills of playing a musical instrument, dancing and providing sophisticated conversation. The best-known of the 60,000 or so geishas in Japan are as famous as film-stars and earn as much as the general manager of a company.

Geishas can be recognised by their expensive kimonos, their elaborate hair-styles and heavily made-up white faces, together with their uniquely delicate and mincing walk.

Their task is to create a pleasant, relaxed atmosphere in the rather distant, male-orientated Japanese society (including business dinners and the like) where the women tend to stay at home.

Geishas are trained for their profession mainly in "geisha-houses". Initially they are *minarai* or *oshaku*, wine-waitresses who also pass food, sing and dance but are not yet allowed to share in the conversation.

After their period of training they work either for an agency or on a self-employed basis. Geisha parties are expensive and exclusive but nevertheless continue to play an increasingly important part in the Japanese life-style.

Kimono

Modern Japanese ladies still welcome the opportunity to wear the kimono at weddings and other social occasions, even though it is a rather irksome piece of apparel. To dress in a kimono is not something that can be done on one's own, and is in fact an art which has to be learned on special courses. Because many Japanese couples prefer to hold their wedding receptions in Western hotels many varieties of the kimono can often be seen there at week-ends; they will always be very expensive ones, costing up to the equivalent of some £10,000/US$ 15,000. Anybody who would like to own even a pale reflection of this beautiful garment, however, can buy in the large kimono departments of departmental stores a *yukata* (a simple cotton kimono for the house), which would make a good bath-robe at home and should cost between £40 and £160/US$60 and $240.

Traditional Sports

Japan's traditional sports (with the exception of sumo) are collectively known as *budo* ("knight's way"). All the competitive sports involved are based on the Zen philosophy which strives for complete harmony between body and mind; as far as the participants are concerned, this philosophy is equally as important as the actual sporting aspect.

Akido, a form of self-defence known since the 12th c., was given its present form by Ueshiba Morihei (1883–1970). Weapons are used only if the opponent is also armed; the outcome is decided not by physical strength but by complete bodily control.

Akido

Judo, which has always been popular in the West as well, is a development of ju-jitsu, which was fostered by the Samurai. The object of the sport is to use the the opponent's strength to one's own advantage; only holds and throws are allowed. The grade a *judoka* has attained is shown by the colour of his belt. In international sport there are seven weight divisions.

Judo

Kendo developed from the art of fencing

29

Sumo wrestling is the most popular sport in Japan

Karate

Karate has become known in the West through such spectacular performances as smashing bricks with the side of the hand and so on, the
sporting value of which is, however, open to debate.

The "open hand" fighting technique includes kicks and blows using
all four limbs. There is little doubt that karate originated in China.

Kendo

Kendo developed from the earlier art of sword-fighting; bamboo
staves are used nowadays. The contestants wear protection for the
head and face together with a breast-plate made of leather and
bamboo.

Kendo forms part of police training, which the public are allowed to
watch.

Kyudo

Kyudo, the ancient art of archery, is still very popular. An asymmetrical
bow about 2·25m/7½ft long is used. The purely sporting side is almost
completely overshadowed by the meditative aspect, and schools and
practice-halls often adjoin temples. Over the centuries several different
forms of teaching have evolved.

Sumo

Sumo ranks as Japan's national sport. This form of wrestling is performed by men weighing between 113 and 159kg/250 and 350lb. The
object is to force the opponent out of the circle or to oblige him to make
contact with the floor with a part of his body other than his feet. The
contest, which often lasts only a few seconds, is preceded by a cleansing ritual when salt is scattered in the circle to scare away evil spirits.

Government and the State

Democracy

Japanese democracy is, as Mr Nakasone, a member of the government, once cried out in parliament, an artificial flower, a cut blossom.

By this he implied that it was something that had been forced on Japan by the American Army of Occupation. Resistance to democracy and democratic ideas is still met everywhere. Political parties only came into existence during the present century as a result of an Imperial edict. As for trade unions, they remain astonishingly firm in their support of the State and business firms, something which goes a long way towards explaining the success of modern Japan in the fields of industry and commerce.

The Constitution was promulgated on November 3rd 1946 and came into force on May 3rd 1947. Under its provisions the Emperor is Head of State. The Legislature is divided into an Upper House (Senate) and a Lower House (House of Representatives). There is universal suffrage for men and women on reaching the age of 21.

Constitution

Japan is a parliamentary monarchy. The throne passes to the eldest son, in accordance with the principles of primogeniture. The title *Tenno* is an allusion to the Emperor's "divine" descent. Nowadays, however, the Emperor, formerly revered as a divine being, is simply a symbol of the state and the unity of its people. Under pressure from the Americans he was persuaded to renounce his personal divinity in the course of his New Year's message in 1946. Since then he has ceased to have any political role. Akihito has been the Emperor of Japan since 1989.

Head of State

Since the end of the 1970s there have been a number of attempts to restore the Emperor's "rights". For instance, the Imperial calendar computations have been reintroduced, as has the singing of the Imperial hymn at morning assembly in the schools. Basically, however, most Japanese have come to terms with democracy, and the parties to the left of the political spectrum in particular – the Socialists and the Communists – defend the principle and the Constitution whenever the opportunity arises.

The Senate has 252 members. They are elected for a six-year term, half of them coming up for re-election every three years. 100 of the Senators are elected through nation-wide lists, while the remaining 152 are elected on lists prefecture by prefecture.

Senate
(Sangi-in)

The Lower House (or House of Representatives) has 512 members. They are elected for a term of four years by 123 constituencies and by the island of Okinawa. Between two and five members are returned by each constituency, depending on its size and population.

Lower House
(Shugi-in)

Executive power resides in the Cabinet. It comprises the Prime Minister and other ministers, all of whom must be Japanese citizens, and is answerable to Parliament.

Cabinet

The Prime Minister and half the members of his Cabinet must be members of parliament. He has the right to form his Cabinet as he considers best. However, after a vote of no confidence in Parliament the Cabinet must resign or else the House of Representatives must be dissolved within ten days.

In 1945 the Americans set in train a liberalisation of Japanese political life, with reforms ranging from the founding of trade unions to the granting of equal rights to the sexes. Progress has, however, been only hesitant in these spheres. Naturally, the changes could not occur overnight in the absence of any corresponding historical precedent of any kind. There is a deep-seated, it might be said, undemocratic dread of changes in government. The Liberal Democratic Party which has been in power for three decades has profited from this. Besides, what exactly is meant by a "political party" in Japan? During the feudal period the distribution of power was clearly laid down; it was clear who was at the top and who at the bottom, and everybody knew his exact place in the pecking order.

Parties

Democracy has produced a sense of equality with which Japanese politicians scarcely know how to cope. There is no party in Japan which allows its policies to be determined by a process of consultation between top and bottom and thus become independent of the opinions of individual members of parliament. When it is politically expedient to do so, the number of members of the LDP may well increase from one million to three, only to fall away again just as rapidly. The LDP, like the other parties, is more or less a coalition of various interest groups which come together, to the disgust of many voters, and form a block, conveniently forgetting the mandate given by the electorate. Because no device is neglected in this never-ending power struggle, corruption sometimes rears its ugly head, as it does in many Asian countries. In 1973 Prime Minister Tanaka had to resign after the discovery of his involvement in a gigantic arms scandal with Lockheed. His successors, too, have – if in rather different circumstances – come under suspicion of bribery.

Parliamentary life

Japanese parliamentary life presents a different picture from that found in Western democracies. There are no great debates here, no decisive votes. Because each party is first obliged to go through the long and wearisome process of reconciling all its own various interest groups, most political differences are in fact settled in secret. Even though such matters may subsequently be voted on by the individual parties in Parliament, everything will in fact have been sorted out beforehand. The sole exception are the Communists. As early as 1965 they began to follow the pattern set by the Euro-Communists and are quite prepared to raise radical issues in the House. This is, however, widely regarded as gross and un-Japanese, and the media generally condemn this "extravagant" behaviour.

A politician who goes to extremes or even commits serious blunders need not be afraid of losing his seat on that account. The principles of loyalty and faithfulness which have been inherited from the Samurai philosophy will work positively to his advantage. For instance, Matsuno, the Minister of Defence, was obliged to admit having pocketed 500 million Yen in an armament scandal. Nevertheless, he was re-elected, because the voters simply would not abandon a man to whom they had pledged their loyalty. A consequence is that the proportion of elderly members in the Japanese Parliament is far above the average; not to re-elect them would amount to committing the disgraceful sin of disloyalty.

The interplay of political and social forces

As this account reveals, the keystone of the system of government is its formality. The Cabinet, headed by the Prime Minister and with twenty other members, is responsible to Parliament, but open debate before the public eye remains something of a rarity. Gradually, however, and equally unnoticed, a compromise is also reached between the claims of various social groups. Japan is famous for the way opposing forces within a firm or authority come to a decision only after lengthy debate. As well as reflecting a taste for the democratic process, however, this is also because each person who, following due consideration of the matter, is not entirely convinced, is regarded as a potential source of disharmony who is best conciliated in advance. This is also the way the government treats industry, banks and businesses; they all get a hearing at Cabinet meetings, and similarly government representatives attend employers' association meetings.

In the final analysis all decisions are reached collectively, and that no doubt is the basis of Japan's strength in the world's markets. In Japan, meanwhile, fringe groups are generally kept in their place.

Economy

Tokyo is Japan's major consumer market, partly because of the size of its population and partly because of the high wages and salaries, which are well above the national average. Tokyo is also the most important commercial city in Japan, with the head offices of all the Japanese clearing banks and branches of American and European banks. Two-thirds of all Japanese firms have their headquarters in the city. The Stock Exchange makes it the unquestioned financial centre of the country.

Tokyo forms part of Keihin, Japan's major industrial region; other important centres are Kawasaki and Yokohama. The Keihin industrial region stretches from Sagami Bay in the south to Maebashi in the north.

It is here that the most important Japanese steel plants have been set up; shipbuilding and petro-chemical industries have also developed here, in some cases on specially reclaimed off-shore islands. A third of Japan's total industrial output is produced in this region.

Pipelines run to Tokyo from the natural gas fields of Nigata and Chiba. Manufacturing industries are represented by aircraft and auto-mobile construction, engineering works, ship-building, electronics, mechanical, pharmaceutical and cosmetic firms. Other important industries are textiles, leather, paper, food and luxury goods.

Among the most important business organisations in Tokyo are:
Keidanren, with 1085 firms, acting for the development of all organisations within the economy; it corresponds approximately to the C.B.I.
Nikkeiren, with 488 firms, supporting the development of employers' organisations.

The Stock Exchange in Tokyo

Nissho, combining 488 chambers of industry and commerce.
The total number of private enterprises in Tokyo is about 790,000.

Service industries

With Japan becoming more and more a country where visitors come from abroad as tourists and to attend congresses – and in this development Tokyo is at the forefront – the service industries are assuming ever greater importance. The hotel and catering trades are profiting from this upswing, together with those industries whose wares are sold as souvenirs and especially those whose products, such as cameras, T.V., video and audio systems, etc., are famous the world over.

Transport

Harbours

Tokyo harbour is part of a port complex extending along Tokyo Bay from Yokohama in the west to Chiba in the east. Freight handled amounts to more than 70 million tonnes annually, of which about 80% consists of imports. This makes it the seventh most important port in Japan. As for container traffic, Tokyo is at present fifth in the world.

The intensive building programme which characterised in particular the period after the Second World War is still continuing unabated. To provide sites for industrial plant which has economic links with the harbour's trade, the area around the harbour is constantly being extended by means of land reclamation schemes. The disadvantage is that quality of life is being eroded by these immense building schemes. That is why, as they plan to extend the port still further, the municipal authorities are considering plans for "marine parks" which will allow the inhabitants of the city to see the sea once again.

Airports

Tokyo has two major airports. For many years there was only Haneda; nowadays, with the exception of flights carrying visiting VIPs, it is used for domestic flights only.

The international airport is Narita. However, it lies 60km/38 miles east of the city, to which it is linked by rail and bus shuttle services. Although work was completed as early as 1973, it did not come into use until 1978, as the local inhabitants and environmentalists attempted to prevent its opening by means of demonstrations, often on a gigantic scale, some of which were marked by violent clashes with the police. The government had dispossessed a number of farmers without offering adequate compensation. The construction of a second runway is planned for the late 1990s, but unfortunately this will not result in more reasonable charter flights between Europe and Japan.

Railway

Japan's highly developed railway network is among the most modern in the world.

The broad-gauge Shinkansen line worked by JR (Japan Rail) links the capital with Kyoto, Osaka, Kobe and Fukuoka. Trains depart every 30 minutes and reach average speeds of 200kph/125mph. The Shinkansen is the most important link in Japan's transport system on the north–south axis. Apart from this railway there is just one road of motorway standard which is generally blocked by traffic jams.

Long distance trains leave Tokyo Main Station for destinations in south-west Japan, from Ueno Station for the north and from Shinjuku for the west.

Underground

The underground, or subway, is the most important form of transport for people within the city of Tokyo. The network of routes covers 203km/126 miles.

At rush hours (between 7 and 8am and around 5pm) the trains are desperately overcrowded. More than 5 million commuters use the city's public transport every day. Some districts of the city are almost completely deserted at night, an indication that places of work are all concentrated together.

Private railways are another sector of public transport. Their operations are based at Tokyo Main Railway Station which, for example, is the terminus of the Yamanote Line, a circle line of some 34·5km/22 miles which circuits the city centre in two directions and stops at all the major railway stations.

Private railways

Most buses in the city centre are run by the municipality, while those in the outlying districts are under private ownership.

Buses

The bus network is very well developed, but using it is so complicated that even locals have problems, and visitors are best advised to seek other means of transport.

From Tokyo motorways lead across the island in all the main directions. However, these motorways are not easy to find, the tolls are high, and at weekends they are so crowded that generally average speeds are no more than 40kph/25mph, especially as there are so many goods vehicles.

Motor traffic

In Tokyo itself the traffic is chaotic. In an attempt to by-pass the points where traffic jams regularly build up on account of the antiquated pattern of streets, so-called expressways on piers have been constructed since 1964. Users are charged a toll, but traffic jams often completely block these routes as well.

Famous People

Note	The following alphabetical list includes people who through birth, residence, achievements or death are connected with Tokyo and have attained recognition beyond the country's borders.
Matsuo Basho (1644–94)	The Japanese poet Matsuo Basho was the master of the typical Japanese art of *haiku*, a verse form which consists of a single stanza of three lines and just seventeen syllables altogether. The full meaning of lyrics in this form is revealed only when it is appreciated how much is just implied by "reading between the lines".
Shirai Gompachi Samurai and robber (b. 1661)	Only his date of birth is known – 1661. He began as a samurai and ended as a robber, a notorious and sinister character who still appears in horror stories today. When finally caught he was crucified.
Suzuku Harunobu Artist (1725?–70)	The artist Harunobu was born in Tokyo. He is considered the first classical master of the coloured woodcut, making a significant contribution to the development of polychromatic printing. In his coloured woodcuts elegant female figures, such as his "Beauties of Yoshiwara", are especially impressive. The discreet charm of his calendar pictures and intimate erotic prints makes them most fascinating.
Ando Hiroshige (1797–1858)	The painter Hiroshige was born and died in Tokyo. He is particularly revered as a master of the coloured woodcut. Hiroshige became well acquainted with the Japanese landscape as a result of his extensive travels through the country. He portrayed Japan in every mood at every hour of the day and every season of the year. His knowledge of European painting is reflected in his artistic and, to some degree, starkly asymmetrical coloured woodcuts. Hiroshige's most famous woodcuts are: "Views of the Capital of the East" (1830), "53 Views of the Tokkaido Route" (1834), "Famous Sites in Kyoto (1834) and "Eight Views of Lake Biwa" (1834–35).
Katsushika Hokusai Artist (1760–1849)	Katsushika Hokusai, probably the best-known Japanese painter and woodcarver of modern times, was also born in Tokyo. European art had a great influence on his work, which included individual paintings, series of landscapes and figures, book illustrations and caricatures. In the late 19th c. his work was widely acclaimed in Europe also.
Kondo Isami (1834–69)	Kondo Isami was a daring swordsman and mercenary, who raised a private army against the Emperor. He was defeated in a decisive battle in what is now the Ueno district of the city. When he was captured his throat was cut.
Yukio Mishima Author (1925–70)	Yukio Mishima is one of the few Japanese authors to have achieved world-wide fame. In the face of considerable controversy he modernised the classical Noh plays. Mishima found it impossible to accept his country's adoption of democracy after the Second World War and bitterly regretted the collapse of tradition. By that he meant above all the Samurai spirit and their unconditional loyalty to their lord, which in his case meant the Imperial dynasty. With the help of a private army of fanatics he tried to organise resistance to developments which he felt were un-Japanese and decadent. His actions did not win him many friends, and so he committed hari-kiri, the traditional Japanese form of suicide.

Moronobu, a painter and master of the woodcut, devoted his energies primarily to the portrayal of social life, with genre pictures and studies of modern beauties. He illustrated many books in black and white and, by producing the first single-sheet prints, he established the woodcut as an indpendent art form. Moronobu taught in Edo, where he also died.

Hishikawa Moronobu
Artist
(1618?–94)

Raiden was a sumo wrestler who weighed 370lb. He threw virtually all his opponents and lost only 10 of his 264 bouts, a record which has never been equalled in the world of sumo wrestling. Visitors who see with what enthusiasm the Japanese follow the fortnight-long wrestling tournaments will appreciate that Raiden's name is still not forgotten.

Raiden
Sumo wrestler
(1767–1825)

The Forty-seven Ronins are historical figures and legendary Japanese heroes. These samurai were followers of Daimyo Asano, who was appointed to the court of the shogun. At an audience in 1701 he was insulted by the courtier Yoshinaka Kira; in defence of his honour Asano immediately struck the courtier with his sword, although only enough to wound him slightly. However, to draw arms at court was considered a serious crime, and Asano was sentenced to slay himself. His forty-seven samurai plotted revenge against Yoshinaka Kira for the death of their lord. They pretended to dissociate themselves from their dead master and became *ronins* or lordless, wandering samurai. Further to lure Kira into a false sense of security they discarded all their knightly virtues and embarked on an unrestrained and undisciplined life. Two years after Asano's death they struck; they forced their way into Kira's house, hacked off his head and placed it by the grave of their master. Following this act of revenge, evidence of their unflinching allegiance to Asano, all forty-seven of them committed ritual suicide hari-kiri.

The Forty-seven Ronins
(17th/18th c.)

Kenzo Tange, perhaps Japan's most important architect, occupies the chair of municipal architecture at Tokyo University and has designed many government buildings and museums. He was responsible for St Mary's Catholic Cathedral in Tokyo and for the daring design of the swimming pool built for the 1964 Olympics. His town planning projects include the reconstruction of the Macedonian town of Skopje following its destruction by an earthquake in 1963.

Kenzo Tange
Architect
(b. 1913)

History

12th c. A.D.	There was a marshy, wooded area where present-day Tokyo now stands occupied by a warrior family which was supposedly called Edo. This name was later given to the city before it becomes Tokyo.
1457	Construction of the first stone fortress when General Ota builds Edo Castle.
1590	The feudal lord Tokugawa makes the insignificant fishing village the provincial capital.
1603	The Emperor appoints Ieyasu as Shogun (or Field Marshal), with the duty of stopping foreign barbarians from invading the country. As Shogun he seizes political power, reducing the Emperor who resides in Kyoto to a mere semi-religious symbolic figure. Under the Shogunate of the Tokugawa dynasty Edo grows into a large city. Craftsmen, traders, officials, artists and warriors are attracted to the Shogun's court. For the next 264 years of the Tokugawa Period power lies with the aristocracy. Japan shuts itself off from the outside world.
1634	The Shogun commands all Daimyos (feudal magnates) to reside with their families in Edo. The object is to ensure the loyalty of the magnates to the Tokugawa dynasty.
1635	From this year on all Daimyos have to undertake a period of attendance at court in Edo.
1657	Almost half of the city is laid waste by a catastrophic fire. Reconstruction begins immediately.
1705	With its 1,100,000 inhabitants Edo is larger than London.
1707	Fuji erupts. Ash rains down even on the streets of Edo.
1853	A US naval squadron under Matthew Perry puts in at the port of Edo. In the name of the American President Fillmore he demands the opening of Japanese ports to foreign trade. At first, by the Kanagawa Treaty, the ports of Shimoda and Hakodate are opened for trade with foreigners; other ports follow suit. Japan is obliged to modernise.
1868	The Imperial dynasty wins back its authority. The last Shogun of the Tokugawa dynasty is forced to abdicate. The Emperor with his family and court moves to Edo. The city is proclaimed the capital of Japan, and its name is changed to Tokyo. The Meiji Period begins with the Emperor Matsuhito.
1869	The first telegraph link between Tokyo and Yokohama is inaugurated.
1871	The postal system is introduced.
1872	The first rail link between Tokyo and Yokohama is inaugurated. The European calendar is introduced.
1912	Emperor Matsuhito dies. The Meiji Shrine is built in his honour. With its extensive grounds it becomes one of the symbols of Tokyo.
1914–18	Japan fights alongside the Allies in the First World War and captures the German garrison in Tsingtau (China).

More than 140,000 in Tokyo lose their lives as a result of the great earthquake in the Kanto region. Nearly all the major buildings are destroyed, as well as some 700,000 dwellings, mainly by the fires that rage after the earthquake. The city is rebuilt in a record time of 7½ years. — 1923

Hirohito becomes Emperor — 1926

Tokyo's population has grown to 2,070,913. — 1930

After boundary changes Tokyo's population reaches the new record figure of 6,369,919. — 1941

The "Prefecture" of Tokyo is proclaimed the "Tokyo Metropolitan Area". — 1943

Tokyo becomes an inferno. On March 9th the Americans launch an air attack on the city with 300 Super Fortresses, each with a bomb load of 7–8 tonnes. 700,000 bombs rain down on the city which becomes a sea of flames. 197,000 people are killed or reported missing. — 1945

Tokyo is rebuilt on its former lines, after a commission of experts comes to the conclusion that the population will under no circumstances exceed 3·5 million. — 1946

Tokyo Tower is built; at the time it is the tallest free-standing tower in the world. — 1958

Tokyo hosts the XVIIIth Summer Olympics. — 1964

The population of Tokyo exceeds 10 million. — 1965

Sunshine City, with 60 storeys and 240m/792ft high, is built in Ikebukuro. It is the highest building not only in Japan but in the whole of Asia. — 1978

Pope John Paul II stops in Tokyo during his visit to Japan. — 1981

A worldwide economic summit meeting is held in Tokyo for the second time. — 1986

A serious earthquake occurs in the Tokyo region on December 17th, measuring 6·6 on the Richter scale. Narita airport is badly damaged. — 1987

On January 7th Emperor dies at the age of 87; his son Akhito becomes the new "Tenno"; his official motto is "Heisel" (Bring about Peace). — 1989

During a state visit the Soviet Foreign Minister Shevardnadze sets down a Ten Point Programme of measures aimed at forming a basis of mutual trust between the two countries; no agreement is reached regarding the Soviet claim to the Kuril Islands.
   Massive fall in share values on the Tokyo stock exchange.
   On November 12th Akhito is enthroned amidst great celebrations. — 1990

Russia indicates its provisional readiness to compromise over the Kuril Islands question; however, no concrete outcome has yet been reached. — 1992

Crown Prince Naruhito marries the diplomat Masako Owada. — 1993

Quotations

Japanese

Sir Rutherford
Alcock
(1809–87)

The Japanese appear to be content and a very happy race, apart from one thing – every one of a certain rank carried two terrifying swords in his belt. One of these two swords is a heavy two-handed weapon sharply pointed and with an edge as keen as a razor; the other is somewhat shorter . . .

Japan is essentially a country of paradoxes and anomalies, where all – even familiar things – put on new faces, and are curiously reversed. Except that they do not walk on their heads instead of their feet, there are few things in which they do not seem, by some occult law, to have been impelled in a perfectly opposite direction, and a reversed order. They write from top to bottom, from right to left, in perpendicular instead of horizontal lines; and their books begin where ours end, thus furnishing examples of the curious perfection this rule of contraries has attained. Their locks, although imitated from Europe, are all made to lock by turning the key from left to right. The course of all sublunary things appears reversed. Their day is for the most part our night; and this principal of antagonism crops out in the most unexpected bizarre way in all their moral being, customs and habits. I leave to philosophers the explanation – I only speak to the facts:

There old men fly kites while the children look on; the carpenter uses his plane by drawing it *to* him, and their tailors stitch *from* them; they mount their horses from the off-side – the horses stand in stables with their heads when we place their tails, and the bells to their harness are always on the hind quarters instead of the front; ladies black their teeth instead of keeping them white, and their anti-crinoline tendencies are carried to the point of seriously interfering not only with grace of movement but with all locomotion, so tightly are the lower limbs, from the waist downwards, girt round with their garments; and finally, the utter confusion of sexes in the public bath-houses, making that correct, which we in the West deem so shocking and improper, I leave as I find it – a problem to solve

The Capital of the Tycoon, 1863

Tokyo (formerly Edo)

Richard Cocks
(16th century)

About 3 a clock in the after nowne there hapned an exceading earthquake in this citty of Edo in Japan, which contynewed, from the begyning to the end, about the eight part of an hower; but about the halfe tyme it was soe extreame and I thought the howse would have falne down on our heads, and was so glad to run out of doares without hat or shewes, the tymbers of the howse making such a nois and cracking that it was fearefull to heare. It began by littell and littell, and so encreased till the middell, and in lyke sort went away againe.

Diary, August 30th 1616

François Caron
(17th century)

If a lord orders the building of a wall, either for the king or for himself, then his servants often beg the privilege of being allowed to be buried beneath it. For their opinion is that no misfortune can befall anything which is built over human flesh. If they are granted the boon they seek,

Colourful procession on Children's Day

they go happily to the appointed spot and lie down there, allow the foundation stones to be placed upon their bodies and are immediately crushed to death by the weight.

The climate is magnificent. The capital city itself is some twenty miles across, and its population is probably several million. Tokyo can moreover boast of something which no European city possesses – delightful roads that fan out in every direction from the city centre and pass over wooded slopes, smiling valleys and shady avenues . . . It would be virtually impossible to besiege the city except with an army the size of the one Xerxes commanded.

Sir Rutherford Alcock (1809–87)

The street signs do little to relieve the monotony of the low, grey houses, nor do the shops (except the toy-shops which are gorgeous) make much show, with their low fronts half-concealed by curtains. Confectioners usually display a spiked white ball a foot and a half in diameter; *sake*-dealers a cluster of cypress trimmed into a sphere; the sellers of the crimson pigment with which women varnish their lips a red flag, goldbeaters a great pair of square spectacles, with gold instead of glass; druggists and herbalists a big bag resembling in shape the small ones used in making their infusions; kite-makers a cuttle fish; sellers of cut flowers a small willow tree; dealers in dried and salt fish, etc. two fish, coloured red and tied together by the gills which it is usual to make to betrothed persons; but the Brobdignagian signs in black, red and gold, which light up the streets of Canton are too "loud" and explicit for Japanese taste, which prefers the simple and symbolical.

Isabella Bishop (née Bird) (1831–1904)

Unbeaten Tracks in Japan 1880

Quotations

Lorenz Stucki
(1925–81)

As far as I am concerned, Tokyo is the most human great city that I know . . . The village lives on behind and next to the office block. The little fish shop, the little greengrocer's, the little butcher's shop, the pharmacy and the little snack bar where you can eat "Yakitori" (little roasted portions of chicken) or the mini-fish restaurant which can only take seven diners – these all help replace the impersonality of a great city with intimacy. There are few customers and scarcely any shop assistants who, despite their shy reserve, do not pause for a moment's chat. Even when communication is no more than a few words and a shy smile the other person is never just a statistic, but rather a fellow human being, and that is shown again and again in little things. For instance, my broken camera strap is sewn up for me in a photographic shop, and all payment is refused. Or on another occasion, when I buy a bottle of whisky I am given a glass, and in a restaurant I am presented with a saki beaker. People even round down the official price of your purchases, just because they feel like it.

Apart from a few districts entirely built up with shops and banks, even in overcrowded Tokyo, in the lanes behind the high-street façades, people always have a little piece of nature close to them. The front garden may be only a couple of square yards, but in it you can see one or a number of dwarf fir trees, bamboos or an azalea growing amidst a few natural stones. From a bamboo pipe a foot long water splashes into a basin no bigger than a wash bowl set in the grass amidst toy rocks. An alleyway between two wooden houses and scarcely wide enough for a man to pass leads into a secluded courtyard with a cherry tree where a sign hanging from a lamp standard shows the way to a café. Likewise, just a couple of minutes away from the Underground Station in the main shopping street with its four and six lanes of traffic, you come upon a little Shinto shrine or Buddhist temple in a tiny park.

Japan's hearts beat to another rhythm

Japanese poets
Matsuo Basho

With each puff of wind
The butterfly is alighting
Differently there

The mountain village
is cheered at the daytime's close
As plum trees blossom

By light of new moon
The land is inundated
With buckwheat blossom

Kaibara Ekiken

Heaven and earth know the rest and the turmoil of the tempest and the thunder, and yet nature knows about harmony and quiet.

If misfortune and illness are rife among men, they too are subject to change and give way finally to happiness and contentment.

Manyoshu

In spite of everything that comes in the way of a stream in spate, all the waters which part to go round banks and snags finally join together once again and rejoice.

On red carnations
The whiteness of butterflies
Who gave them their souls?

Shiki

Right in the middle
Mount Fuji reaches the skies:
Japan's spring has come.

Sho-u

© Baedeker

CHIYODA-KU

SHINJUKU-KU

Hanzo Moat

Hanzomon

Otemon

Wadakuram

Imperial Household Agency

Sakashitamon

Imperial Palace

Biology Laboratory

Kokyo Gaien

National Theatre

Akasaka Palace Meiji Shrine

Supreme Court

Aoyama-dori

Sakurada Moat

Nijubashi

Batsaski M

National Library

Constitutional Memorial Hall

Sakuradamon

KASUMIGASEKI

Gaisen Moat

Hibiya Moat

Imperial Theatre

Police

Parliament

Ministry of Transport

Ministry of Construction

Ministry of Home Affairs

Ministry of Justice

6

Hibiya-Park

Sakurada-dori

Kasumigaseki

Ministry of Foreign Affairs

Ministry of Health

7

Hibiya-dori

Prime Minister's Office

Schnellstraße Nr. 3

4

Ministry of Finance

9

8

11

10

12   13   15   14

Library

Patent Office

3

Ministry of Education

2

5

Hibiya Hall

Imperial Hotel

MEGURO-KU, MINATO-KU, SHIBUYA-KU

1

Nippon Press Center

Uchi-Sawai-cho

Sotobori-dori

Sotobori-dori

Watanabe

Konpira Shrine

Sakurada-dori

Ginza-Tokyu Theatre

Seinenkan

Hibiya-dori

Sotobori-dori

Shimbashi Railway Station

Okura Shukokan-Museum

New Shimbashi Building

Yokohama   Haneda Airport

1 Prime Minister's Residence	3 Kasumigaseki Building	5 Ministry of Posts & Telecommunications
2 Toranomon Hall	4 Environment Agency	6 Tokyo High Court

7 Ministry of Agriculture, Forestry & Fisheries
8 Tokyo Family Court

44

Tokyo
Centre

250m

Internat.
Post
Office

Postal
Services
Museum

Bank of Japan

Mitsukoshi
Department
Store

Nippon
Building

Nippon
Steel

Etai-dori

akura-
i

JNR

17 16

Marunouchi
Bldg.

Mitsubishi
Building

Tokyo Central
Post Office

MARUNOUCHI

Main
Railway
Station

Daimaru
Department
Store

Sotobori-dori

Etai-dori

Chuo-dori

Maruzen
Bookshop

Takashimaya
Department Store

Showa-dori

Yamatone
Museum

Yaesu-dori

Bridgestone
Art Gallery

Yaesu-dori

City
Hall

Sotobori-dori

akucho
ailway
Station

JNTO

18 Asahi
Press

Tokyo-
Theater

Ginza-yu

Namiki-dori

Central
Art
Gallery

Showa-dori

CHUO-KU

Ginza
Church

Fuji Bldg.

Chuo-dori

Harumi-dori

Sony
Building

Nichido
Gallery

Ginza Tower

Asahi Building

Canon Building

GINZA

Kabukiza-
Theater

Harumi-dori

Jisaku

ori-dori

Ginza
Tokyu-
Hotel

Togeki
Building

Showa-dori

Minolta Bldg.

Nissan Bldg.

19

Nishi
Honganji

SUMIDA-KU

KOTO-KU

KOTO-KU

9 Ministry of Trade
   and Industry
10 District Court
11 Hibiya Concert Hall

12 Nissei Theatre
13 Takarazuka
   Theatre
14 Yurakuza Theatre

15 Hibiya Theatre
16 Shin-Marunouchi
   Building
17 Tokyo Kaijo Building

18 Nichigeki
   Theatre
19 Shimbashi
   Embujo Theatre

Tokyo from A to Z

Because of the communication difficulties likely to exist between foreign tourists and native Japanese, who in only exceptional cases have any command of a foreign language (usually English), the entries for the sights of Tokyo from A to Z in the following section of the guide are accompanied by the corresponding Japanese characters printed in blue. These can at least enable the visitor to make himself understood where necessary (for instance, to a taxi driver).

Note

The transcriptions of the Japanese names have been made using the internationally recognised "Hebonshoki" system (see Introduction, Language).

Helpful suggestions for planning a short visit to Tokyo can be found under Sightseeing in the Practical Information section.

Short stay

Akasaka Palace

D 4/5

赤坂離宮

Japanese
equivalent

Akasaka Palace, which extends as far as the Outer Garden of the Meiji Shrine (see entry), was built in 1899–1909 for the Crown Prince using earthquake-proof technology.

Prior to that the area had been the site of the Kii-Tokugawa residence, in which the Emperor had lived while the Imperial Palace (see entry) was being rebuilt. Since 1974 Akasaka Palace has been used for receiving state visitors.

The palace was modelled on the architectural styles of late 18th c. Europe, such as Buckingham Palace in London, but some parts of it also call to mind the Palace of Versailles in Paris.

District
Minato-ku

Underground
Yotsuya
(Marunouchi Line)

Railway station
Yotsuya
(Chuo Line)

★Akihabara (City District)

F 3

秋葉原

Japanese
equivalent

Akihabara is Tokyo's Electronic City. In the tiny streets here there are vast numbers of shops selling recorders, radios, microphones, television sets, video and computer equipment. There are large stores, too – many of them having a floor specially catering for foreign tourists.

These are the only places where it is possible to buy export goods designed for a 220 volt AC power supply. They also have a reasonable number of sales assistants who have sufficient English to explain and advise on technical specifications.

Akihabara is in any case well worth a visit because it reveals how keenly the Japanese "play" with electronic products of all kinds. DIY enthusiasts can obtain everything here from computer chips to soldering irons, while it is frequently possible to "negotiate" prices.

District
Chiyoda-ku

Railway station
Akihabara
(Keihin-Tohoku
Line;
Yamanote Line;
Chuo Line)

Underground
Akihabara
(Hibiya Line)

◄ *The new city hall in Shinjuku district*

Street in Akasaka (See page 47)

"Electronic Eldorado" in Akihabara (See page 47)

★★Asakusa Kannon Temple

浅 草 寺

Japanese
equivalent

Asakusa was once a marshy district and therefore the part of the city where
the poor people lived. Even today it is still the place where the old traditional life style is maintained. At the end of the long street of shops where
masks, carvings, combs made of ebony and wood, toys, kimonos, fabrics
and precious paper goods are on sale, stands the Kannon Temple. It is the
centre of Asakusa. Around it, everywhere within the 20ha/50 acre temple
precinct, there is a warren of lanes with little temples, booths and also
places where the Japanese can indulge their passion for betting, especially
on horse races.

District
Asakusa

Underground
Asakusa
(Ginza Line)

The Kannon Temple (Senso-ji) belongs to the Buddhist Sho Kannon sect
and is dedicated to the Kannon, the Buddhist goddess of mercy. It has been
in existence since the foundation of the city. Although the buildings have
been destroyed on numerous occasions, they still retain their original
appearance, having been restored authentically after each catastrophe.
This is exemplified by the Main Hall and the Scarlet Pagoda.
  According to legend the Temple was founded in 628 (or more likely in
645) by three fishermen who had found a small statue of the goddess in
their nets when they hauled them. In its honour they founded the temple.
The main entrance is the Kaminari-mon Gate, with a 3.3m/10ft high red
paper lantern, weighing 100kg/220lb, which bears an inscription meaning
"Thunder Gate". The great Kannon Hall of 1651 was rebuilt in reinforced
concrete in 1958, using the original design, following its destruction during
the Second World War. The temple treasures are housed in the Hozomon
Gate, also newly restored.

Kannon Temple
(Senso-ji)

To the north-east of the Temple stands the Asakusa Shrine, known as
Sanjasama, which was built by Tokugawa Iemitsu (1604–51), in memory of
the three fishermen. In the courtyard in front of the main temple stands the
famous and much-loved Incense Vat which is reputed to drive away

Asakusa Shrine

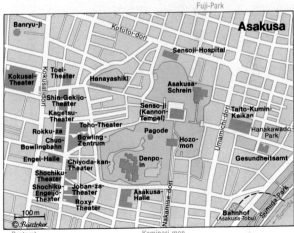

Asakusa Kannon Temple

Asakusa Kannon Temple

The famous paper lantern over the temple doorway

ailments. Sick people need only to cup their hands around the smoke and apply it to the part of their body which is unwell.

The temple doves are considered to be the Kannon's sacred messengers. Nowadays they also tell fortunes if that is what the visitor desires. With its beak a dove pulls out from a heap of cards the one which foretells the enquirer's future.

Asakusa Kannon Temple is one of the most popular in Tokyo. Accordingly the annual festival of Sanja Matsuri (May 15th–17th approx.) is the largest in the city, others being the Sanno Matsuri at the Hie Shrine (see entry) and the Kanda Matsuri at the Kanda Myojin Shrine (see entry).

City Halls

Old City Hall

都庁

The Old City Hall of Tokyo is situated just a few minutes' walk to the south of the Main Railway Station. Built by the Japanese architect Kenzo Tange, it was the seat of the city administration of Tokyo until 1991.

In front of the building stands a bronze statue of the feudal chief Ota Dokan (1432–86), who built the Chiyoda (Edo) Castle, today the Imperial Palace (see entry), and is generally considered to be the founder of Tokyo.

★★New City Hall

東京都庁

In the western district of Shinjuku-ku, in the middle of a cluster of skyscrapers, stands the highly impressive New City Hall (New Tokyo Metropolitan Government Office). Built by Kenzo Tange, it was officially opened in 1991.

With its 243m/797ft high twin towers, it is – after Tokyo Tower (see entry) – the highest building in Tokyo at the present time. Both of the towers possess viewing platforms on the 45th floor, and entry to these is free of charge on public holidays (as a rule, very crowded).

★★Fuji-san (Fujiyama)

富士山

Fuji-san (the name Fujiyama, by which it is generally referred to in the West, is not used in Japan) is 3776m/12,390ft high and is without doubt one of the most famous mountains in the world. It is generally shrouded in clouds and only seldom can it be glimpsed in all its dazzling whiteness. Those fortunate enough to see it in this latter guise will not easily forget the sight.

Every year over a million Japanese climb up to the volcano, which last rained down ash over Tokyo in December 1707. Visitors wishing to climb Fuji-san during their stay in Tokyo must allow for a two-day excursion, and it is only possible to undertake it during the period from July 1st to August 31st.

Sunrise on the summit of Fuji-san is reputed to be among the most impressive natural phenomena which it is possible to experience. It is also

F 5

Japanese equivalent

District
Marunouchi

Railway station
Main Station
(Yamanote Line)

A–B 4

Japanese equivalent

District
Shinjuku-ku

Underground
Shinjuku
(Marunouchi Line)

Japanese equivalent

Location
80km/50 miles
south-west of
Tokyo

said that anyone who has had this experience acquires a deeper understanding of and greater sensitivity towards Japanese landscape painting.

Access

The main JR Chuo line connects Shinjuku Station with Fujioshida (it may be necessary to change trains at Otsuki). From there there is a bus service to the fifth stopping point on the mountain (Go-gome).

It is also possible to travel by bus from Tokyo directly to the fifth stopping place on Fuji-san, either from Hamamatsucho Bus Terminal or Shinjuku Bus Terminal. Hamamatsucho Bus Terminal is located in the World Trade Center Building (1st floor), directly opposite Hamamatsucho Railway Station (JR); Shinjuku Bus Terminal is in Yasuda Seimei 2nd Building (west side), about two minutes' walk from the west exit of Shinjuku Railway Station (JR).

Seat reservations can be made through the Japan Travel Bureau and other agencies.

Ascent of
Fuji-san

Six mountain paths, each with ten stopping places, lead up Fuji-san. All these paths are well worn and disfigured with litter, though more and more heed is being paid to the need to keep the landscape clean and tidy. The steady stream of people making their way up the mountain shows the way clearly. Generally walkers start from the fifth stopping place (Go-gome). It is also possible to go up as far as the seventh stopping place (Shichi-gome) on horseback. But the path is steep.

For those wishing to experience sunrise from the mountain summit there are three different ways of making the ascent. One is to climb from the fifth stopping place as far as the eighth on the afternoon of the first day, and then spend the night in a mountain hut (hard wooden bunks) and start off on the last leg of the ascent at two o'clock in the morning.

The second, recommended, method is to set off in the evening from the fifth stopping place and walk on through the night. The third alternative is

Fuji-san – Japan's sacred mountain

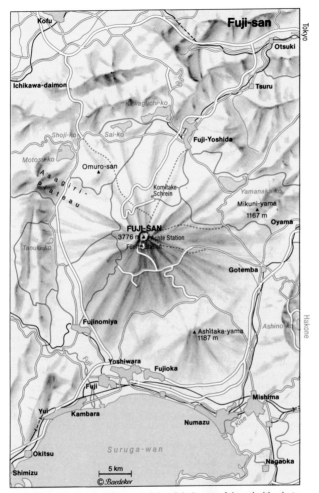

to go during the day and then spend the night in one of the primitive huts near the summit; in which case all one has to do in the morning is await the sun's rays.

Another alternative, well worth considering, is to make the ascent from Fujiyoshida, but then descend via Gotemba. On this route down, there is a short cut between the seventh and second stopping places known as Suna-bashiri ("sandslide"), which involves sliding down a 7km/4 mile long slope of volcanic ash in about half an hour. (Beware: possible falls of stone!)

Anyone wishing to climb Fuji-san should ensure that they are suitably dressed before setting out. Because of the volcanic ash, stout shoes are essential. Warm, wind-proof clothing is also an absolute necessity, as even in the summer months there can be frost on the summit and weather conditions can change very rapidly. A sun-hat and torch or flashlight are also required, as is a supply of food, although provisions can be bought in the mountain huts.

★★Fuji Lakes/Fuji-goko

At the northern foot of Mount Fuji the visitor will find the delightful scenery of the five Fuji Lakes (Fuji-goko), which is a popular recreational area all the year round for the citizens of Tokyo, as well as representing a much-prized holiday destination for foreign visitors. This lakeland plateau lying at an altitude of more than 600m/2000ft has an agreeably cool climate, with cherry-trees and azaleas in bloom in spring, while in autumn the woodland is a mass of glowing colours. In summer large numbers of water-sports enthusiasts come here, in winter skiers and skaters.

Scenery

The lakeland plateau encompasses the northern base of Mount Fuji in a wide arc. At the eastern end lies Lake Yamanaka, followed in a westerly direction by Lakes Kawaguchi, Saiko, Shoji and Motosu. For visitors coming from the Tokyo direction the town of Gotemba is the best starting-point for visiting the region, for those coming from the Osaka, Kyoto and Nagoya area, the town of Fujinomiya to the south-west of Fuji.

From Gotemba to Fujinomiya

This route takes in all five Fuji Lakes as well as the various starting-points for footpaths up Fuji-san.

Lake Yamanaka

Lake Yamanaka is, at 982m/3220ft, the highest of the five lakes and, with a surface area of 6.5sq.km/2.5sq.miles, the largest. The surrounding area is very popular with health-conscious people seeking somewhere to go and stay. On the southern shore of the lake lies Asahigaoka, which can be reached by bus either from Gotemba or direct from Tokyo. Trips around the lake can be arranged, while in the immediate vicinity are Fuji Golf Course and various camping sites. The lake is home to the round green alga known as "marimo", which also occurs in Lake Akan on Hokkaido, as well as eels, carp and salmon. A favourite sport in winter is ice-angling for a type of fish known as "wakasagi". The nearby river of Katsura is good for trout-fishing.

Fuji-Yoshida

To the north of Lake Yamanaka is the town of Fuji-Yoshida (pop. 54,000; rail and bus connections with Tokyo), which is famous for its silk fabrics (kaiki).

To mark the end of the official season for ascending Mount Fuji, the festival of Himatsuri takes places here on August 26th. In the evening torches and bonfires are lit along the Fuji-Yoshida path and there is also a procession which involves carrying a shrine weighing 1125kg (just over one ton).

Fujikyu Highland

South of the town is the amusement park Fujikyu Highland (connection with the Fuji-Kyuko Railway; overnight accommodation available), one of the largest in this region.

Kawaguchi-ko ★Tenjo

North-west of Fuji-Yoshida (bus service; rail link with Tokyo) lies the second largest and most beautiful of the Fuji Lakes, Kawaguchi-ko (822m/2697ft; 6.1sq.km/2.4sq.miles). A cable car ascends from the east shore of the lake to the 1084m/3556ft high mountain of Tenjo, from where there is an impressive view over the lake, with Mount Fuji reflected in its waters.

Unoshima

In the centre of Kawaguchi-ko is the densely-wooded island of Unoshima with a shrine dedicated to the goddess of good fortune, Benten, as well as numerous holiday and leisure amenities. About 1km/½ mile north-west of Kawaguchi-ko Station is the Fuji Museum (local history, collection of erotica), while near the tollbooth for the Fuji-Subaru road can be found the visitors' centre for the Yamanashi prefecture (previously known as the Fuji National Park Museum), which has a collection devoted to the natural history of Fuji.

Kawaguchi-ko is a starting-point for one of the routes up Fuji-san. In addition there are boat trips round the lake (1 hour). At its eastern end the lake is spanned by a 1260m/1380yd bridge Kawaguchi-ko O-hashi (toll).

The next lake to the west is Saiko (12sq.km/4½sq.miles; buses from Kawaguchi-ko), much frequented by anglers in spring and autumn (trout). Like Lakes Shoji and Motosu, Saiko has no visible drainage outlet. It is thought that all three lakes have underground connections with the source of the River Shiba and supply it with water. There is a boat service linking the town of Saiko on the north-east bank with Neba on the north-west bank.

Saiko

Excursions into the area to the south of the lake are well worth while, for instance to Koyodai ("maple hill"; bus or footpath (20 mins.) from Kawaguchiko Station), which offers a superb view over the surrounding woodland.

★Koyodai

Not far away to the south-west can be found the ice-cave of Narisawa Hyoketsu and further west (footpath 20 mins; also bus from Kawaguchiko Station) the cave of Fugaku Fuketsu with its lava and ice formations (inside very cold!).

Between Lake Saiko and the next lake to the west Shoji-ko stretches the primeval area known as the Jukai ("sea of trees"). In this wilderness, 16km/10 miles in circumference, the magnetic eruptive stone plays havoc with the accuracy of compass readings, with the result that walkers here are forever getting lost.

Jukai

Lake Shoji opens out in a southerly direction and is surrounded by wooded rounded mountain tops. With a surface area of 0.75sq.km/185 acres it is not only the smallest of the five Fuji Lakes but also the most idyllic (bus connections with Fuji-Yoshida, Kawaguchiko and Fujinomiya). In winter "wakasagi", a kind of salmonide, are caught.

Shoji

From the north bank the ascent to the summit of Eboshi (1257m/4124ft; also Shoji-Panorama-dai) takes 1½ hrs. From here there is a rewarding view across the lake to Mount Fuji and the Jukai ("sea of trees").

★Eboshi

The arc of the five lakes is completed at the western end by the deep-blue Lake Motosu (bus connections with Fuji-Yoshida and Fujinomiya). At 126m/413ft it is the deepest of the lakes and does not freeze over in winter.

Motosu

★Fujinomiya Toll Road

The 22km/14 mile long Fujinomiya Toll Road, which leads on to Fujinomiya (bus, 1¼ hrs), is well worth travelling along for the views it affords of Mount Fuji. Halfway along the road the visitor comes to the Shiraito waterfall, where the River Shiba, with a breadth of 130m/140yds, plunges over a 26m/85ft precipice into the depths below.

On the other side of the road is the Otodome-notaki waterfall.

To the south lies the Temple of Taisekiji, founded in 1290 and one of the main shrines of the Nichiren sect as well as the main seat of the sister organisation of Soka Gakkai. There is a modern assembly hall with 6000 seats.

In Fujinomiya (pop. 112,000) stands the Sengen shrine (1km/½ mile to the north-west of the Railway Station), which was built in 1604 and is the main

Fujinomiya

Sengen shrine in the Fuji area. It is consecrated to the goddess Konohana-Sakuyahime-nomikoto.

From Fujinomiya one can take the JR Minobu line southwards to Fuji Station where there are connections with the main JR Tokaido line to Tokyo.

★★ Ginza (shopping district)   F 5

Japanese equivalent

銀 座

District
Chuo-ku

Railway station
Yurakucho
(Keihin-Tohoku
Line; Yamanote
Line)

Underground
Ginza
(Marunochi Line;
Hibiya Line)

Ginza is Tokyo's most famous shopping area, with its rows of exclusive shops and imposing palatial department stores, selling literally every conceivable thing from anywhere in the world, and interspersed with tea-shops, cafés, bars and restaurants.

At weekends, in particular, when everything is open, Ginza represents a shopper's paradise, because it is then closed to traffic. Gigantic advertising panels on many of the buildings bathe Ginza in bright light in the evenings, while the crowds of moving people sweep the visitor along and the din is almost frightening.

In among all the bustle of the shopping streets can be found the Kabuki-za Theatre, in which Kabuki performances take place. "Earphones" are available here for foreign visitors to hire, enabling them to receive a résumé of the stage action in English. There is also the Shinbashi Embujo Theatre, in which the traditional Azuma-odori dances or Bunraku performances may be seen. The Ginza district was the commercial centre of the country in the Edo period. It was here that the Chonin, craftsmen and merchants, lived. In

The renowned shopping mile – Ginza

The "Japanese Bridge" Nihonbashi

1612 Tokugawa Ieyasu had the silver mint (in Japanese "ginza") moved to Edo (present-day Tokyo) and it was sited south of the Kyobashi bridge. The Nihonbashi (= Japan Bridge), which was built in 1603 and restored in 1911, was at that time the starting-point of the five main highways serving the rest of the country: the Oshu Road to Sendai, the Nikko Road to Nikko, the Tokaido Road to Kyoto, the Koshu Road to Kofu and the Nakasendo Road to Nagano. Today the bridge is itself spanned by a flyover forming part of the urban motorway network. In the middle of the bridge can be seen the zero milestone used for measuring distances on the national road network.

★Gokokuji Temple

D 2

Japanese equivalent

The Gokokuji Temple is one of the largest temple complexes in Tokyo. It belongs to the Buzan School of the Shingon Sect.

The temple is dedicated to the goddess Kannon, whose statue is reputed to be of Indian origin. Among the treasures of the temple are a Mandara which is said to date from the Kamakura period (1192–1333). Important personages from recent Japanese history have been laid to rest in the temple, while to the east of the temple building is to be found the grave of the Anglo-American writer Lafcadio Hearn (1850–1904).

District
Bunkyo-ku

Underground
Gokokuji
(Yurakucho
Line)

Behind the temple is a knoll which has been the burial place of the Imperial house since 1873. For the Emperor and Empress, however, there are other special burial places; these are to be found chiefly in Kyoto and Nara (see entries).

57

★Hakone

Japanese
equivalent

箱根

Location
about 100km/
60 miles south-
west of Tokyo

The area of Hakone, bounded on the north by Fuji-san (see entry) and in the
south by the peninsula of Izu (see entry), is one of the most popular holiday
areas in Japan and is much visited both in summer and winter. The region
has volcanoes, a large number of thermal baths and a number of historic
monuments. Lake Ashi is particularly attractive.

Access

By rail from Tokyo Main Station in 45 mins (JR Tokaido Shinkansen Line) to
Odawara; from Shinjuku Station in about 2 hrs (Odakyu private line) via
Odawara to Hakone-Yumoto.

Transport
services in the
Hakone area

Hakone-Tozan rail line from Odawara via Hakone-Yumoto, Tonosawa,
Miyanoshita, Kowakidani to Gora (about 1 hr).
Hakone-Tozan bus line from Odawara via Hakone-Yumoto, Tonosawa,
Miyanoshita, Sengoku and Sengoku-kogen to Togendai (about 1 hr). Izu-
Hakone railbus line from Odawara via Hakone-Yumoto, Miyanoshita,
Kowakidani, Sounzan, Owakudani and Ubako to Hakone-en (about 1½ hrs).

Izu-Hakone cable cars from Hakone-en to Komagatake (8 mins). Another
cable car from Gora via Sounzan and Owakudani to Togendai.
Boat service on Lake Ashi from Togendai via Hakone-machi to Moto-
Hakone (30 mins); from Kojiri via Hakone-en to Moto-Hakone (30 mins).

Recommended
circular trip

From Tokyo (Shinjuki Station) Odakyu line to Hakone-Yumoto; Hakone-
Tozan line to Gora; cable car to Togendai; boat to Moto-Hakone; on foot via
the Hakone Museum to Hakone-machi; bus to Odawara; JR rail service
back to Tokyo (about 6 hrs).

Scenery

Hakone lies within the crater area of the extinct Hakone volcano, the centre
of which subsided some 400,000 years ago to form a caldera. The crater
area measures some 40km/25 miles in circumference. Later eruptions
formed the volcanoes Kamiyama (highest mountain in the Hakone area at
1438m/4718ft), Komagatake (1327m/4354ft) and Futago (1091m/3579ft).
Lake Ashi was formed from the original crater lake. Its drainage rivers
Hayakawa and Sukomo have created romantic gorges.

Trip through Hakone

The circular trip described below can be made without difficulty using
public transport, given that the region is well served by trains, buses, cable
cars and boats. Anyone reluctant to undertake the trip on their own can join
an organised party.

Odawara

The starting-point is the old castle town of Odawara, situated on Sagami
Bay at the eastern foot of the Hakone Mountains. The castle itself stands
400m/¼ mile from the railway station. Its five-storey main tower was
restored in 1960 and now houses a museum of weapons, and objects
relating to the history of the area. Within the castle grounds there is also a
zoo and a folk museum.

Yumoto

To the west of Odawara (rail and bus connections) lies Yumoto, the oldest
spa town in the region (thermal springs, 35–74°C/95–165°F). South of the
station is the Sounji Temple belonging to the Rinzai sect (the portrait on silk
of the temple founder Hojo Soun is of interest).

The castle of Odawara

The solfatara at Owakudani

Hakone

Tonosawa

To the west of Yumoto lies Tonosawa at the head of the beautiful gorge formed by the River Hayakawa. 1 mile/2km to the north rises the mountain Tonomine (556m/1824ft) with the 17th c. Amida Temple, from which there are fine views.

Miyanoshita

Miyanoshita, an important traffic junction 12km/7 miles west of Odawara, forms, together with Sokokura and Dogashima, one of the liveliest towns in the region. The climate remains mild even in summer; the main hot springs have temperatures between 62 and 78°C/144–172°F. To the north of the station stands the oldest Western-style hotel in Japan, the Fujiya Hotel opened in 1878; south of this lies the 802m/2631ft high mountain of Sengen (ascent 1 hr; splendid view over Hakone).

Kowakidani

Kowakidani ("valley of the small steam"; 5 minutes by bus from Miyanoshita) is a long-established spa town which also attracts people in April when the azaleas and cherry trees are in blossom. The hot steam which occurs here is used, among other things, to heat greenhouses.

Kowakien Garden

Not far from the bus-stop at Kowakien-mae (2 minutes from Kowakidani) lies the leisure centre known as Kowakien Garden, with a hotel, "ryokan" (traditional Japanese inn), open-air swimming baths and a botanical garden.

Gora

The route leads from Kowakidani northwards to Gora on the eastern slopes of the mountain of Sounzan (beautiful view across to the upper reaches of Hayakawa). From Owakudani ("valley of the great steam") thermal waters are piped to Gora. To the south of the town stands the Hakone Open-air Museum (Chokoku-no-mori) with sculptures by European masters (Moore, Rodin, Bourdelle, etc.)

The Hakone Museum of Art (Chinese and Japanese porcelain; paintings) is to be found to the south-west of Gora in Gora Park, which is also much visited for its azaleas.

From Gora a cable-car connects with the north shore of Lake Ashi to the west. Visitors can break their journey at certain of the stations along the route.

Owakudani

At Owakudani Station there is a viewing platform with a fine panorama across to Mount Fuji. In addition the many solfataras in the region can be reached in a short time from the station. The Natural History Museum offers an insight into the local fauna, flora and geology.

The cable-car ends at Togendai on the north shore of Lake Ashi. From here and from Kojiri there are boat services to Hakone-en (east shore) and Moto-Hakone and Hakone-Machi (south shore).

★Lake Ashi

Lake Ashi (also known as Lake Hakone) is the main scenic attraction in Hakone and is famous for the reflection of Mount Fuji in its waters. The Ashinoko Skyline Drive, a toll road running along 12km/7 miles of its western shores, offers a superb view of Fuji and the bays of Sagami and Suruga.

Togendai

The main centre on the northern shore of the lake is formed by the towns of Togendai and Kojiri. By following the eastern shore road, the visitor will come to Hakone-en, where the large holiday centre of Hakone-en Park is situated. It comprises swimming pools, ice-rinks, golf courses and camping sites as well as an "international village" with typical houses from 29 countries and a folk-art exhibition. To the north-east the skyline is dominated by the 1327m/4354ft high mountain, Komagatake, which has cable-car connections both with Togendai and with the base of the mountain on its south-eastern side. The mountain offers a panoramic view across to Fuji and the peninsula of Izu.

Fuji-san and Lake Ashi

On the south shore of the lake lies Moto-Hakone (bus connections with Miyanoshita and Odawara), one of the harbours for the boat service which operates on the lake. Together with the more southerly Hakone-machi it forms an important tourist area.

Moto-Hakone

Standing among dense woodland on an eminence to the west of the town is the Hakone Shrine, founded in 757 and restored in 1667. In the Treasury next to the Main Hall there is a picture scroll depicting the foundation of the shrine, a wooden statue of the shrine's founder and a sword belonging to Soga Goro (12th c.), one of the Soga brothers, who took their own lives while avenging the death of their father. The anniversary celebrations of the shrine take place on July 31st and August 1st.

Hakone Shrine

From the old post station of Moto-Hakone a 2km/1 mile avenue of crescent pines leads to Hakone-machi. Just a short distance outside the village is the former control point on the Tokaido Road, with a reconstructed watch-house. Next to it is the Hakone Palace Garden, originally part of an Imperial villa, and at the entrance is the Historical Museum (Hakone-shiryokan) with exhibits devoted to the history of the Tokaido Road and the control station.

Hakone-machi

The Hakone Museum, situated opposite the Hakone Hotel, is somewhat similar to the Historical Museum, with its old coins, seals, documents and maps. The holiday area around Hakone-machi attracts plenty of visitors both in winter as well as summer.

From Hakone-machi the Hakone Bypass Road (bus service) leads back through the beautiful valley of the River Sukomo back to Odawara.

See entry.

Izu

61

Hamarikyu Park   F 6

Japanese equivalent

浜離宮

District
Chuo-ku, on the
Sumida River

Railway station
Shinbashi
(Keihin,
Yamanote Line)

Opening times
9am–4.30pm
daily

Hamarikyu Park is ten minutes' walk from Shinbashi Railway Station. Its particular charm lies in the wonderful view it affords out over the mouth of the River Sumida, the harbour and Tokyo Bay.

The marvellously tended gardens and park with lake and villa ("Garden of the Imperial Hama Villa") were formerly used as the summer residence of the Tokugawa. They are a typical example of the princely gardens of that period, the so-called Daimio-Teien.
 The lagoon spanned by a bridge makes a special impression.

After coming into municipal ownership the garden was opened to the public in 1946.

South-east of the gardens is the Takeshiba Pier. Steamers for Oshima Island ply from here, and this is the starting-point for sightseeing cruises on the River Sumida.

Happo-en Park   D 7

Japanese equivalent

八芳園

District
Minato-ku

Underground
Meguro
(Yamanote Line)

This small, beautifully laid-out park near Meguro Underground Station has an incredible attraction for bridal couples. When the lunar calendar shows that the days are favourable, there is a practically endless procession of weddings here. The bride and groom sit patiently with their families in the hall until their names are announced over the loudspeakers. The ceremony itself is short, the preparation and artistic arrangement of the group photographs taking a good deal longer. Visitors are welcome to take their own photographs if they wish.

Harajuku (City District)   C 5

Japanese equivalent

原宿

District
Shibuya-ku

Underground
Meijingu-mae
(Chiyoda Line)

The district of Harajuku, situated between the Inner and Outer Gardens of the Meiji Shrine (see entry), is a popular place for younger people wishing to go shopping or just stroll around, as Western-style clothes and accessories, in particular, are available in its shops.
 Many rock and pop groups put in an appearance in the main streets (Meiji-dori, Omotesando, etc.) – their music usually played at a deafening volume.

Hibiya Park   E 5

Japanese equivalent

日比谷公園

District
Marunouchi

Hibiya Park lies close to the Imperial Hotel, which was designed in 1922 by the famous American architect Frank Lloyd Wright, and was built on rollers in order to make it earthquake-proof. It remains to this day one of the most prestigious hotels in Tokyo.

Until 1903 the site of Hibiya Park was used for military manoeuvres but it was then laid out as a park along European lines. It covers an area of some 16ha/40 acres. At midday it is full of people who come from the nearby office blocks to eat their lunch in the open air. Demonstrations often take place here and it is also less frequently the site of popular festivals. In November there is a major chrysanthemum show.

The buildings in the park include the Hibiya-kokaido Concert Hall and the Hibiya Library.

★★Hie Shrine   D 5

日 枝 神 社

South-west of the National Theatre and the Parliament Building (see entry) and only five minutes' walk from the Akasaka Underground Station lies the Hie Shrine. The shrine, which is also known as the Sanno-sama shrine, dates from the early Edo period and is dedicated to the divinity Oyamakui-no-Mikoto. After being destroyed in the Second World War it was faithfully restored.

District
Chiyoda-ku,
south-west of
the Parliament
Building

Underground
Akasaka
(Chiyoda Line)

It is situated on a hill at the foot of which stands a torii. A zigzag path leads up to the sanctuary. The divinity Oyamakui used to be the protector of Kyoto, the former capital. When Ota Dokan built his palace in Edo (see Imperial Palace) he nominated Oyamakui as tutelary divinity of his castle. Later Tokugawa Ieyasu erected this protective shrine in its honour.

The Hie Shrine

Hie Shrine

Sunshine City in Ikebukuro-ku

Under the Tokugawas the festival of this shrine was among the capital's most important religious occasions. Even today the annual Sanno Matsuri celebrations, between June 10th and 16th, are among the largest in Tokyo. The culminating point of these is the procession, which takes place every two years, with the image carried on bearers.

Ikebukuro (District)   C 1/2

Japanese equivalent

池袋

District
Toshima-ku

Railway station
Ikebukuro
(Yamanote Line)

The extension of the Yamanote Line in 1903 did much to further the development of Tokyo's most northerly shopping and pleasure centre. Ikebukuro Railway Station has become a major public transport centre. Here there is an underground shopping mall (Ikebukuro Shopping Park), while the Sunshine City skyscraper with its 60 storeys is one of the tallest buildings in Japan. It houses a hotel, aquarium, planetarium, etc.

Nearby lie an estimated 150 "love hotels", 50 cabarets and theatres and three dozen gaming dens.

Ikegami Hommonji Temple   south of the area covered by the city plan

Japanese equivalent

池上本門寺

District
Meguro-ku

It is necessary to change at Gotanda Underground Station on to the Tokyu-Ikegami railway line. Near Ikegami stands the Ikegami Hommonji Temple, an important centre of the Nichiren sect. On the thickly-wooded site are to be found the graves of the Nichiren disciples, Nichiro and Nichirin, as well as the painter Kano Tanyu (1602–74). Of the old temple buildings only the five-storey pagoda (1607) and the Sutra Hall have survived the Second World War.

The great festival of Oeshiki, which commemorates the death of Nichiren, is celebrated in October.

★★Imperial Palace   E 4

皇 居

The chief attraction of the Marunouchi district (see entry) is undoubtedly the Imperial Palace with its parks surrounded by walls and moats (which date from 1613). The residence of the Imperial family stands on the site where in 1457 the feudal lord Ota Dokan built a first fortress, which served as a focal point from which the city of Tokyo (or Edo, as it then was) gradually spread outwards. After capturing the fortress in 1590, Tokugawa Ieyasu rebuilt it, making it the strongest in the land. Subsequently it was burnt down in a disastrous fire in 1657 and only partially restored. Until 1868 the splendid palace was the residence of the Tokugawa Shoguns. With the restoration of Imperial authority and the transfer of the seat of government from Kyoto to the city which had now been renamed Tokyo (i.e. Eastern Capital), it became the Imperial residence. After destruction in 1873 and again in 1945, the palace has been rebuilt in the traditional "flat" style.

District
Chiyoda-ku,
1–1 Chiyoda

Railway station
Main Station
(Yamanote Line)

Underground
Otemachi
(Chiyoda, Mita
and Tozai
Lines)

Higashi-Gyo-en Garden: Tue.–Thur. 9am–4pm. Palace Gardens: 2.1., 23.12

Opening times

Imperial Palace

The Nijubashi Bridge in the palace grounds

The Nijubashi Bridge leads into the palace interior. Its name, meaning "double bridge", refers to its appearance as reflected in the water. The wall surrounding the palace, which is 2m/7ft thick, is penetrated by various gates. Of these the southern Sakurada-mon used to form the main entrance to the palace, the Sakashita-mon today houses the Imperial Household Office, and the three gates Ote-mon, Hirakawa-mon and Kita-Hanebashi-mon open out into the Higashi-Gyo-en (eastern section of the park), which is open to the public. Up until the end of the last war it was customary for all passengers on buses and trams passing the palace walls to comply with the conductor's order "Kyojo mai ni!" ("Bow!").

The individual buildings of the Palace comprise the Main Building (Kyu-den), the Residential Building (Fukiage-gosho) and the three Palace Buildings (Kashikodokoro, Koreiden and Shinden). Within the Palace are to be found a hospital, an air-raid shelter, tennis courts, stables for horses, a cemetery, a paddy field, a kitchen garden, a hen-house and a silk-worm farm. 245 families, which make up the Imperial household, all live in the Palace.

The Palace is not accessible to the general population. The Palace Gardens, however, are open to the public on just two days in the year, January 2nd and December 23rd (the Emperor's birthday). On these days people flock past in order to catch sight of the Emperor (Tenno Heika), who lets himself be seen several times in the course of the day, and to wish him good fortune. On other days permission for a visit must be obtained from the Imperial Household Office (Kunaicho, 1–1 Chiyoda, Chiyoda-ku).

The eastern Higashi-Gyo-en Garden or Imperial Palace East Garden can, however, be visited from Tuesday to Thursday between 9am and 4pm (no entry after 3pm). It contains several old buildings worth seeing.

Formerly the Kinomaru Park formed part of the Palace grounds, but it is now cut off by a motorway.

In April and October the Music Room (Togakudo) of the Palace is open to the public for Bunraku and Gagaku performances. To obtain an entrance ticket it is necessary to send a written request accompanied by a stamped addressed envelope to the Imperial Household Office (Kunaicho, see above). The exact dates of performances are announced in the press; the Japan Travel Bureau will also provide information.

★★Izu

伊豆

Japanese equivalent

The Izu Peninsula, lying to the south of Mount Fuji (see entry), extends out into the Pacific, with Suruga Bay to the west and Sagami Bay to the east. Izu is a popular holiday area, not just because it enjoys a mild climate throughout the year, but also on account of its varied scenery: a coastline made up of small bays, wooded uplands, large numbers of hot springs and romantically situated bathing places. The name Izu is derived from the older name Yu-Izu (Yu = hot water, Izu = spring).

Location
about 120km/
75 miles west of
Tokyo

The backbone of the peninsula is formed by the Amagi Mountains, a continuation of the mountain of Hakone (see entry). The highest point is Mount Amagi (1407m/4616ft), which is also the source area of the River Kano, flowing northwards through the peninsula and reaching the sea at Numazu on Suruga Bay.

The best starting-points for excursions into the region are the towns of Atami, Mishima and Numazu, all accessible from Tokyo. The best road access is the Tomei Express Highway, which passes close by Mishima and Numazu. The peninsula itself is served by the Izu-Kyuko and Izu-Hakone railway lines as well as several coach routes.

From Tokyo (Main Station) JR Tokaido-Shinkansen Line to Atami (50 mins) and Mishima (1¼ hrs); also to Shimoda (2¾ hrs); also JR Tokaido Main Line to Atami (1¾ hrs), Mishima (2¼ hrs) and Numazu (2½ hrs); from Tokyo (Main Station) JR Ito Line via Atami to Ito, then Izu-Kyuko Private Railway to Shimoda; from Mishima Izu-Hakone Private Railway to Shuzenji.

Access

From Tokyo (Takeshiba Pier) boat connection to Okada (Oshima Island; 4–7 hrs); from Yokohama to Okada (Oshima; 6 hrs); from Atami to Motomachi (1–2 hrs); from Shimoda to Motomachi (1½ hrs) and to the islands Kozu, Shikine, Niijima and Toshima.

East Coast of Izu Peninsula

Atami

Right at the northern end of the east coast of Izu is the seaside resort of Atami (pop. 49,000), situated on a magnificent stretch of coastline. It is one of the most modern resorts in the country. The apricot garden (Atamibaien), with some 1300 trees, is well worth visiting (bus from railway station, 15 mins). The cactus garden (Atami saboten-koen), with its large greenhouses, is situated on a mountainside with a view across the town (bus from railway station, 15 mins).

The Atami Museum of Art (Atami-bijutsukan; bus from station) is housed in the headquarters of the Church of World Messianity and has on display an art collection pertaining to this "new religion", including coloured wood engravings (Ukiyo-e), ceramics, precious metal and lacquerwork. Many of the exhibits are classified as "national treasures" or "important items of cultural heritage".

★★Museum of
Art

The beautiful Atami-Himenosawa Park (bus from station, 20 mins) is particularly worth a visit when the azaleas and cherry trees are in blossom.

The Atami Museum of Art

Cape Uomi

Cape Uomi is the location of the Atami Koraku-en Leisure Centre (bus from station, 10 mins), with its swimming pool, angling ponds, reptile garden, etc.

The best view of Atami can be obtained from the Atami Pass situated to the north of the town.

Ito

There is an attractive coast road, running parallel to the Ito railway line, which leads southwards to the town of Ito (pop. 71,000), the second largest town on the peninsula. Here there are some 700 hot springs which are used by both private households and public baths. Some of these springs have been used in this way for several hundred years. 1.5km/1 mile south of the station lies the Jonoike Pool, and to the east of it the Butsugenji Temple of the Nichiren sect, whose founder lived here in exile from 1261 to 1263.

2km/1 mile south-east of the station stands a memorial to William Adams (1584–1620), who built the first Western-style ship in Japan (commemorative celebrations in August).

Omuroyama-shizenkoen

A bus service (20 mins) connects Ito Railway Station with the nature park of Omuroyama-shizenkoen, which occupies the surroundings of a 231m/758ft high volcanic hill. There is a fine view of the Amagi Mountains and of the offshore island of Oshima to the east.

Ippeki

South-west of the nature park lies the crater lake of Ippeki (4km/2½ miles in circumference; bus from the station 25 mins), in which the Amagi Mountains can be seen reflected. The shoreline is famed for its cherry blossom. To the east is the Jogasaki Beach, a 10km/6 mile long stretch of ria coastline of volcanic origin. The focal point of this region is the Izu Ocean Park (bus from Izu-Kogen Station 10 mins), with several swimming pools.

Of interest is the Ikeda Museum of 20th Century Art (Ikeda-nijusseiki-bijutsukan; bus from station 25 mins) with pictures by Picasso, Chagall, Matisse as well as Japanese coloured-wood engravers.

At the foot of Mount Omuro (581m/1906ft), which lies to the south of the crater lake, is the Izu Cactus Garden (Izu-saboten-koen; coach from Ito 40 mins) with peacocks and a viewing platform.

Cactus Garden

Shimoda

At the extreme southern end of the east coast lies the harbour town of Shimoda (pop. 32,000; Izu-Kyuko railway line, 1 hr from Ito), departure point for boat crossings to several of the Seven Izu Islands.

It was in the Bay of Shimoda that the "Black Ships" of the American admiral Matthew Perry (1794–1858) dropped anchor in 1854, their presence there inducing Japan to become a signatory to the Treaty of Kanagawa (March 31st 1854) and to open the harbours of Shimoda and Hakodate to foreign vessels. The first American diplomatic representative in Japan, Townsend Harris (1804–78), lived here from 1856 to 1857, but then transferred his official residence to Yokohama, which opened its docks to foreign ships as a result of a new trade treaty signed with the USA in 1858.

History of the town

The Gyukosenji Temple, once the official residence of Townsend Harris, is situated 2km/1 mile east of the town in the village of Kakisaki. It contains, apart from a portrait and some mementoes of Harris, the eight-volume diary kept by a village resident and relating to the life of the diplomat. Nearby are the graves of American and Russian sailors. In mid-May the three-day festival of Kurofune-matsuri commemorates Admiral Perry's landing.

Kakisaki

On a hillside close by the harbour lies Shimoda Park with a beautiful view over to Cape Suzaki in the east. At the railway station is to be found the valley station of a cable-car which ascends Mount Nesugata, from where there is a view over the southern tip of the Izu Peninsula. This was also the location of the look-out post from where a watch was kept on the Black Ships when they anchored in the bay.

Shimoda Park

Not far from the station is the Hofukuji Temple, dedicated to Okichi Tojin, presumed to be Harris's mistress. An extension to the temple contains a portrait and mementoes.

Hofukuji Temple

South of the station stands the Ryosenji Temple, where negotiations for the Japanese-American treaty were held. The temple houses a collection of historic documentation relating to the love-life of the Japanese.
    The Japanese-American treaty and the agreement with Russia were both signed in the adjacent Chorakuji Temple.

Ryosenji Temple

Well worth seeing is the underwater aquarium built into a cave, which boasts several hundred species of local marine fauna.
    Near Shirahama Beach, stretching away to the east, can be found the Shimoda Kaiko-Kinenkan memorial hall with mementoes of the Black Ships period.

Aquarium

Yumigahama Beach lies to the south-west of Shimoda (bus from station 20 mins). With its white sand and large numbers of pine-trees it is one of the most beautiful beaches on the island.

Yumigahama Beach

Shimogamo-onsen	Somewhat further south-west and also accessible by bus (from Shimoda Station 25 mins) is the resort of Shimogamo-onsen with its tropical garden.
★Cape Iro	The most southerly point on the Izu Peninsula is Cape Iro (coach from Shimoda 40 mins), from where there is a splendid view across to the Seven Izu Islands. Close by the cape is the Jungle Park (Jungle-koen; opposite the lighthouse) with over 3000 types of plants.

Central Izu

Mishima	The centre for this area is Mishima (pop. 99,000), which is also the location of the Mishima Taisha Shrine (bus from station 5 mins), the oldest shrine on Izu. The site, which is completely surrounded by woodland, has a treasure-house with documents from the time of Minamoto Yoritomo (1147–99, founder of the Kamakura Shogunats) as well as antique weapons. Ten minutes' walk to the south of the station is the Rakuju-en landscape garden, which was laid out during the Meiji Period on the site of the former residence of the daimio Mito Mitsukuni. The extensive grounds contain a pond which is fed by melt-water from the Fuji area, as well as a hall with folk art.
Nirayama	The Izu-Hakone railway line begins in Mishima. It leads southwards to the small resort of Nirayama (pop. 14,000), which has the remains of a Hojo castle and a well-preserved furnaceworks, which was built in 1853 for the manufacture of firearms and was run by Egawa Tarozaemon (also known as Tan'an), the provincial governor of Izu. 1.5km/1 mile east of the station stands Egawa-no-ie (family home of the Egawas), which was built 700 years ago. Further to the east is the large pleasure park Izu-Fujimi Land (bus from the station 20 mins; also coach from Mishima 50 mins), with tropical gardens, sports facilities, etc.
Shuzenji	The Izu-Hakone railway line ends at Shuzenji. 3km/2 miles south-west (bus service) is the resort of Shuzenji-onsen (pop. 18,000), which has been renowned since the 9th c. and is attractively situated in the valley of the River Katsura. After Atami and Ito it is the most popular resort on the island. The town has numerous thermal springs (37–74°C/99–165°F), while in the centre stands the Shuzenji Temple, which is thought to have been founded at the beginning of the Heian Period by Kobo-daishi. The Treasure Hall contains items from the house of Minamoto and an old No mask. The mask is connected with the Kabuki drama "Shuzenji-monogatari", which portrays the murder of Minamoto Yoriie (1182–1204), the son of Yoritomo, by Hojo Tokimasa (1138–1215). The temple was also the site of the murder of Minamoto Noriyori (1156–93) at the hands of his brother Yoritomo, founder of the Kamakura shogunate. Noriyori and Yoriie are both buried here; alongside the latter's grave on the opposite side of the river is the tiny Shigetsuden Temple.
★Daruma	To the west of the town rises the 982m/3222ft Mount Daruma (coach from Shuzenji Station to the foot of the mountain 30 mins; ascent 1 hr). From the summit there is a view of Fuji and Suruga Bay. A picturesque footpath runs parallel to the Nishi-Izu Skyline Drive.
Yugashima	From Shuzenji a road (with coach service) leads southwards into the Amagi Mountains. At the north-western foot of the mountains nestles the tiny town of Yugashima (pop. 9000; coach from Mishima Station 1¼ hrs) with several hot springs (45–58°C/113–136°F) and attractive scenery. 2.5km/ 1½ miles to the south are the 25m/82ft high Joren Waterfalls, which can be viewed from a cave situated behind the water curtain.

The Amagi Mountains, a group of extinct volcanoes, extend to the south-east of Yugashima. The road from the north reaches the Amagi Pass (800m/2625ft), where a road turns off to the east into the mountains. The highest peak is the 1407m/4616ft high Banzaburo; Banjiro reaches 1300m/4265ft, Hoko 1024m/3360ft. The thickly-wooded mountain-tops form a popular hunting area on accounts of their large stocks of game.

Amagi Mountains

A rewarding walk (about 6 hrs) takes one from Amagi-kogen Golf-jo (bus from Ito 1 hr) to Banjiro, then on over Banzaburo to the romantic mountain lake of Hacho-ike, close to the peaks, which is particularly lovely in autumn, and then on to the Amagi Pass.

Walks

West coast of the Izu Peninsula

The town of Numazu (pop. 210,000), in the north-west of the peninsula, is the starting-point for boat trips round the coast and also for coach trips around Izu and to the Fuji Lakes. 1.5km/1 mile south-west of the station is Sembon-Matsubara Beach ("beach of the thousand pines"). The trees are said to have been planted in the 16th c. by the priest Zoyo.

Numazu

Situated about 10km/6 miles south of Numazu on a small island in the Bay of Uchiura is the Awashima Marine Park (Awashima-kaiyo-koen; coach from Numazo 35 mins) with a large number of leisure facilities.

Awashima Marine Park

Nearby (on the same coach route) is the town of Mito. On the beach is the Mito Aquarium (Mito-tennen-suizokukan) with many pools, a dolphin show and a free-water area separated from the sea by nets.

Mito

Coastal landscape of Izu

Izu

Excursion

An excellent excursion can be made to Cape Ose (also by bus from Numazu 1½ hrs), which consists of a narrow tongue of land extending far out to sea. There is a splendid view of Mount Fuji. The Ose Shrine, dedicated to the god of seafarers, is also worth seeing. There is an attractive promenade running right round the cape.

Toi
Matsuzaki

The only spa town on the west coast is Toi (pop. 7000; boat service to Numazu 1½ hrs; rail to Shuzenji 1 hr) with its beautiful beach. From there it is worth making the coach trip south along the marvellous coastline to the town of Matsuzaki, which is famed for its beaches and mild climate.

Orchid Centre

4km/2½ miles to the south (bus 10 mins) is the Dogashima Orchid Centre (Dogashima-yoran-center) with 23 hothouses. The neighbouring coastline displays bizarre rock formations as well as caves formed by the action of the surf. In prehistoric times these caves are supposed to have been inhabited.

Cape Hagachi

From Matsuzaki there are connections by coach (twice daily; 40 mins) and boat (45 mins) to Cape Hagachi with its precipitous cliffs which are several hundred metres high. These cliffs are inhabited by wild monkeys (Hagachi-zaki Wild Monkey Park).

The Seven Izu Islands

The Seven Izu Islands (Izu-Shichito), which extend southwards into the Pacific Ocean, are a geological continuation of the chain of volcanoes which includes Fuji and Hakone. The group, which administratively belong to Tokyo, include (from north to south) Oshima, Toshima, Niijima, Kozushima, Miyakejima, Mikurajima and Hachijojima.

Oshima

The largest of the islands is Oshima (pop. 35,000), with an area of 90sq.km/35sq.miles, which is situated 117km/73 miles south-west of Tokyo and 25 miles/41km east of Shimoda. Ships from Tokyo dock at Okada on the north coast, from where there are bus services to the other parts of the island. The administrative and communications centre of the island is the harbour town of Motomachi, port of call for ships coming from Atami and Ito.

Mihara

Buses run from both towns to the active volcano of Mihara, which is the highest point on Oshima (following its violent eruption in 1986 it has increased from 758 to 762m/2487 to 2500ft in height . From the summit there is a fine view across to Fuji and the Seven Islands.

Oshima Park

Oshima Park with its zoo, camping site and leisure facilities can be reached in 15 minutes by bus from Okada. At the south end of the park is the Gyoja Cave with a stone sculpture, which represents the Buddhistic ascetic En-no-Ozunu (7th–8th c.).

Habuminato

In the south of the island lies Habuminato, the most important fishing harbour on the island, situated on a bay formed from a subsided crater.

Trips round the island take place daily. Departure points are Okada and Motomachi and the trip lasts about 6 hours.

Toshima

20km/12½ miles south-west of Oshima lies Toshima (boat service from Oshima three times a week). Maehama Beach on the north coast provides excellent bathing. The island, which is only 8km/5 miles in circumference, is famous for its beautiful camellia blooms (February/March).

Niijima

Niijima (boat service to Oshima three times a week) also possesses superb bathing beaches, particularly on the north and west coasts.

Kozushima (boat service to Oshima three times a week, in summer also direct from Tokyo) not only has beaches such as Tako-wan and Nagahama in the north and Sawajiri in the east, but also offers the opportunity for deep-sea fishing (apply at the office of the Boat Union at Maehama Quay).

Kozushima

Miyakejima (boat service to Oshima and also direct to Tokyo) is formed from lava, which means that its beaches are made of black sand. The best places for bathing are on the north coast, while the south offers good opportunities for angling.

Miyakejima

From Miyakejima it is possible to reach the island of Mikurajima, which has only 200 or so inhabitants. In the west there is a 100m/330ft high waterfall, while the south coast consists of steep cliffs.

Mikurajima

There is no public transport of any description on Mikurajima.

The island at the southern end of the chain is Hachijojima (pop. 11,000; boat service to Oshima and also direct to Tokyo, from where there are also flights). The island, at 70sq.km/27sq.miles, is the second largest in the archipelago and its highest point is the 854m/2802ft high Nishi (also called Hachio-Fuji), which, like the 701m/2300ft high Higashi (also called Mihara), is an extinct volcano.

Hachijojima

Bus trips start from the town of Hachijo.

★★Kamakura

 鎌倉

Japanese equivalent

The former capital of Japan, Kamakura, lies to the south-west of Tokyo on Sagami Bay. It is surrounded by wooded hills on three sides, while the Miura Peninsula extends out into the Pacific in a south-westerly direction.

Location
50km/30 miles south-west of Tokyo

Rail: from Tokyo (Main Station) JR Yokosuka Line via Yokohama (1 hr).

Access

Thanks to its many sights and monuments, Kamakura is a highly popular destination with tourists, while the mild climate and beaches attract visitors in summer from the Tokyo-Yokohama conurbation. Yet only 30 years ago Kamakura was still just a small resort; since then it has developed into a dormitory suburb of Tokyo and Yokohama and has become the home of large numbers of intellectuals.

★Townscape

There are 65 temples and 19 shrines in Kamakura, as well as large numbers of artistic treasures. The town is divided into two by the Wakami-ya-oji, a road running from the coast northwards.

The town's most renowned product is its lacquered wood-carving work "Kamakura-bori" (demonstrations of the production methods are given in the Kamakura-bori-Kaikan Hall).

Minamoto Yoritomo (1147–99) emerged as victor in the battle waged in 1185 at Dannoura between the Minamoto and the Taira. In 1192 he made the town of Kamakura the seat of his military government (Kamakura-bakufu) in order to escape the decadent court life of Kyoto. What is more, by doing this, he was able to strengthen his grip over the east of the country, which was already completely under his control. He founded an austere culture of chivalry and Kamakura was to remain the centre of this feudalism imposed on the military nobility up until 1333. After Yoritomo's death his sons Yoriie and Sanetomo assumed the shogunate but after their murder the Minamoto line died out. The Hojo clan seized power but their eventual

History

73

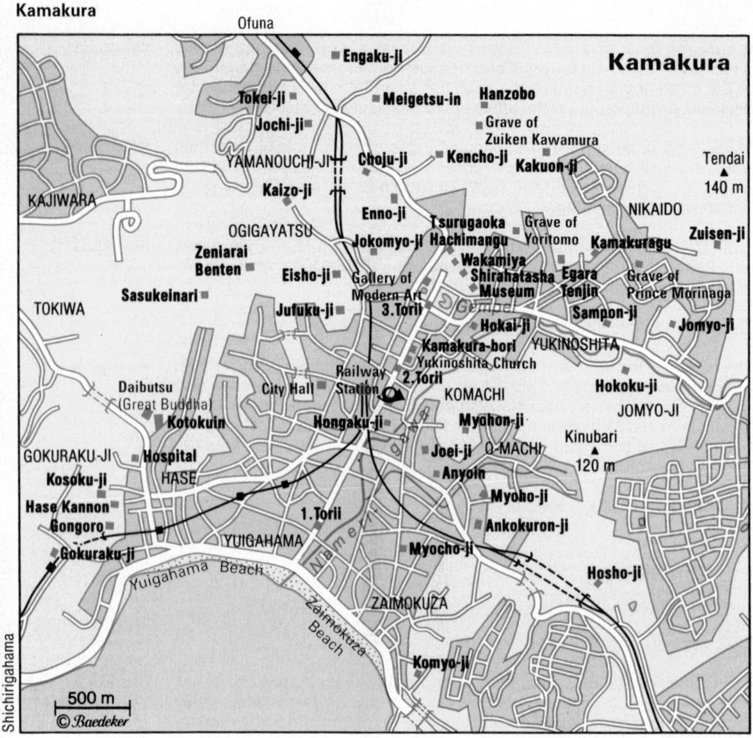

Map labels: Ofuna, Engaku-ji, Kamakura, Tokei-ji, Meigetsu-in, Hanzobo, Jochi-ji, Grave of Zuiken Kawamura, YAMANOUCHI-JI, Choju-ji, Kencho-ji, Kakuon-ji, Tendai 140 m, KAJIWARA, Kaizo-ji, NIKAIDO, Enno-ji, Tsurugaoka, Grave of Yoritomo, Kamakuragu, Zuisen-ji, OGIGAYATSU, Jokomyo-ji, Hachimangu, Zeniarai Benten, Eisho-ji, Wakamiya, Shirahatasha, Egara, Grave of Prince Morinaga, Gallery of Modern Art, Shirahatasha Museum, Tenjin, Sasukeinari, 3.Torii, Sampon-ji, TOKIWA, Jufuku-ji, Hokai-ji, Kamakura-bori, Jomyo-ji, Kamakura-bori, YUKINOSHITA, Daibutsu (Great Buddha), Railway Station, Yukinoshita Church, Gembei, City Hall, 2.Torii, KOMACHI, Hokoku-ji, Kotokuin, Hongaku-ji, Myohon-ji, JOMYO-JI, GOKURAKU-JI, Hospital, Joei-ji, O-MACHI, Kinubari 120 m, Kosoku-ji, HASE, Anyoin, Myoho-ji, Hase Kannon, 1.Torii, Gongoro, Myocho-ji, Ankokuron-ji, Gokuraku-ji, YUIGAHAMA, Namerigawa, Myocho-ji, Hosho-ji, Yuigahama Beach, Zaimokuza Beach, ZAIMOKUZA, Komyo-ji, 500 m, © Baedeker, Shichirigahama

downfall as rulers was accompanied by fierce fighting, in the course of which Kamakura was largely destroyed. During the ensuing Muromachi Period (1338–1573) Kamakura experienced a renaissance under the rule of the Ashikaga shogun as an administrative capital of the eastern province. However, with the transfer of the administration to Odawara, the town quickly returned to its former obscurity as a quiet fishing village.

Sights

Jufukuji Temple

The Jufukuji Temple of the Rinzai sect is only 500m/¼ mile north of Kamakura Station. It was founded in 1200 by Masako, the wife of Yoritomo, and once counted as one of the five large Zen temples situated on hills, the others being Kenchoji, Engakuji, Jochiji and Jomyoji. The only thing surviving from the original temple site is the reconstructed Main Hall with a wooden statue of Jizo, the patron god of children. On the hill behind the temple site are the graves of Masako and her son Minamoto Sanetomo (1192–1219).

Eishoji Temple

A short distance to the north stands the Eishoji Temple with a nunnery which belongs to the Jodo sect and was founded in 1636 by Eisho, the consort of Tokugawa Ieyasu.

The Great Buddha of Kamakura ▶

Kamakura

Zeniarai Benten Shrine

The Zeniarai Benten Shrine, which is dedicated to Benten, the goddess of good fortune, is situated some 20 minutes' walk to the west of Kamakura Station. If a sum of money is washed in the shrine's spring at the time of the snake (one of the oriental zodiac signs), it is, according to popular belief, supposed to double or treble itself. The torii leading to the consecrated cave are the donation of grateful believers.

★★Tsurugaoka Hachiman Shrine

North-east of the station stands the Tsurugaoka Hachiman Shrine (bus 3 mins). The road leading to the shrine, Wakamiya Oji, is divided up by three torii and becomes narrower as it goes north, thereby strengthening the impression created by perspective of great distance. Between the second and third torii the road is lined by cherry-trees and azaleas.

The Tsurugaoka Hachiman Shrine was founded in 1063 by Minamoto Yuriyoshi (998–1075), but was not moved to its present location by Yoritomo until 1191. It is dedicated to the war-god held in particular veneration during the Kamakura Period, Hachiman, who is linked with the legendary Ojintenno and was the tutelary god of the Minamoto. The present-day shrine buildings, built in 1828, embody the lavish style of the Momoyama Period (1573–1600). Within the shrine there are valuable artistic treasures, including weapons, swords and masks. To the left of the stone steps leading to the shrine stands a 22m/72ft high ginkgo tree with a trunk circumference of 7m/23ft. It marks the spot where Sanetomo, the third Kamakura shogun, was assassinated by his nephew Kugyo in 1219.

To the right of the steps is the secondary shrine of Wakamiya (1624), dedicated to Nintoku-tenno, the son of Ojin. A popular theme of Japanese literature is the dance which Shizuka, the lover of Minamoto Yoshitsune (1159–89), had to perform here for the edification of the latter's brother Yoritomo. She is supposed to have been forced to reveal the whereabouts of the fugitive Yoshitsune.

Close by this secondary shrine lies the Shirahatasha, the memorial for Yoritomo and Sanetomo. The name of the shrine means "white banner" and is derived from the banner of the Minamoto.

★Museum

To the right of the shrine is the Municipal Museum (Kamakura Kokuhokan). Built in 1928 in the style of the Shosoin of Nara, it contains artistic treasures from local temples and shrines, private collections from the Kamakura and Muromachi Periods and a large number of Ukiyo-e wood-carvings. Alongside stands the Museum of Modern Art, built in 1951 and extended in 1966.

Tomb of Yoritomo Kamakura Shrine

Just over 500m/¼ mile north-east of the shrine, a pagoda surrounded by a 1.60m/5¼ft high stone wall marks the burial-place of Yoritomo, the founder of the Kamakura-bakufu. Walking eastwards from here we reach the Kamakura Shrine (also buses from Kamakura Station 10 mins), which was erected in 1869 in the middle of a grove and dedicated to the Prince Morinaga (1308–35). The shrine's treasure-house is well worth seeing. Morinaga, the son of the Godaigo-tenno, was murdered in a nearby cave by the brother of the ruling shogun, because of his attempts to win back power for the Imperial House. His tomb is to be found on the hill of Richikozan, 200m/220yds to the east.

Kakuonji Temple

Just under 700m/½ mile to the north of the Kamakura Shrine lies the Kakuonji Temple of the Shingon sect (Sen-yuji School), which was built in 1218 under Hojo Yoshitoki.

In the Aisendo Hall are to be found a wooden statue of the seated Yakushi-nyorai, with two bosatsu at his side, and a statue of Jizo, the tutelary god of children.

The caves (yagura) in the hill behind the temple are thought to be ancient burial-grounds, as remains of human bones have been found there.

Zuisenji Temple

One kilometre/½ mile east of the Kamakura Shrine stands the Zuisenji Temple (Zen temple) of the Rinzai sect (Engakuji School), which is situated in green hills. Its garden, which was laid by Muso Kokushi (also Soseki,

1275–1351), is a famous example of landscape gardening from the closing years of the Kamakura Period, with its strong influence of Zen Buddhism. The temple itself is also the work of Muso Kokushi, but was renovated in the 14th c. The 1m/3ft high wooden statue of Muso Kokushi, kept in the founder's hall, is one of the most beautiful works of art of the Muromachi Period.

From the hill behind the temple there is a fine view of the town.

To the south of the Kamakura Shrine lies the Samponji Temple (also Sugimoto-dera; bus from Kamakura Station 7 mins), which is thought to have been founded in the 8th c. It houses three statues of the Eleven-headed Kannon (two of which are believed to date from the Heian Period). Having once been a departure point for pilgrimages to the 33 Kannon temples of the Kanto region, the temple is still known by the name "Sugimoto Kannon".

Samponji Temple

350m/400yds east of here (bus from Kamakura Station 8 mins) an avenue lined with cherry trees leads to the Jomyoji Temple, one of the five great Zen temples of Kamakura, which was founded in 1188 by Ashikaga Yoshikane (d. 1199).

Jomyoji Temple

Several temples of the Nichiren sect are to be found to the south-east of Kamakura Station. The Nichiren Shonin (1222–82), who came from Kominato on the Boso Peninsula, spent three years as a monk in Kyoto and then returned to his homeland to impart his teaching. As a result of being expelled from there because of his beliefs, he founded the Nichiren Hokke sect in 1253, set up the hermitage and within the space of just three years wrote his polemics. His criticism of governmental power and attacks against other sects led to his banishment to the Izu Peninsula (1261–63). On his return he took up the task of disseminating his teachings again. Narrowly escaping the penalty of execution, he was exiled to the island of Sado in 1271 where he wrote further works, including the "Kaimokusho" (1272). From 1274 until his death he lived in the secluded temple of Kuon-ji on the slopes of Mount Minobu (west of Fuji) and in the Hommonji Temple, founded by him, in Ikegami (now Tokyo).

Ten minutes' walk away is the Myohonji Temple, which was founded by Hiki Yoshimoto (later Priest Nichigaku), a Nichiren disciple.

Myohonji Temple

A short distance from here stands the Ankokuronji Temple, which was founded in 1274 on the site of the hermitage of Nichiren (also bus from station 5 mins). Among its most important treasures is an old copy of the polemical writing "Risshoankokuron", written by Nichiren and attacking other sects.

Ankokuronji Temple

Nearby to the north is the Myohoji Temple with the Hokke-do Hall.

Myohoji Temple

In the far south-eastern part of the town (bus from Kamakura Station 10 mins) lies the Komyoji Temple belonging to the Jodo sect. Founded in 1243, it contains a collection of valuable pictures and pictorial scrolls, while on the temple site there is a beautiful lotus-pool.

Komyoji Temple

The most famous monument in Kamakura, the Great Buddha (Daibutsu), stands in the south-west of the town (bus from Kamakura Station 10 mins). It belongs to the Kotokuin Temple of the Jodo sect.

★★ Great Buddha

The Great Buddha, a representation of the seated Amida made in bronze, is the second largest statue in Japan after the Daibutsu of Todai-ji in Nara (see entry). It is 11.40m/37ft high and weighs 93 tonnes. Considered the most beautiful and perfect Buddha statue in the country, it was cast in 1252 by either Ono Goroemon or Tanji Hisamoto. An enormous hall was built around the statue, but this was destroyed by a storm in 1369 and the ruins were then washed away by a tidal wave in 1495.

Kamakura

The second largest Buddha statue in Japan

The position of the Buddha's hands (mudra) expresses steadfastness of belief.

★Hase Kannon

The Hase Kannon Temple of the Jodo sect is a short distance to the south-west. In its main hall stands the statue of the Eleven-headed Kannon. The 9.3m/31ft high gilded wooden statue is believed to have been carved in 721 by the priest Tokudo out of one half of an old camphor tree, the other half being used for the Kannon statue at the Hase-dera in Nara (see entry). The third oldest bell in the town, cast in 1264, also belongs to the temple. From the temple there is a fine view of the beaches in the south of Kamakura.

Gokurakuji Temple

Further to the south-west lies the Gokurakoji Temple (Enoden private railway line from Kamakura Station). Apart from various temple treasures, such as the Shakyamuni statue, scarcely anything has been preserved of the shrine, which was founded in 1259 by Hojo Shigetoki (1198–1281).

Beaches

To the south, on the other side of the railway line, are the beaches of Yumigahama (east) and Shichirigahama (west), the latter with a splendid view of Enoshima. The 2km/1 mile long Yumigahama Beach, one of the finest around Tokyo, is the setting for the boisterous town carnival, held at the beginning of August.

★★Engakuji Temple

Kita Kamakura Station, just to the north of the city limits, is the starting-point for a visit to the Engakuji Temple, a short distance to the east. This temple, belonging to the Rinzai sect and centre of the Engakuji School, was founded in 1282 by Hojo Tokimune and run by a Chinese abbot. In spite of severe damage caused by the earthquake of 1923, the Hall of Relics (shari-den), which was built in 1285, remains the best example of the powerful architecture of the Kamakura Period. Here there is a precious quartz reliquary hall (only open from January 1st–3rd) with one of Buddha's teeth.

In the belltower to the right of the two-storey gateway there is a bell cast in 1301, which at 2.60m/8½ft high is the largest in the town. Behind the main building is the tomb of Tokumine. The tea-house (butsunichian) with its tea-room (ensoku-an) and adjoining garden is very pleasantly situated.

To the south of Kita Kamakura Station (5 mins' walk) is the Tokeiji Temple of the Rinzai sect (Engakuji School). According to a law passed by Hojo Sadatoki (1271–1311), women who had been maltreated by their husbands could be considered as divorced when they entered this nunnery. This led to the temple acquiring the name "enkiridera" (temple of divorce). The first abbess was the temple's foundress, Sadatoki's widow. The Main Hall contains a wooden statue of the Sho Kannon.

Tokeiji Temple

A footpath leads to the Jochiji Temple of the Rinzai sect, situated a short distance to the south in an old cypress wood. This temple, which was founded in 1283 by Hojo Morotoki, is another of the five great Zen temples of Kamakura. The wooden statue of Jizo, the tutelary god of children, which is the work of the sculptor Unkei, was the only one of the temple's treasures to survive the earthquake of 1923. Next to the temple gate is one of the town's "ten clear springs".

Jochiji Temple

South-east of Kita Kamakura Station, and surrounded by high cedar-trees, is the Kenchoji Temple (bus 4 mins; also connection with the Tsurugaoka Hachiman Shrine 6 mins). Hojo Tokiyori (1227–63) was the founder of the temple, which was built in 1253 for the Chinese priest Tai Chiao (Japanese: Daigaku-zenji). In 1415 the temple buildings burned down, but were restored in the 17th c. at the behest of the Tokugawas. The gate and main hall are examples of the Chinese style of the Sung Period. The temple treasures include the second oldest bell in Kamakura, cast in 1255, and the wooden statue of the temple's founder, a masterpiece of the Kamakura Period. The grave of Tai Chiao, who was active under the Hojos as a political adviser and spiritual leader, is situated on a slope behind the temple.

Kenchoji Temple

Kanda (City district)   F 4

神 田

Japanese equivalent

Kanda is famous as Tokyo's bookshop district. There are more than 100 secondhand bookshops in Yasukuni-dori Street between Surugadai and Kudanshita. This makes Kanda not only Japan's largest bookshop district but one of the largest in the whole world.

District
Chiyoda-ku

Underground
Jinbocho
(Toei Mita Line)

Here those who take delight in such things can purchase xylographs (in the Ohya-shobo shop, for instance), buy popular artistic books (in the Sancha-shobo shop, for example) or search for examples of calligraphy (in the Iijima-shoten shop, for example). Works on Japanese and Chinese history can also be discovered (in Isseido's shop and elsewhere).

Kanda Myojin Shrine   F 3

神 田 明 神

Japanese equivalent

On a knoll by the River Kanda stands the Shinto Kanda Myojin Shrine. Its origins are said to date from the 8th c. The present-day, gaily-coloured religious building was erected in 1934.

District
Chiyoda-ku

Railway station
Ochanomizu
(Chuo Line)

In this shrine Masakado Taira, a knight from the Kanto region, is venerated. In popular belief Taira is the tutelary god of townsmen.

The anniversary festival of Kanda Matsuri, which is celebrated every odd-numbered year on May 14th and 15th, is, along with that of Sanno Matsuri (see Hie Shrine), one of the most important Shinto religious festivals.

★ Koraku-en Park   E 3

Japanese
equivalent

後楽園

District
Bunkyo-ku

Underground
Koraku-en
(Marunouchi Line)

Railway station
Suidobashi
(Chuo Line)

Opening times
daily 9am–5pm

Koraku-en Park, one of the most beautiful parks in Tokyo, lies five minutes north of Suidobashi Railway Station and five minutes south of Koraku-en Underground Station. It covers an area of 7ha/18 acres. Koraku-en Park was laid out in 1626 by Tokugawa Yorifusa, ancestor of the Tokugawa branch in Mito, and subsequently improved by his son. It is the oldest garden in Tokyo. The lake was added later. It was created at the behest of Iemitsu, the third Tokugawa Shogun.

As well as the artistic displays of Japanese and Chinese plants, the little temple on the island in the lake also deserves to be seen. It is dedicated to Benten, the goddess of good fortune. Also of interest is the Kantokutei teahouse, which is a smaller reproduction of the original teahouse, which was destroyed in the 1923 earthquake.

In the eastern part of the park is the huge Koraku-en Games and Sports Centre, where there is skating, billiards, table-tennis, swimming and also the inevitable Pachinko and electronic games.

Foreign films in their original versions are shown at the cheap student cinemas.

★★ Kyoto

Japanese
equivalent

京都

Location
about 500km/300
miles south-west
of Tokyo

The city of Kyoto is surrounded by hills and lies in the central part of the Japanese main island of Honshu near the south-western end of the lake Biwa-ko. Situated in the southwards-facing basin between the rivers Katsura (west) and Kamo (east), the city covers an area of over 600sq.km/230sq.miles. It is the fifth biggest city in the country and one of its most important industrial centres. Kyoto is also capital of the prefecture of the same name and the main centre of learning in West Japan with several universities and colleges. Despite being one of the most important places to visit in Japan and regularly receiving over 10 million visitors each year, the city has retained much of its old atmosphere. This is because Kyoto – as the only city with over a million inhabitants – was left unscathed by the Second World War.

For close on 1100 years, from 794 to 1868, Kyoto was the Imperial residence and therefore the most important cultural centre in the country – a place where architecture, sculpture, painting and many other arts enjoyed their finest flowering. Quite early on Buddhism gained an influence over this artistic creativity, with the result that a large number of the works of art which have survived are to be found in the old temples. Even today Kyoto occupies a dominant position in Japan's religions; thirty of the city's

The Nijo Castle complex ▶

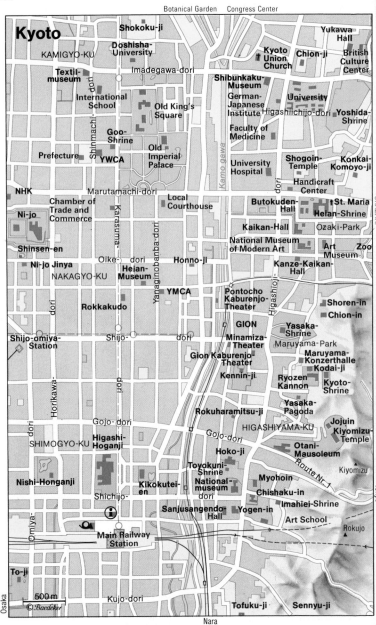

Kyoto

Kyoto

Botanical Garden   Congress Center

KAMIGYO-KU

Shokoku-ji

Doshisha-University

Imadegawa-dori

Textil-museum

International School

Old King's Square

Goo-Shrine

Prefecture

YWCA

Old Imperial Palace

NHK

Marutamachi-dori

Chamber of Trade and Commerce

Local Courthouse

Ni-jo

Shinsen-en

Ni-jo Jinya

Oike- dori

Honno-ji

NAKAGYO-KU

Heian-Museum

Rokkakudo

YMCA

Shijo-omiya-Station

Shijo-   dori

Shijo-omiya-Station

Kamo gawa

Yukawa Hall

Kyoto Union Church

Chion-ji

British Culture Center

Shibunkaku-Museum

German-Japanese Institute   Higashiichijo-dori

University

Yoshida-Shrine

Faculty of Medicine

University Hospital

Shogoin-Temple

Konkai-Komoyo-ji

Handicraft Center

Butokuden-Hall

St. Maria

Heian-Shrine

Kaikan-Hall

Ozaki-Park

National Museum of Modern Art

Art Museum

Zoo

Kanze-Kaikan-Hall

Pontocho Kaburenjo-Theater

Shoren-in

Chion-in

GION

Yasaka-Shrine

Minamiza-Theater

Maruyama-Park

Gion Kaburenjo Theater

Maruyama-Konzerthalle

Kodai-ji

Kennin-ji

Ryozen Kannon

Kyoto-Shrine

Yasaka-Pagoda

Rokuharamitsu-ji

HIGASHIYAMA-KU

Jojuin

Kiyomizu-Temple

Gojo- dori

Higashi-Hoganji

SHIMOGYO-KU

Gojo-dori

Hoko-ji

Otani-Mausoleum

Route Nr. 1

Kiyomizu

Nishi-Honganji

Kikokutei-en

Toyokuni-Shrine

National-museum   dori

Myohoin

Chishaku-in

Shichijo

Sanjusangendo-Hall

Yogen-in

Imahiei-Shrine

Art School

Rokujo

Main Railway Station

To-ji

Osaka

500 m

© Baedeker

Kujo-dori

Tofuku-ji

Sennyu-ji

Nara

Horikawa   dori

Karasuma-   dori

Shinmachi-   dori

Yanaginobamba-dori

Higashioji

Omiya-   dori

temples are centres for different Buddhistic sects, while furthermore there are some 200 Shinto shrines within the city's boundaries.

Kyoto is the junction of the JR Tokaido Shinkansen and main lines, the JR San-in and Nara lines. From Tokyo (main station) the journey is on the JR Tokaido Shinkansen Line (Hikari 3hrs, Kodama 4hrs).

Access

In 794, ten years after the removal of the seat of government from Nara to Nagaoka, Emperor Kammu had the new capital of his empire laid out on the site of a village to the north-east, Uda. The capital was first called Heiankyo ("capital of peace"), then Miyako ("imperial residence"), and finally, from the time of the Meiji reform, Kyoto ("capital").

History

Following the pattern of Chinese urban planning, the city was laid out on a right-angled checkboard-type groundplan and was surrounded by walls and a double ditch. The old city measured 5.2km/3¼ miles from north to south and 4.4km/2¾ miles from east to west. To the south of the Imperial palace Daidairi the 83m/272ft wide street Suzaku-oji formed the dividing line between the eastern half of the city (Saskyo) and the western half (Ukyo). Access to the city was afforded by 18 gates. It is believed that the city already had 400,000 inhabitants in the year that it was founded. On several occasions parts of the city have been destroyed by earthquake or fire. The imperial palace burned down in 960, 1177 and 1227 and was not rebuilt after the last conflagration.

Even as early as the beginning of the 9th c. the Imperial house was becoming increasingly involved in non-political affairs and allowing itself to be overshadowed by the Fujiwara family, which took control of all the key political positions. Later the Empire came increasingly under pressure from the militant monasteries in the surrounding areas. Unrest led to power being usurped by the Tairas, who in turn were annihilated by the Minamotos in the Battle of Dannoura (1185). Minamoto Yoritomo (1147–99), having been appointed Shogun by the Emperor, transferred the seat of government to Kamakura, and the Imperial house, deprived of its power, was reduced to the role of fostering art and culture, court life thereby reaching a zenith of refinement.

Emperor Godaigo (1288–1339), who had ascended the throne in 1318, set out to defend himself against the Kamakura shogunate. His military commander, Ashigaka Takauji, despite having been victorious against the shogunate, marched into Kyoto in 1336, drove out Godaigo and installed Komyo (d. 1380) as anti-emperor. In 1392 the southern dynasty, which Godaigo had established in exile in Yoshino, relinquished its claim to power, with the result that Kyoto remained unchallenged as the seat of government. In 1467 the dispute over Ashigaka's successor led to new hostilities and at the end of this Onin War (1477) Kyoto had been reduced to rubble and ashes. At the Imperial behest Oda Nobunaga moved into Kyoto in 1568 and set about the task of rebuilding the old Imperial palace and the city itself. After his death the work was continued by Toyotomi Hideyoshi. The peace which he secured for the Empire made a new cultural heyday possible and Kyoto became the focal point of the Japanese Renaissance. Nevertheless administrative power remained in the hands of the shoguns and the city's political importance faded when Tokugawa (1542–1616) moved the seat of government to Edo, present-day Tokyo. Parts of the city were again destroyed as a result of fires (1708 and 1788), while the earthquake of 1830 inflicted grievous damage.

The decision of the shogunate in Edo to open Japan to the outside world after centuries of isolation had the effect of strengthening the position of the Imperial house, which had opposed this measure. With the abolition of the shogunate in 1867 the Imperial house came back into power. However, as Emperor Meiji also moved his seat of government to Edo in 1869, the position of Kyoto did not change at all. However, by decree of the Emperor, it continued to be the coronation city of the Japanese rulers.

Description of the city

Shimogyo-ku

Kyoto Tower
Building

Only a short distance to the north of the Main Station in the district of Shimogyo-ku stands the nine-storey Kyoto Tower Building, which is, when including the Kyoto Tower erected on its roof, 131m/430ft high. The Tourist Information Center is on the ground floor and there is also a viewing platform.

Higashi-
Honganji Temple

Not far to the north (Karasuma Shichijo) lies the Higashi-Honganji Temple of the Jodo Shinshu sect, founded in 1602, which after repeatedly being destroyed was most recently rebuilt in 1859.

The foundation of the Jodo Shinshu sect in 1224 can be traced back to Shinran-shonin (also Keishin-daishi, 1173–1262). He had spent several years at the mountain monastery of Hiei, north-east of Kyoto, and then became a disciple of Ho-nen, the founder of the Jodo sect, who encouraged him to found the Jodo-shinshu sect. The central tenets of the new teaching were the belief in the salvation-bearing Amida Buddha and the rejection of celibacy. The increasing influence of these sects persuaded Tokugawa Ieyasu to divide up the Honganji Temple in 1602; he had the Otani School founded with its seat in the Higashi-Honganji Temple.

The only parts of the complex freely open to the public are the Founder's Hall and the Main Hall; to visit the other buildings, and also the abbatial residence (Shosei-en), it is necessary to apply at least one day in advance.

The two-storey gate, Daishi-do-mon, leads through to the Founder's Hall, Daishi-do, which is supported by massive wooden pillars and contains a statue of the Shinran supposedly carved by the founder of the sect himself. On either side there are portraits of abbots of the Otani School. To the south the hall is joined by a gallery to the Main Hall, Hondo, which contains an Amida statue by the hand of the artist Kaikei. Of interest is the smaller sealed-off north gate Chokushi-mon (gate for Imperial envoys), a copy of a gate from the Fushimi Palace of Toyotomi Hideyoshi. Besides Amida statues by Shotoku-taishi and Jocho and paintings by Eshin, the temple possesses the original version of the sect's teaching (Kyogyoshinsho) written by Shinran.

The abbatial residence Shosei-en (also Kikokutei), located to the east of the temple on the street Kawaramachi-dori, was originally part of Fushimi Palace. The 17th c. garden, laid out by Jozan and Kobori Enshu, is also impressive.

★★ Nishi-
Honganji Temple

To the west of the temple, on the Horikawa-dori (Nishi-Rokujo), stands the Nishi-Honganji Temple, the main temple of the original Jodo-shinshu sect and an outstanding example of Buddhist architecture. This temple is also only partially accessible to the public; it is necessary to apply to the temple office for a more extensive visit.

The Main Hall, Hondo, newly built in 1760, includes sumptuous rooms with gold-ground paintings of unknown masters of the Kano School and contains an Amida statue by a master of the Kasuga School. In the rooms lying off to the side there are statues of Shotoku-taishi (573–621) and the priest Ho-nen (1133–1212). The Founder's Hall, Daishi-do, built in 1636, houses one of the sect's most holy relics: a statue of Shinran in a seated position, assumed to be a self-portrait dating from 1244. After the death of Shinran the statue was given a coat of lacquer, into which his ashes were mixed. On both sides there are portraits of the abbots who came after him. Over the hall entrance there is an inscription in the Emperor Meiji's hand with the two characters "Ken-shin". In front of the Founder's Hall is the beautiful gateway of Seimon.

Of particular interest is the Treasure Hall of Daishoin, formerly belonging to Fushimi Palace in the extreme south of the city, but brought in 1632, together with the richly carved Kara-mon gate, to its present site. The individual rooms are named according to the wall and ceiling paintings with which they are decorated and which are predominantly of the Kano School. The Sparrow Room (Suzume-no-ma) was decorated by Maruyama Ozui and Kano Ryokei; the (severely damaged) paintings in the Wild Geese Room (Gan-no-ma) are the work of Kano Ryokei; in the Chrysanthemum Room (Kiku-no-ma) can be seen the flower pictures in gold and white by Kaiho Yusetsu (17th c.) and works by Kano Hidenobu and Kano Koi; the Stork Room (Ko-no-ma) is decorated by Kano Tanyu, Kano Ryokei and Maruyama Okyo and was used as an audience chamber by the abbot; the Shimei-no-ma (also Siro-shoin) likewise started life in Fushimi Palace and contains works by Kano Koi, Kaiho Yusetsu and Kano Ryotaku.

Close by stands the Kuro-Shoin Hall with sliding-doors painted by Kano Eitoku; in addition there is a Noh stage which was brought here from Fushimi Palace.

In a somewhat out-of-the-way position in the south-eastern corner of the temple area stands the Hiunkaku Pavilion (16th c,) with paintings by Kano Tanyu, Tokuriki Zensetsu, Kano Eitoku, Kano Sanraku and Kano Motonobu; it also includes the Hideyoshi's tearoom.

Minami-ku

To the south of Nishi-Honganji, on the far side of the railway line, in the district of Minami-ku, stands the Toji Temple (also Kyoo-gokokuji), which was founded in 796. In 823 the holy place was entrusted to the founder of the Shingon sect, Kobo-daihsi. After the destruction which took place during the civil wars of the 15th c. the temple was rebuilt. Its main hall, which was built in 1603 by Toyotomi Hideyori, is one of the greatest Buddhistic buildings to have survived from the Momoyama Period. The construction of the 56m/184ft high five-storey pagoda can be traced back to Tokugawa Iemitsu. Also of interest are the Founder's Hall (1380), the Rengemon Gate (1191) and the lecture-hall built in 1598. The temple museum, built in 1197 using the temperature-regulating techniques of Azekura-zukuri (see Nara), houses important works of art.

★Toji Temple

Higashiyama-ku

Going east from the main railway station we come to the district of Higashiyama-ku. The first place of interest on the other side of the River Kamo is Sanjusangen-do (also Rengyoin Temple; founded in 1164), whose buildings were rebuilt in 1266 after a fire. The name of the temple (Sanju-San = thirty-three) is derived from the 33 spaces or chambers lying between the supporting pillars. The temple's most important work of art is the wooden picture of the seated Thousand-handed Kannon, which is flanked by the statues of 28 disciples and another 1001 small Kannon statues. All these sculptures are the work of Unkei, Tankei and their pupils. In the rear gallery there are other sculptures from the Heian and Kamakura Periods.

★★Sanjusangen-do

Standing opposite to the north is the National Museum, built in 1897, which has three sections, devoted to history, art and handicrafts.

★National Museum

To the east, on the other side of the street Higa-Shioji-dori, can be found the Chishaku-in Temple, the main shrine of the Chizan School, which belongs to the Shingon sect. The temple, which was originally erected in the province of Kii (today the prefecture of Wakayama), was moved here in 1598 at the command of Tokugawa Ieyasu. In 1947 most of the old buildings were destroyed by a fire. The temple garden is the work of Sen-no Rikyu (1522–91).

Chisaku-in Temple

Sanjusangen-do

Veranda of the Kiyomizu Temple

The Myohoin Temple of the Tendai sect adjoins to the north. It was transferred here from Mount Hiei. In the Great Hall there are pictures by Kano
Eitoku (1543–90) and Kano Shoei (1519–92). The temple itself contains
more works of art belonging to Toyotomi Hideyoshi. Over 500 stone steps
lead to the Hokokubyo (tomb of Hideyoshi), with its five-storey pagoda and
the burial shrine, which was restored in 1897.

Myohoin Temple

Further away in the north-east rises the hill of Kiyomizu, on which the
Kiyomizu Temple stands (bus to the Gojo-zaka stop). The road leading up to
the temple, Kiyomizu-zaka, contains a large number of shops selling
ceramics. The shrine, dedicated to the Eleven-headed Kannon, was
founded in 798 and restored in 1633 by Tokugawa Iemitsu.

★★Kiyomizu
Temple

The temple area is entered by the two-storey Seimon Gate (west gate). Its
side niches contain guardian figures (Kongo-Rikishi). Nearby stand the
belltower and the three-storey pagoda. Further on, the Hall of Scriptures
(Kyodo) is reached, followed by the Founder's Hall (Tamurado) and then
the Asakura Hall (Asakurado), built by Asakura Sadagake (1473–1512).
Behind lies the Main Hall, Hondo, with a wooden veranda built over the
steep drop, which offers a fine view over Kyoto and the surrounding
uplands. The Japanese often call an act of mad daring a "jump from the
veranda of the Kiyomizu Temple". In front of the hall lie two iron sandals,
which are supposed to have belonged to the giant who was vanquished by
the dwarf Issun-boshi. Inside there is a statue of the Eleven-headed
Kannon.

In the eastern section of the temple area stand the halls of Shakado and
Amidado, and below these is the Otowa waterfall, where the deity Fudo-
Myo-o, who punishes the evil, is venerated.

On the western foot of the hill stands the 39m/128ft high five-storey Yasaka
pagoda (14th/15th c.; restored 1618). Close by to the north-east is the
Kodaiji Temple, built in 1606 by the widow of Toyotomi Hideyoshi. Its
founder's hall (Kaisando) is decorated inside with pictures of the Kano
School. In the nearby burial shrine (1606) there is fine lacquerwork
(Tata-makie) to be seen. The two small pavilions standing on a hill used to
belong to Fushimi Palace. The landscaped garden of Kobori Enshu is worth
seeing.

Yasaka Pagoda
Kodaiji Temple

★Gionmachi

A bus service operates between the main station and the Gionmachi Quarter, situated further to the north-east, where numerous entertainment
facilities are to be found (night-life very expensive). Worth mentioning are
the Minamiza Theatre, one of the oldest stages in Japan (built in the early
17th c.), and the Gion Corner (displays of traditional arts such as tea
ceremonies, puppet shows, music and dancing, flower arranging). In the
narrow streets and alleys there are a large number of restaurants.

In the south of Gionmachi stands the Kenninji Temple, founded in 1202 by
the priest Eisai. Only the Chokushi-mon Gate remains from the time of the
temple's foundation, the other buildings dating from 1763. The temple
owns picture scrolls by Kaiho Yusho (1533–1615).

Kenninji Temple

Further north-east (bus-stop Gion) is to be found the Yasaka Shrine (also
Gion Shrine), which is dedicated to the deities Susanoo-no-mikoto, his wife
Inadahime and their son. The buildings, which are copies of the original
architecture, were erected in 1854. The main shrine is covered with shin-
gles of cypress-wood; to the south there is a 9.5m/31ft high stone torii. The
shrine's artistic treasures include the wooden Koma-inu (lion-like animal
figures), which are attributed to the sculptor Unkei. The Gion-matsuri,
which is celebrated in July, is one of the largest festivals in the country.

Yasaka Shrine

Kyoto

Maruyama Park

The area to the east of the shrine site is occupied by Maruyama Park, which stretches out at the foot of Higashiyama Hill and looks especially delightful during the cherry-blossom season (evening illuminations).

Chion-in Temple

Following the road which separates the Yasaka Shrine from Maruyama Park northwards, we come to the Chion-in, one of the most extensive temple sites in the country. The temple was founded in 1234 by the priest Genchi as the centre of the Jodo sect. The Main Hall and priests' dwellings date from the 17th c. The 24m/79ft high main gate of Sammon is the largest temple gate in Japan. The Main Hall and the Assembly Hall are connected by a corridor, the floor of which is constructed in such a way that any footstep on it produces a squeaking sound. In this way it was impossible for anyone to draw near unobserved. Behind the Assembly Hall (also called "Hall of the Thousand Mats", even though it only has 360 mats) are the priests' living quarters, with screens decorated with works of the Kano School. The adjoining garden is believed to be the creation of Kobori Enshu, but was more likely laid out at a later date. South-east of the temple stands a belltower with what is reputed to be the largest bell in Japan (cast in 1633). It is struck on April 19th to commemorate the founder of the sect, and also at the New Year. The sutra library of Kyozo, which was built in 1616, contains sutras from the time of the Sung dynasty. The Kara-mon Gate, built in the same year, and the Honen tomb are also worth seeing.

Shoren-in Temple

Just to the north is the Shoren-in Temple (also called Awata Palace), where the abbots of the Enryakuji Temple (Mount Hiei) used to reside. The Main Hall (restored in 1895) contains screens with works by Kano Mitsunobu, Kano Motonobu and Sumiyoshi Gukei. The beautiful, well-tended landscape garden, which was created by Soami and Kobori Enshu, is also worth seeing.

Sakyo-ku

Heian Shrine

A short distance to the east of the Kumano-jinja-mae bus-stop in the district of Sakyo-ku is the Heian Shrine, which was built in 1895 to commemorate the eleven-hundredth anniversary of the foundation of the city. It is dedicated to the founder, Emperor Kammu, and also to the last emperor who resided here, Komei. The buildings are a copy, on a smaller scale, of the first Imperial palace of 794. Passing through the great entrance gate (of reinforced concrete) and the red Ote-mon gate, the visitor reaches the Great State Hall (Daigokuden), the east and west main halls (Honden) and the laterally-standing pagodas. At the back of the site there is a delightful landscaped garden.

The municipal museum of traditional handicrafts in the south of the shrine site is worth visiting on account of its demonstrations of old craft techniques.

Okazaki Park Museums

Just to the south-east of the Heian Shrine lies Okazaki Park, bounded by a water-channel linking Lake Biwa-ko with the River Kamo. The park, which covers an area of 8.7ha/21½ acres, contains the National Museum of Modern Art, the Municipal Art Museum, the city hall, a library and a zoo. In front of the library stands a memorial to the German Gottfried Wagner, who was active here round about 1878 in the art of ceramics and textile-dyeing techniques.

Nanzenji Temple

Not far to the east of Okazaki Park lies the Nanzenji Temple of the Rinzai sect, which was founded in 1293 and stands in the middle of a spruce grove. The present-day buildings are reconstructions from the time of Tokugawa Ieyasu. In the Main Gate (Sammon), which was built in 1628, there are

Heian Shrine

ceiling paintings of the Kano School. The Main Hall was rebuilt after a fire in 1895. The priest's quarters, Daihojo, which were formerly the hall of residence of the Imperial palace before passing into the ownership of the temple in 1611, also contain works of the Kano School. The famous picture "Tiger in the Bamboo Grove" by Kano Tanyu (1602–74) is to be found in the smaller Shohojo Room, which used to belong to Fushimi Palace. From the veranda there is a view of the famous Zen Garden (beginning of 17th c.). On the temple site there are twelve smaller shrines, including the Nanzen-in, for a short time the residence of the Emperor Kameyama (1249–1305), with a 14th c. garden. In the 17th c. the Garden of Konchi-in was created. Near the Tenjuan Temple are the graves of Daimei-kokushi, the founder of the Nanzenji, and Hosokawa Yusai.

A road continues northwards along the side of the hill to the Ginkakuji Temple (also called the Silver Pavilion or Jishoji; bus-stop Ginkakuji-mae).

★★Ginkakuji Temple

The complex was built in 1482, originally as a country seat for Ashikaga Yoshimasa, and after his death was turned into a temple; despite its nickname, however the temple was never actually given a coat of silver paint. The buildings frame a Zen garden of white sand which was laid out by Soami. In the two-storey pavilion stands a gilded Kannon statue (not accessible); in the Buddha Hall, Butsuden, there is a Buddha statue, while in the easterly Jogudo Hall a statue of Yoshimasa can be seen. The small tearoom in the north-eastern part of the hall is reputed to be the oldest in the country.

A short distance to the west of the temple is the Ginkaku-ji-michi bus-stop, from where it is possible to travel northwards on Line 5 to the Shugakuin-rikyu-michi Station. From here it is about 1km/½ mile to the former Imperial summer villa of Shugakuin-rikyu at the south-western foot of Mount Hiei.

Shugakuin-rikyu

Ginkaku-ji

Visits to the villa (guided tours) are only possible by prior application to the Imperial Household Office.

★★Garden

The villa and its garden, which is laid out on three levels, were commissioned by Emperor Go-Mizunoo, later to become the monk, Enjo, after his abdication in 1629. A suitable site having been found by him in 1655, the upper and lower garden sections were completed just four years later in 1659. The middle section of the garden with the villa belonging to the Emperor's daughter, Ake, was not added until later and, on her entry into a convent, became the Rinkyu-ji Temple. In 1855, as the Middle Garden, it was incorporated into the overall complex.

The visitors' entrance in the Lower Garden (Shimo-no-chaya) is a small gate on the north side, which in turn leads to a second gate, Chumon. To the left of the path there is a covered veranda, to the right the Emperor's house, which was built in 1659 and restored in the early 19th c. (not open to the public).

Passing through the east gate and along a path between rice-fields and an avenue of pines, the visitor reaches the Middle Garden (Naka-no-chaya) with the Rinkyuji Temple (water-garden and cascade). In the middle of the garden stands the villa with its reception hall, Kyaku-den, and a smaller building, Rakushi-ken (1668). In the reception hall there are paintings worth seeing, including the motive of the Gion festival and on wooden sliding-doors depictions of carp, covered by a net. It is said that the net was added to the painting in the 18th c. by Maruyama Okyo, because the painted fishes kept escaping back to the garden pool at night. The Upper Garden (Kami-no-chaya), the largest section of the estate, was created following the principle of "borrowed landscape" (Shakkei-zukuri), in which surrounding scenery is included in the overall composition. To the left of the entrance, behind a hedge and an earthwork which it conceals, stands the Rinun-tei Pavilion (restored in 1824), which by virtue of its raised position offers a fine view across the garden and its lake.

On an island below the Rinun-tei stands the Kyusui-tei summer-house, restored to its original plan in 1824.

About 1.5km/1 mile south of the villa stands the Shisendo Temple, originally the residence of the poet and soldier Ishikawa Jozan (1583–1672). It contains paintings by Kano Tanyu, including in the study (Shisen) the likenesses of 36 Chinese poets. In front of the Shisen is a sand-garden from the Edo Period. The temple site lies in quiet woodland.

Shisendo Temple

On the north-eastern edge of Kyoto lie the wide expanses of Takaragaike Park (Keifuku-Eizan railway line to Takaragaike Station). Takaragaike Lake lies in the northern section of the park. The International Conference Hall, which was built in 1966, is situated nearby.

Takaragaike Park

The eastern continuation of the Keifuku-Eizan railway line ends 5km/ 3 miles further on in Ohara (also bus from main station, 1 hr). This is the location of the Sanzen-in Temple, which belongs to the Tendai sect and was rebuilt in 860 by the priest Joun. The Main Hall Ojo-gokuraku-in ("Paradise of Rebirth") is the work of the priest Enshin (942–1017). The hall ceiling, which is shaped like the keel of a boat, is decorated by 25 Bodhisattva pictures. On the walls there are mandara pictures by Enshin, while the gilded Amida statue dates from 1148. Other buildings in the temple area were built in the early 17th c. from sections of the ceremonial hall of the Imperial palace Shishinden.

Ohara
Sanzen-in
Temple

Not far to the west of the Sanzen-in stands the convent of Jakko-in, where the mother of the child emperor Antoku lived, after her son had perished in the Battle of Dannoura in 1185.

Jakko-in

The western branch of the Keifuku-Eizan railway line goes to Mount Kurama (750m/2460ft; Kurama halt), situated to the north of Kyoto. Half-way up the mountain stands the Kurama Temple, founded by the priest Kantei in 770 (restored in 1872; main hall destroyed in 1945). The temple possesses a painting by Kano Motonobu.

Kurama

Nakagyo-ku

From Kyoto Main Station there is a bus (line 9 or 52) to the district of Nakagyo-ku. Directly to the west of the Nijojo-mae stop lies the castle of Nijo-jo, which has been in municipal ownership since 1939.

★★Nijo-jo

The castle was erected in 1603 by Tokugawa Ieyasu. At the beginning of the Meiji era it was for a short time the seat of government, and it was here that the Emperor passed the edict to abolish the shogunate. From 1871 to 1884 the prefectural administration was housed here and it was at this time that severe damage occurred to large numbers of works of art.

The castle is surrounded by ditches and stone walls with corner towers. The inner area is reached through the east gate Higashi Otemon and the Karamon gate. The latter has elaborate carvings by Hidari Jingoro, as well as beautiful metalwork. It was originally part of Fushimi Palace. On the other side of the Inner Gate Mikuruma-yose, which also possesses works by Hidari Jingoro, stands Ninomaru Palace. It consists of five buildings placed opposite one another, with corridors linking them. The inner rooms were decorated with paintings by Kano Tanyu and his pupils. The main room is the Jodan-no-ma (the Imperial messenger's room), while in the adjoining apartments, Ni-no-ma and Tozamurai-no-ma, there are pictures of tigers. The connecting passages (like those at Chion-in) have floors which produce a noise whenever anyone steps on them and thereby give forewarning of any imminent visitor.

Passing through the second part of the building, with its three rooms, we come to the third complex, the great Audience Hall, which has a gallery running all the way round it. On the sliding-doors there are large pictures of spruces on gold ground, while in the side-rooms there are elaborate carvings by Hidari Jingoro. In the fourth group of buildings Kuro-shoin there are depictions of animals by Kano Naonobu and in the adjoining private apartments of the shogun there are pictures of mountain landscapes.

The garden to the west of the palace buildings was originally conceived without trees, the creators wishing to spare the observer any sight of foliage, which was considered a reminder of the transitoriness of existence. The plants which can be seen today were put in only recently.

Kamigyo-ku

Imperial Park

About 1km/½ mile north-east of the castle, in the district of Kamigyo-ku lies the 84ha/208 acre large Imperial Park (also bus from main station, lines 36, 204 or 206B), which is surrounded by the roads Karasuma-dori (west), Marutamachi-dori (south), Teramachi-dori (east) and Imadegawa-dori (north). The Old Imperial Palace (Kyoto-gosho) stands in the middle of the park.

Visits are allowed by prior application to the office of the Imperial Household Office in the north-west part of the park.

When Kyoto was founded, Emperor Kammu had Daidairi Palace built in the north-west part of the town. Having suffered fire damage on numerous occasions, the palace was rebuilt on its present site in the late 18th c. to designs which were absolutely faithful to the original. However even this building burned down and had to be rebuilt yet again in 1855, the designs once again being as close to the original as possible.

The rectangular inner area, which is surrounded by an earthwork (Tsuiji-bei), is accessible to visitors via the west gate, Seisho-mon. The south gate, Kenrei-mon, was reserved for the Emperor, the east gate, Kenshu-mon, for the Empress and Empress's mother, the southern west gate, Gishu-mon, for the princes, and the north gate, Sakuhei-mon, for the wives of the Imperial family and the ladies of the court. There are a total of 18 buildings in the palace complex and these are connected by a system of galleries. Between the various buildings there are charming gardens. Turning to the right after passing through the west gate one comes after about 200m/220yds to the Shodaibu-no-ma building with its three waiting-rooms for noblemen. To the east stands the great hall of ceremonies Shishin-don (also called Shishii-den), where enthronements and new year festivities were held. The central point of the 22×33m/72×108ft inner hall is occupied by the throne, Taka-mi-kura. Above it there is an octagonal baldachin embellished by a phoenix figure; the Imperial insignia are kept to one side. To the right is the smaller throne, Michodai, belonging to the Empress. The walls of the hall display pictures of Chinese sages, which were the work of Kano Sukenobu using 9th c. models.

Outside the south façade of the hall, in the inner courtyard, stand an orange-tree (Ukon-no-tachibana) and a cherry tree (Sakon-no-sakura), whose names refer to bowmen and cavalrymen's lodgings, which once stood on this site.

In the north-western section of the group of buildings is to be found the former residential quarter, Seiryo-den, later a ceremonial hall. As ritual dictated, the floor in one corner of the room consisted of closely-stamped earth for the Emperor to stand on when he was worshipping his ancestors. The throne, Michodai, is flanked by two animal figures (Koma-inu), while the wall-screens have pictures and calligraphy of the Tosa School.

The north-east section is occupied by the small palace, Kogosho (restored in 1958), with three apartments and the hall of studies, Gogaku-monjo (outer frontage in the Shinden-zukuri style). The palace buildings situated further to the north are not generally open to the public.

East of here is the water-garden, Oike-niwa, which was not incorporated into the palace complex until the 17th c.

To the south of the enclosed palace area, the park contains additional old palace buildings (to visit apply to the Imperial Household Office). Particularly charming are the gardens of Sento-gosho and Omiya-gosho, which were the residence of the ex-Emperor from 1629 to 1854. There is only very slight visible evidence of the actual residences. The gardens, which include ponds and the tea-pavilions of Seikatei and Yushintei, were the creation of Kobori Enshu (17th c.).

To the north of the park area, on the other side of the road Imadegawa-dori, lies the Doshisha University and behind it the Shokokuji Temple of the Rinzai sect.

Shokokuji Temple

Sakyo-ku

North-east of here, in the district of Sakyo-ku, lies the Shimogamo Shrine (also bus from main station, lines 4 or 214A). The majority of the buildings date from 1628, the Main Hall from 1863. The shrine is famous for its temple festival, Aoi-matsuri (mid-May).

Shimogamo Shrine

Further to the north-west on bus route 4, can be found the botanical garden, which was laid in 1923 to commemorate the accession to the throne of Emperor Taisho. South of here is the University of the Prefecture of Kyoto.

Botanical Garden

Nishijin

If we continue westwards from Doshisha University along the road Imadegawa-dori, we reach the weavers' district of Nishijin with its tiny old wooden houses where to this day the traditional crafts are still practised. There is an exhibition of textiles (with shop and kimono-show) in the Nishijin Textile Museum. In the immediate vicinity of the museum is the Horikawa-Imadegawa bus-stop, from where bus route 9 continues northwards.

Textile museum

Kita-ku

Not far to the west of the next bus-stop Kitaoji-Horikawa, in the district of Kita-ku, stands the Daitokuji Temple, one of the main shrines of the Rinzai sect.

★★Daitokuji Temple

The temple was founded in 1324, but was destroyed during the civil wars of the 15th c. The present building dates from the 16th and 17th c. There are 22 buildings in all, of which seven are open to the public. Of special interest are the Zen Gardens in the Karesan-sui style.

The main entrance to the temple site was formerly the Chokushi-mon gate (now closed), originally the south gate of the Imperial palace and transferred here in 1640. Next comes the Kara-mon gate, designed in the Chinese style with splendid carvings. It previously belonged to Fushimi Palace and remains an outstanding work of the Momoyama Period. The two-storey main gate of Sammon was built in 1589 by Sen-no-Rikyu. The ceiling paintings in the lower storey were carried out by Hasegawa Tohaku. On the upper floor there are statues of Shakyamuni, the sixteen rakan (disciples of Buddha), plundered by Kato Kiyomasa on his Korean campaign, and a picture of Rikyu (thought to be a self-portrait).

The Main Hall, Butsuden (also Daiyu-den), built in 1664, contains a Shakyamuni sculpture with the pupils Anan and Kayo, as well as a statue of Daito-kokushi, the first abbot of the temple. Behind the Main Hall stands the lecture-hall, Hatto (1636), based on a Chinese model, while to the north-east is the abbatial residence, Hojo. This contains paintings by Kano Tanyu and a wooden panel inscribed by Emperor Godaigo with the words "incomparable temple of Zen". The adjoining garden was created by Kobori Enshu.

The old abbatial residence of Shinju-an (restored in 1638), and once the residence of Ikkyu (1394–1481), is only accessible by prior arrangement. Inside there is a statue of Ikkyu and fragments written in his hand. The wall pictures are the work of Soga Dasoku (d. 1483). Here can also be found the graves of the Sarugaku dancer Kan'ami (1333–84) and his son Zeami (1363–1443), who as master of the No Theatre achieved the highest regard.

To the west of Shinju-an stands Daisen-in, the garden of which is thought to have been created in 1513 to a design by its founder Kogaku Soko (1465–1548) and ranks as an outstanding example of a Zen garden. The overall concept can trace its models to Chinese water-colour painting. The garden is divided into four areas. By the most sparing use of plants, and the employment mainly of sand and stone, a mountain-style landscape, complete with waterfall, has been created and the artistry of its layout conveys the impression of vast depths. The sliding-doors in the interior of the building have paintings by Kano Motonobu, Soami and Kano Yukinobu, the scenes from rustic life, Shikiko-saku-zu, being particularly interesting.

In Shuko-in, to the west of the abbatial residence, lies the grave of Senno-Rikyu, and to the west of it, in Soken-in, the tombs of Oda Nobunaga, his sons and the widow of Hideyoshi.

The most westerly part of the site is occupied by Koho-an, a famous Zen garden laid by Kobori Enshu, in which are to be found the graves of Enshu and his family.

Kamikamo Shrine

About 2km/1 mile north of the Daitokuji site (bus route 9 to the Kamika-mo-jinja-mae stop) lies the Kamikamo Shrine, which dates back to the period when the city of Kyoto was founded and where in May traditional horse-races and the Aoi-matsuri take place.

Tofukuji Temple

From the main railway station the JR Nara line goes southwards. Close to Tofukuji Station stands Tofukuji Temple, founded in 1236 and belonging to the Rinzai sect. The Sammon gate, erected in the 13th c., contains sculptures which have been attributed to the sculptor Jocho (d. 1057). The ceiling paintings are thought to be the work of Mincho (1352–1431) and his pupil Kandensu. In the expansive gardens stand the Founder's Hall (with a picture of the temple's founder) and the Main Hall, which was burnt down in 1882 and rebuilt in 1932. The artistic treasures of the temple include a 12×8m/39×26ft picture scroll by Mincho, which depicts the entry of Buddha into Nirwana (only open to the public on March 15th).

Fushimi-ku

Further south the JR Nara line reaches the district of Fushimi-ku, where Fushimi Palace belonging to Toyotomi Hideyoshi existed until the late 16th c. During the years of Tokugawa rule it was dismantled and the building material used for the construction of the many temples in Kyoto, with the result that no trace of the former palace is to be found here.

★★Fushimi-Inari Shrine

Immediately to the east of Inari Station, which is on the JR Nara line, stands the Fushimi-Inari Shrine, founded in 711 and one of the most important in Japan. It is dedicated to the goddess of rice cultivation, Ukanomita-ma-no-mikoto. The main building (1499) displays the building style typical of the Momoyama Period. Of note is the 4km/2½ mile long avenue of red torii, which were erected by believers. On the site there are numerous sculptures of foxes, the fox being the messenger of the gods.

From Momoyama Station Momoyama Hill, with its large numbers of peach-trees, can be easily reached. This is the site of the former Fushimi Palace.

The mausoleum of Emperor Meiji and his consort, Shoken, is reached by 230 steps. The monument is surrounded by three walls and was built out of blocks of granite which had been hewn on the island of Shodo. The way to the Nogi Shrine is a right turning off the path leading to the mausoleum. This shrine is dedicated to General Nogi Maresuke, who had his head-quarters here during the Russian-Japanese War of 1904/1905. Loyally devoted to the Emperor, the General was a national hero on account of his military service. At the age of 64 and in the company of his wife, he committed suicide in the year of Emperor Meiji's death.

The places of interest in the western and north-western edges of the city can be reached from the centre of Kyoto by two private railway lines.

The departure point for the south-westward running Hankyu private line is Hankyu-Omiya Station (bus routes 26, 28 or 38 link it with the main railway station).

Not far to the east of Nishi-Kyogoku Station is the Yuzen Hall of Culture, where the cloth printing techniques of Yuzen Zome are demonstrated.

Nishikyo-ku

The next station, Katsura, in the district of Nishikyo-ku, is the best starting-point for a visit to the Imperial villa, Katsura-rikyu, situated on the west bank of the River Katsura. In order to visit the villa it is necessary to apply to the Imperial Household Office.

The villa was originally built for Prince Hachijo Toshihito (1579–1629), the brother of Emperor Goyozei. Large sections of the buildings were completed by 1624, the rest being completed in 1658. The design of the landscape garden is purported to be the work of Kobori Enshu, but can only really be credited with any degree of certainty to his circle of followers. It is also assumed that Prince Toshihito, a great connoisseur of the arts, must have taken part in the planning stages himself. Reports also have it that Kobori made three conditions when he took on the commission: firstly, that no limits should be put on the costs of the project; secondly, that no deadline should be stipulated for its completion; thirdly, that during work on the garden none of his clients should visit the site. It would thereby be impossible to impose any alterations to the plans at a later date.

The whole garden is conceived in such a way that, wherever the observer stands, he is presented with only a front view. Tiny gardens are arranged around the lake; in the distance the hilltops of Arashiyama and Kameyama are visible. The three sections of the building, which are located opposite one another, are in the Shoin-zukuri style of architecture and have had an influence on modern trends in building, both in Japan and even abroad.

The visitors' entrance is the Miyuki-mon gate (1658). The garden paths, partly made out of river pebbles, partly out of square housebuilding bricks, are lined with moss and undergrowth. Two more gates take the visitor through to the interior of the garden, in the centre of which the Goten group of buildings stands. This comprises three sections: Furu-shoin, Naka-shoin and Miyuki-den. The veranda of Furu-shoin was especially designed for looking at the moon.

The three rooms of Naka-shoin contain valuable paintings by Kano Tanyu (first room, including the widely-known picture of a crow), Kano Naonobu (second room) and Kano Yasunobu (third room).

The hall for Imperial visits, Miyuki-den, also contains a picture by Kano Tanyu. The ornamental fittings (Kugi-kakushi) used to cover the nail-heads in the construction are also worth seeing. They have floral shapes and are thought to be the work of the goldsmith Kacho.

To the east of the main group of buildings, on a rise, stands the simply conceived Gepparo, while on the other side of the pond is the Shokin-tei, comprising several rooms and with a tearoom which is skilfully designed so that the light penetrates right into its furthest corners. A pebble-covered tongue of land protrudes into the pond and is to a large extent a stylised copy of the coastal scenery of Ama-no-hashidate. In the south-west of the garden is the Shoiken building containing ten rooms.

Saihoji Temple
★★ Garden

From Katsura Station the Arashiyama stretch of the Hankyu railway line goes off northwards. Close to Kamikatsura Station lies the Saihoji Temple of the Rinzai sect, thought to have been founded in the 12th c. and restored in 1339 by the priest Muso-kokushi, who at the same time was an important landscape gardener. In the lower part of the Zen garden which surrounds the temple there is a lake full of little bays as well as a teahouse thought to date from the Momoyama Period. The garden is particularly famous for its forty or so different types of moss, which have led to the temple acquiring the nickname "Kokedera" (temple of moss). Owing to the escalating number of visitors wishing to see the garden, it was decided to set a limit of 200 people per day. As a result it is essential to apply to visit in writing (at least 3 months in advance).

Matsunoo Shrine

From the next station of Matsuno-jinja-mae it is only a few minutes' walk westwards to the Matsunoo Shrine, which is famous for its rice-planting ceremony (Otaue-matsuri).

Horinji Temple

Near the terminus station of Arashiyama is situated the Horinji Temple, thought to have been founded in 713 and well known for the festival of Jusan-mairi, which takes place in April.

Katsura

From Arashiyama Station a bridge leads across the River Katsura, also known hereabouts as Hozu or Oi. The riverside scenery here is especially attractive (also direct access from Shijo-Omiya Station, close to the previously mentioned Hankyu-Omiya Station, on the Arashiyama section of the Keifuku private line). Above the river rises Arashiyama Hill, covered in cherry-trees and dense maple copses and famous for its cherry blossom and autumn colours. The ex-Emperor Kameyama (1248–1304) had cherry-trees brought from Yoshino and planted here.

Daihikaku
Temple

Leaving Arashiyama Station we pass over Togetsukyo Bridge and climb up the hill to a small pool and then on a side path to the Daihikaku Temple. This has a picture of the Thousand-handed Kannon and a wooden statue of Suminokura Ryoi (1554–1614), who succeeded in making long stretches of the river navigable.

Arashiyama Park

Arashiyama Park (also known as Kameyama Park) extends along the river, while further downstream is the landing stage for boats conveying those wishing to accompany and observe the cormorant-fishing boats (early July to mid-August).

Tenryuji Temple

To the north near the bridge over the Katsura stands the Tenryuji Temple, founded in 1339 by Ashikaga Takauji, the first Ashikaga Shogun, in memory of Emperor Godaigo. The temple is the chief seat of the Tenryuji School, which belongs to the Rinzai sect. Muso-Kokushi, the first abbot of the temple, created the garden, which is situated behind the priests' quarters. The present temple buildings date from around 1900.

★ Seiryoji
Temple

A bus route runs further north to the Seiryoji Temple (also called Shaka-do). In the main hall of the temple stands the highly remarkable Shakyamani statue, which is 1.6m/5¼ft high and made from sandalwood. It is reputed to have been carved in 987 by the Indian master Bishu Katsuma and brought

The famous moss-garden of Saihoji

by the priest Chonen from China to Japan. The statue can only be viewed on April 8th (Buddha's birthday) and April 19th (cleansing ceremony).

A short distance to the north of Seiryoji is the Daikakuji Temple, formerly residence of Emperor Saga and in 876 turned into a temple. The Main Hall contains statues created by Kobo-daishi (Godai-Myo-o), while the entrance-hall, Kyaku-den, was originally the throne room. The temple's paintings are the work of Kano Motonobu, Kano Tanyu, Kano Sanraku and Watanabe Shiko.

★★Daikakuji
Temple

At the terminus station of Arashiyama transfer to the Keifuku private line and travel to Katabiranotsuji Station, a short way to the east. Nearby stands the Koryuji Temple (also called Uzumasa-dera) (or travel on the Keifuku railway line from the city centre to Uzumasa Station).

★★Koryuji
Temple

The temple was founded in 622 by Hata Kawakatsu, but the present buildings are of a later date. The lecture-hall, built in 1165, is the second oldest building in Kyoto. It contains three old statues – the centrepiece being a statue of the seated Buddha; next to it a Thousand-handed Kannon and a Fukukenjaku Kannon. In the rear hall of Taishi-do (1720) there is a wooden statue of Shotoku-taishi (thought to be a self-portrait; 606).

In the north-western part of the temple area stands the octagonal hall of Keigu-in (also Hakkaku-do: 1251) with a statue of the 16-year-old Shotoku-taishi and statues of the Nyoirin Kannon (gift of a Korean ruler) and the Amida. Other sculptures of interest are in the temple museum Reiho-kan, including some in wood by Yakushi-nyorai (864) and Miroku-bosatsu (oldest preserved sculpture in Kyoto, 6th/7th c.; possibly by Shotoku).

Kyoto

Film Studio

About 5 minutes from Uzumasa Station lies the 28,000sq.m/7 acre large site of the Toei Uzumasa Film Studios with a hall of cinematography and production rooms. There is the opportunity of seeing films being shot.

Myoshinji Temple

From Katabiranotsuji Station the Kitano branch-line of the Keifuku private railway leads northwards to Omuro Station. A short walk to the south will bring the visitor to the Myoshinji Temple, the main shrine of the Myoshinji School, which belongs to the Rinzai sect. The shrine has many temples subordinate to it.

The temple was built in 1337 on the site of the former residence of Emperor Hanazono. To the west of the Buddha hall there is a belltower with a bell cast in 698. In the Buddha hall, Butsuden, there is a Shakyamuni statue. The ceiling paintings in the lecture hall, Hatto, were executed by Kano Tanyu. To the east, in the Gyokuho-in hall, there is a picture of Hanazono. To the west of the priests' quarters stand some smaller temple buildings, of which Reiun-in (also called the Motonobu Temple) merits examination on account of its many paintings by Kano Motonobu. The Tenkuyan Temple contains works by Kano Sanraku, while in the Kaifuku-in there are screen pictures by Kano Tanyu in the form of caricatures.

★Ninnaji Temple

To the north of Omuro Station stands the Ninnaji Temple, originally famous as Omuro Palace and begun in 886. After his abdication Emperor Uda (9th c.) was the first abbot of the shrine. The buildings which are visible today date from the first half of the 17th c. To the right of the Central Gate there is a 33m/108ft high five-storey pagoda. In the main hall stands a wooden Amida statue. The temple site is particularly attractive in April when the many cherry-trees are in blossom.

Ryoanji Temple ★★Garden

Not far to the north of the Ninnaji Temple stands the Ryoanji Temple, famous for its garden. The Zen garden (dry-climate garden), to a large extent a stylised creation of blocks of rock and raked white sand, was the work of an anonymous artist. The grave of the founder of the temple, Hosokawa Katsumoto, is to be found on the site.

Toji-in Temple

South-east from here, near Toji-in Station (Keifuku private railway) stands the Toji-in Temple, which was founded in 1341 by Takauji, the first Ashikaga shogun. The buildings were restored most recently in 1818. In the Main Hall are the statues of all the Ashikaga shoguns (with the exception of the fifth and tenth) and water-colour paintings by Kano Sanraku (1559–1635). The landscape garden which surrounds the temple is also delightful.

★Kitano Shrine

The Keifuku railway line (Kitano section) ends at Kitano-Habukai-cho Station. To the north-east, in the district of Kamigyo-ku, the Kitano Shrine (also Kitano-Tenjin) is worth a visit. Its present buildings were constructed in 1607 by Toyotomi Hideyori.

The shrine is dedicated to Sugawara Michizane and was founded in 947. Michizane, appointed chancellor in 899, was banished to Dazaifu in 901 as a result of a calumny. He died there two years later. When, after his death, a spate of catastrophes occurred in Kyoto, he was posthumously rehabilitated in 933. In order to assuage the spirit of the dead man, he was worshipped as the god of learning, Tenjin.

The most important buildings at the shrine are, in addition to three gates, the Main Hall, Honden, and the hall of worship, Haiden. The artistic treasures include a picture scroll relating the history of the shrine by Tosa Yukimitsu, dating from the 14th c., three other picture scrolls on the same theme by Tosa Mitsuoi (17th c.). The shrine is surrounded by numerous plum-trees, these being the favourite trees of Michizane.

★★Kinkakuji Temple

From Kitano-Hakubaicho Station a bus (route 204 or 214B) goes to the Kinkakuji Temple (Kinkakuji-mae stop). The temple, also known as the "Golden Pavilion", lies at the bottom of the 200m/650ft high Kinugasa Hill. One of the most beautiful buildings of the Muromachi Period (14th–16th c.),

The Golden Pavilion

the pavilion unites three different styles of architecture. Its gilded façades are reflected in a small lake. The ground floor (Hosui-in) displays the Heian Period architectural style of Shinden-zukuri, the first floor the sober Buke-zukuri of the Kamakura Period and the second floor the Chinese Kara-yo temple style of the Muromachi Period. Originally a villa belonging to the nobleman Saionji Kintsune; later it came into the possession of Ashikaga Yoshimitsu (1358–1408), after he had withdrawn from active political life. On his orders the Golden Pavilion and the garden were established in 1394. After Yoshimitsu's death the pavilion was turned into a temple by his son Yoshimochi. The building was destroyed by fire on several occasions, most recently in 1950 as a result of arson. The present building was erected in 1955 and is a faithful reconstruction of the original.

On passing through the entrance gate, Chuo-mon, the visitor enters the temple garden with its lake. On the shore stands the pavilion, crowned by a bronze phoenix. To the right of the path is the Main Hall with statues of the deities Benten, Kannon and Taishakuten, and of Ashikaga Yoshimitsu and the priest Muso-kokushi. In the courtyard there is a 500-year-old pine tree.

On a hill behind the pavilion stands the tiny teahouse, Sekka-tei, dating from the time of Emperor Go-Mizunoo (restored in 1874). In front of it there is a stone pool with a lantern from the shogun's Muromachi Palace. Close to the rear gate is a small temple with pictures of Fudo-myoo and his companions.

It is best to take a taxi to reach the Koetsuji Temple, further to the north, which is particularly popular with visitors when the trees have their autumn colours. The grave of the artist Hon'ami Koetsu (1558–1637) is to be found here, as well as several teahouses, including the Daikyo-an, built by Koetsu.

Koetsuji Temple

Marunouchi (City district)　　　　　　　　　　　　　　　　　E/F 4/5

Japanese
equivalent

丸の内

District
Chiyoda-ku

Underground
Nijubashi-mae
(Chiyoda Line)

Marunouchi is the commercial centre of Tokyo. This is where almost all the large banks and firms have their main offices – in Western-style high-rise blocks which have replaced the old Samurai houses. Tokyo's Main Railway Station is also here, built in 1914 in red brick (east side) after the model of the main station in Amsterdam. An extension was built in 1964 to accommodate the Shinkansen Line. 3000 train services use this station every day. Nearby are the buildings of Japanese Railways (JR), the Japanese Travel Bureau (JTB) and the main post office.

Marunouchi is also, however, the political centre of Tokyo. The Tenno lives in the walled Imperial Palace (see entry). The government district with the Parliament Building (see entry) and ministries extends south of the palace walls. The former City Hall of Tokyo lies only a few minutes away from the Main Railway Station, though the new City Hall (see entry) is actually situated a long way to the west in the district of Shinjuku (see entry). Last but not least Marunouchi is an important shopping district with the Daimaru department store and an underground shopping centre.

★★Meiji Shrine

Japanese
equivalent

明治神宮

The Meiji Shrine is one of the most popular Shinto places of worship in Tokyo. It was founded in 1920, destroyed during the war and restored in traditional style. It is dedicated to the Emperor Meiji (1868–1912). It was he who put an end to the 700-year-long rule of the shoguns and led Japan into the modern era. Around the shrine stretches the 72ha/180 acre Inner Garden.

Inner garden of the Meiji Shrine　　　　　　　　　　　　　　　B 5

District
Shibuya-ku

Railway station
Harajuku
(Yamanote Line)

Underground
Meiji-jingumae
(Chiyoda Line)

Opening times
daily 9am–4pm

The Main Torii is impressive. Almost 12m/40ft high, it is made of ancient Hinoki (Japanese cypress) tree-trunks from Taiwan. Most of the trees and bushes are gifts from all over the country. Gravel pathways lead to the sanctuary with its hall for devotions and Main Hall. The faithful pour water over their hands and symbolically cleanse their mouths at a fountain by the entrance, as religious custom requires. Furthermore they remove their hats and coats before entering the shrine.

A little to one side lies the Treasury. There artistic and ritual objects once belonging to Meiji-tenno are preserved. They illustrate the outlook on life of the period.

In the southern part of the park lies the Iris Garden. At the end of June and the beginning of July its flowers bloom with almost unbelievable magnificence.

The most important festivals are the birthday of Meiji-tenno (November 3rd) and the Celebration of Spring (April 29th–May 3rd), with performances of the old Bugaku court music and traditional archery tournaments, known as Kyudo Taikai. At New Year there is a display of the most expensive kimonos, albeit amid crowds of people.

Yoyogi Sports
Centre

The Yoyogi Sports Centre in the south part of the Inner Garden was built for the 1964 Summer Olympic Games. The vast swimming pool building was

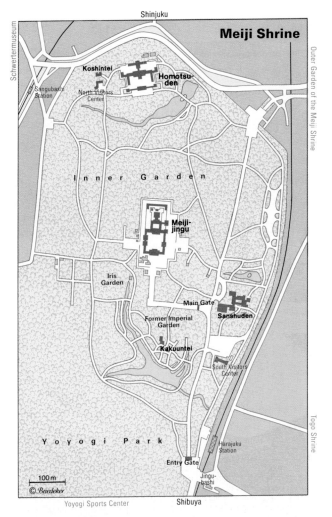

designed by Japan's most famous architect, Kenzo Tange, at a cost of more than 6 million American dollars. The swimming hall and Budokan Hall are occasionally cleared for certain large events (e.g. an international tennis tournament). The swimming pool's roof is suspended on steel cables which are anchored in two rocks. The Budokan Hall, not far from the Imperial Palace (see entry), was designed for martial sports, such as judo, but nowadays it is also used as a festival hall.

In the sports centre stands the bronze bust of the aviation pioneer Tokugawa Yoshitoshi (1884–1963); the double-decker bus used by him can be seen in the Museum of Transport (see Practical Information, Museums).

The Torii of the Meiji Shrine

Main building of the Meiji Shrine

Capturing the magnificent Iris Garden

A short distance to the south-west lies the broadcasting centre of the radio and telecommunications company NHK (Nihon Hoso Kyokai) with a concert hall able to seat an audience of 4000 and a museum of broadcasting technology.

NHK

Outer Garden of the Meiji Shrine

C 5

The Outer Garden of the Meiji Shrine is connected with the Inner Garden and the Meiji Shrine by an expressway. In this precinct are to be found the Crown Prince's Palace (see entry for Akasaka Palace), the Memorial Picture Gallery and the National Stadium.

District
Shinjuku-ku

Railway station
Shinanomachi

The National Stadium lies in the west part of the Outer Garden. It was originally erected for the Asiatic Games of 1958 and then enlarged for the 1964 Olympics. 80,000 spectators can watch football matches and athletics events here.

The Memorial Picture Gallery is in the north part of the park. It was opened in 1925. Its exhibits come from the period of Meiji-tenno's reign.

Meiji Memorial
Picture Gallery

Museum of Communications Technology

F 4

逓信総合博物館

Japanese
equivalent

The Museum of Communications Technology is just five minutes' walk from the Main Railway Station and is a veritable Aladdin's Cave for philatelists. Every devotee will be fascinated by this collection of some 200,000 postage stamps, in which Japan and the other Asiatic countries are particularly well represented.

Location
2-3-1, Otemachi,
Chiyoda-ku

Nara

Railway station
Main Railway
Station

All those who are interested in the techniques of communication will also
find a great deal to absorb them here.

Opening times
Tue.–Sun.
9am–4pm

The museum has on show a complete collection of exhibits and documents
illustrating the history of Japanese postal and telecommunications technology, while there is also a special library with around 24,000 books.

★★Nara

Japanese
equivalent

奈 良

Location
about 500km/
310 miles south-
west of Tokyo;
about 40km/
25 miles south of
Kyoto

The prestigious prefectural city of Nara (pop. 310,000) was from 710 to 784
the first capital city of Japan. Previously the seat of government had always
been transferred from place to place after the death of each ruler. Nara still
possesses many old temples, some from the 7th c., museums and temple
treasure-houses, which contain outstanding examples of Buddhist art.

The old buildings of Nara lie in particularly beautiful natural surroundings, a situation which can be best appreciated from the top of Mikasayama
Hill. The climate undergoes considerable changes with the seasons, but on
the whole it is mild.

In terms of area and population Nara may well rank as a relatively small
city and it possesses hardly any industries of note. Its most important craft
products include carved wooden dolls, lacquerwork, fans and ceramics.

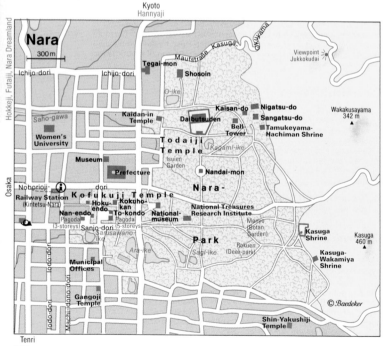

104

By air from Haneda Airport in 1 hr to Osaka and then by rail from Nanba Station (JR Nara Line) in 30 mins to Nara; by rail from Tokyo Main Station (Tokaido and Sanyo-Shinkansen Line) in 3 hrs to Kyoto and then by JR in 40 mins to Nara.

Access

★★Nara Park

The visit will start from Kintetsu-Nara Station, where on the 3rd and 4th floors there is an excellent exhibition with objects from the Jomon to the Nara Period. Go through the shopping street of Noborioji-dori or the road running parallel to the south, Sanjo-dori, to Nara Park, which with an area of just over 525ha/2sq.miles is the largest of its kind in Japan. Besides its enormous old trees, the park contains numerous historic buildings, while a further attraction are the many tame deer which live here.

To the right of the entrance is Sarusawa Lake (360m/390yds in circumference), in which the five-storey pagoda of the Kofukuji Temple is reflected. On the north-west shore is the Uneme Shrine.

From the eastern shore of the lake a path leads northwards to the Kofukuji Temple, one of the Seven Great Temples of Nara. The sanctuary was founded in 669 by Kagami-no-Himehiko, the wife of Fujiwara-no-Kamatari. It was the family's tutelary temple and was the main temple of the Hosso sect. Originally erected in Kyoto under the name Yamashina-dera, the temple was transferred in 678 to Umasaka (south of Nara) and then, with the founding of the capital city in 710, brought to its present site by Fubito, one of the Kamatari sons, and renamed "Kofukuji". The importance of the temple grew with the power of the Fujiwara and in its heyday it consisted of 175 buildings. Most of them, however, were destroyed during the wars between the Minamotos and Tairas in the 12th c.

★★Kofukuji
Temple

From where the great south gate once stood can be seen the buildings which have survived. These include the octagonal hall, Nan-endo, built in 813 by Fujiwara Fuyutsugu and restored in 1741. Its most important treasure is the statue of the Fukukenjaku Kannon, made in 1188 by Kokei, the father of Unkei. Also of interest are the statues of the four celestial guardians and those of the patriarchs of the Hosso sect. Outside the hall there is a 9th c. bronze lantern with an inscription thought to be by Kobo-daishi. To the south-west stands the three-storey pagoda, an attractive building of the Fujiwara Period.

To the north of Nan-endo stands the North Hall, Hoku-endo, also with an octagonal groundplan. It was originally commissioned by the Empress Gensho in 721 in memory of Fubito, the founder of Kofukuji, and was subsequently restored in 1208. Inside there is a wooden statue of Miroku-bosatsu (1212), thought to be by Unkei.

To the east is the hall, Chu-kondo, which was founded in 710 and rebuilt in 1819. It contains a wooden Shakyamuni statue.

The eastern Main Hall, To-kondo, was faithfully rebuilt to the original design in 1415, after having been destroyed on many occasions. It contains a statue of Yakushi-nyorai (15th c.), which is surrounded by various other statues including those of Nikko-bosatsu and Gakko-bosatsu (thought to be 8th c.).

Standing opposite to the south is a five-storey pagoda. It was built in 730 by Komyo, the wife of Shomu-tenno, burned down five times and then rebuilt in the old style in 1426. At 50m/164ft high the pagoda is the second highest in Japan and represents a notable example of Nara architecture. Inside there are statues of Amida-nyorai, Shakyamuni, Yakushi-nyorai and Miro-ku-bosatsu. North-east of the hall, To-kondo, stands the Treasury, Kokuho-kan, a new building (1959) with important temple treasures. Particularly worth seeing is a bronze Buddha head (7th c.), a wooden group of figures of Juni-shinsho ("twelve heavenly generals"; Heian Period), two

In the Deer Park at Nara

Kasuga Shrine

Nio statues (Kongo and Misshaku), an Ashura statue in dry lacquer (early Nara Period) and the two guardian figures, Kongo-rikishi.

Along the path leading eastwards from Kofukuji is the National Museum (built in 1895, extended in 1972). It exhibits important artistic works, mainly from the Nara Period. Temporary exhibitions are held which show a selection of the many objects stored here.

★★National Museum

Further east stands the Cultural Heritage Research Institute, behind which a large red torii (Ichi-no torii) leads through to the site of the Kasuga Shrine. A path lined with cypresses and cedars leads past the Botanical Garden on the left and the deer park, Rokuen, on the right. In the former there is a small stage for Gagaku and Bugaku performances. The animals living in the deer park are said to be messengers from God, for according to legend the Fujiwara, who built the shrine, invited the deity Takemikazuchi-no-mikoto to Nara and the deity arrived in the town on the back of a deer.

The path to the Kasuga Shrine crosses the second torii (Ni-no torii) and continues between two rows of 3000 stone lanterns which are lit twice a year for the Mandoro Festival. Then comes the south gate, a single-storeyed building dating from 1179. Ornate lanterns hang in its corridors. Behind this building is the hall of devotions, Heiden (1650), and to the left the hall of festivities, Naoraiden, dating from the same period. Stone steps lead to the central gate, Chumon, which has roofed corridors running on either side which encircle the main buildings of the Kasuga Shrine.

★★Kasuga Shrine

The Kasuga Shrine was founded by Fujiwara Nagate (714–771). It consists of four separate buildings and is dedicated to the deities Takemikazuchi and Futsunushi, and the ancestral gods of the Fujiwara, Amenokoyane and his wife Hime-okami. The buildings are a typical example of the Kasuga-zukuri style of architecture and can be distinguished from older wooden buildings by the red paintwork of their balconies, their white plasterwork and their curved roof-lines. Up until 1863 the buildings were dismantled every twenty years on a rota system and then rebuilt in the old style. Since then this restoration work has only been confined to the roofs.

On the left-hand side stands the removal hall, Utsushi-dono, where pictures of the deities are stored during restoration work on the shrine buildings. The covered walkway leading from here to the main shrine, Nejiri-roka, is the work of Hidari Jingoro (thought to have lived 1594–1634) and is embellished with outstanding carvings. To the north of the removal hall stands the tree Yadorigi. Six other types of tree have been grafted on its trunk. The strips of paper fixed to the branches by visitors to the shrine contain prayers for good luck.

Another pathway passing between stone lanterns leads from the Kasuga Shrine southwards to the Kasuga Wakamiya Shrine, which is dedicated to the god Ameno-oshikumo, son of Amenokoyane, and was probably founded in 1135. The present-day buildings were erected in 1863, also in the Kasuga-zukuri style.

Kasuga Wakamiya Shrine

In the south building of the shrine is to be found the Holy Dance Hall of Kaguraden (1613), where the ritual dances, known as "Kagura" are performed in honour of Amaterasu, the ancestral deity of the imperial house.

The shrine festival, "On-matsuri", takes place in December and is the largest festival in the city, attracting visitors from far and wide. A magnificent procession with people in historical costumes starts from here and makes its way through the city.

The shrine's treasury (Homotsuden) was built in 1973 to the south-west of the main shrine and contains valuable artistic treasures.

To the east of Nara Park rises the 460m/1509ft high Mount Kasuga, venerated as a seat of the gods. The woods covering the sides of the mountain

Kasuga

have been left untouched since prehistoric times and present a beautiful picture, especially in autumn. From the summit there is a fine view of the city and the Nara Basin.

Wakakusa

Another fine panorama is that offered by Wakakusa (342m/1122ft), a grass-covered hill further to the north. The festival of Yamayaki is held here in January.

★★Shin-Yakushiji Temple

About 600m/656yds south of the Kasuga Shrine stands the Shin Yakushiji Temple, which was founded by the Empress Komyo in 747 as a way of entreating the gods to cure her husband Shomu of an eye affliction.

The temple, a classical work of the late Nara Period, owes its name to the Healing Buddha (Yakushi), to whom the sanctuary is dedicated.

Inside there is a statue of Yakushi-nyorai, carved from a single block of wood, and next to it a statue of the Eleven-headed Kannon. Both are surrounded by twelve guardian deities made of clay (Juni-shinsho); all these sculptures are masterpieces of the late Nara Period. The Main Hall, Hondo, is the only part of the temple which has been preserved from the Nara Period; all the other buildings were destroyed quite early on.

Tamukeyama Hachiman Shrine

In the northern section of Nara Park, at the bottom of Wakakusa Hill, stands the Tamukeyama Hachiman Shrine (founded in 749), which is dedicated to the god of war, Hachiman. It was probably originally built next to the Heijo Palace to the west of city, but was then brought to its present location in 1251. The present-day buildings were put up in 1691 by the priest Kokei. The central hall is dedicated to Emperor Ojin (posthumously honoured as Hachiman), the left one to his consort Hime-mikoto and the right one to his parents Jingu-tenno and Chuai. In the south stands the Treasury, Hozo, and in the north the Sutra hall, Kyozo.

Of considerable interest is the building technique, known as "Azekura-zukuri", where wooden beams with a triangular cross-section are joined together without the use of nails. At times of high humidity the wood expands and hinders the passage of air into the inner room, while in dry weather the wood contracts to some extent, thereby allowing sufficient fresh air to penetrate. In this way a relatively stable spatial environment is created, which helps to explain the superb state of preservation of the old artistic treasures, some of which date back over a thousand years. This technique is found not only in the buildings of the Tamukeyama Hachiman Shrine, but also in other places.

★★Todaiji Temple

The area immediately to the west of the shrine is the location of the Todaiji Temple (Great East Temple), one of the Seven Great Temples of Nara. It is the main shrine of the Buddhist Kegon sect and of all provincial temples built as a result of the edict of Shomu-tenno (Koku-bunji).

History

The Kegon sect was founded in 736 by the Chinese priest, Dozen, and is one of the oldest in Japan. Its central tenet of belief is in the possibility granted to every human being of attaining enlightenment. The object of worship is the Rushana Buddha (Vairoçana), the earliest of the Buddhas.
In 745 Emperor Shomu, the most ardent champion of Buddhism at that time, gave orders for the building of the Todaiji Temple. Work was begun in 745 in Nara on the casting of the statue of Daibutsu (Great Buddha) – earlier attempts in 743, on the site of Shigaraki Palace to the south of Lake Biwa-ko, having failed – and the task was completed in 749.

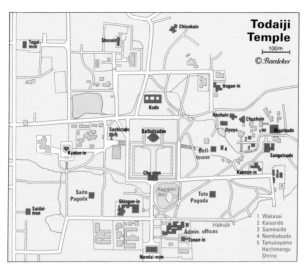

Todaiji Temple

| 100m |
© Baedeker

1 Wakasai
2 Kaisando
3 Sammaido
4 Nembutsudo
5 Tamukayama
  Hachimangu
  Shrine

After its completion the Todaiji Temple was consecrated in 752 with one of the most magnificent celebrations of the century. Those present included the abdicated Emperor Shomu with his wife and daughter, the Empress Koken, the whole of the court and some 10,000 priests and believers. In 855 the head of the Buddha statue was torn off in a severe earthquake (restored in 861). In 1180 the Great Buddha Hall (Daibutsuden) was destroyed by Taira Shigehira and the head and right hand of the statue fell victims to the fire. At the instigation of the abbot Chogen the statue was reconstructed and its completion was celebrated in 1195 by a ceremony in the presence of Emperor Gotoba and the Shogun Minamoto Yoritomo. During a revolt by Matsunaga Hisahide in 1567 the Buddha Hall burned down. The damaged statue was reconstructed in 1692, the hall in 1709.

Entry to the temple area is afforded by the Great South Gate, Nandaimon, a two-storey building supported by 18 pillars. It was originally erected towards the end of the Nara Period, but was then destroyed by a typhoon in 962. In 1199 it was rebuilt. The building displays the powerful architectural style known as Tenjiku-yo, which originated in India. In the outer side niches stand two Nio statues (guardian figures), 8m/26ft in height, which have been ascribed to the masters Unkei and Kaikei (or Tankei). In the rear niches there are two Koma-inu (dog or lion-like animals) standing on a stone base, thought to have been made by the Chinese Chinnakei in 1196 and a typical example of Chinese Sung culture.

Temple area

Passing Kagami-ike Lake (Bugaku performances here during Shomu-sai celebrations) we come to the Hall of the Great Buddha (Daibutsuden). The building was finally rebuilt to a smaller scale than the original (about two-thirds) after having been destroyed on several occasions. Nevertheless it is still the largest wooden building in the world, measuring 57m/187ft long, 50.5m/166ft wide and 48.7m/160ft high. It is also an example of the Tenjiku-yo style of architecture. At the end of the roof ridge there are talismans called "Shibi", which are supposed to protect the building from fire.

★★Hall of the
Great Buddha
(Daibutsuden)

Inside the hall stands the Great Buddha (Daibutsu), a bronze statue of the earliest Buddha, whose original shape is derived from a design by the Korean Kuninaka-no-Kimimaro. The bronze pedestal (20.7m/68ft in circumference) has the shape of a lotus blossom with 56 leaves. The statue itself has a height of 16.2m/53ft and is the largest Buddha statue in Japan. For its casting 437 tonnes of bronze, 130kg/287lb of gold and 7 tonnes of wax were used. The raised right hand displays the mudra "Semui-no-in" (promise of peace), the left hand the mudra "Yogan-no-in" (fulfilment of wishes). The gold wooden aura with depictions of the 16 Buddha incarnations was added in the 17th c. The two figures standing in front of the Buddha, Nyoirin Kannon (fulfiller of all wishes, on the right) and Kokuzo-bosatsu (deity of wisdom and good fortune, on the left), date from the same period. At the back of the hall there are statues of two of the four celestial guardians: on the left Komokuten, the ruler of the west, who is crushing underfoot a demon which symbolises everything which stands in the way of the Buddhist faith. On the right stands Tamonten in a similar pose. Next to Komokuten is the model of the original temple building, while in front of Tamonten there is a massive wooden pillar with a rectangular opening at ground level. According to popular belief, anyone who manages to crawl through this opening, is assured of reaching paradise.

To the right of the Buddha hall there is a wooden statue of Binzuru, which is supposed to cure illnesses if the patient touches it with one hand and the affected part of the body with the other hand. A masterpiece of the late Nara Period (Tempyo Period) is the octagonal bronze lantern standing in front of the hall, which is decorated on the outside with perfect reliefs.

★Kaidan-in
Temple

About 300m/330yds west of the hall stands the Kaidan-in Temple, which was burnt down on numerous occasions after its foundation (754) and was finally rebuilt in its present form around 1730. In the middle of the inner room are statues of Shakyamuni and Taho-nyorai, in the corners statues of the four celestial guardians in full armour. "Kaidan" was originally the name of the terrace used for the ordination of priests. It was built using earth brought by the Chinese priest Ganjin. He is supposed to have ordained 500 monks as priests here.

Treasury

500m/¼ mile to the north stands the Todaiji Treasury (Shosoin), built using the Azekura-zukuri techniques (see above) of controlling the indoor climatic environment. The buildings, which are normally not open to the public, house art objects of inestimable value which originally formed the collection of Emperor Shomu and were handed over to the temple by the Emperor's widow and daughter after his death. Many of the decorative pieces, weapons, pictures and religious objects come from the Near and Middle East. At the end of October and beginning of November the Treasury is thoroughly ventilated and at this time parts of the collection are put on display in the National Museum in Nara. Close by there are two modern extension buildings made of reinforced concrete.

★Belltower

East of the Buddha Hall stands an old belltower. The bell was cast in 749 and severely damaged in a typhoon in 989 (recast in 1239). It measures 3.9m/13ft high and with a diameter of 2.8m/9ft is the second largest bell in Japan.

Hall of the
Second Month

Further east on a hill stands the Hall of the Second Month (Nigatsu-do), which was built by the priest Jitchu, a disciple of Roben (689–773, first abbot of Todaiji). After a fire it was rebuilt in 1669. The interior, which is not open to the public, contains two statues of the Eleven-headed Kannon. The hall owes its name to the water-creation ceremony "Omizu-tori", which used to fall in the second month of the moon calendar (now between March 1st and 14th).

Just to the south is the Hall of the Third Month (Sangatsu-do), built in 733 by Roben and the oldest building still standing in the temple area. The prayer-hall, Raido, was added in about 1200 (Kamakura Period). The two buildings have significant differences in the construction of their roofs. The Hokke Sutra is stored here and the name of the hall is derived from the reading from it which took place in the third month of the moon calendar. In the middle of the inner room is the 3.6m/12ft high Fukukenjaku Kannon, a dry-lacquer statue which is attributed to the abbot Roben. Its crown is decorated with 20,000 pearls and precious stones. It is flanked by the clay figures of Nikko-bosatsu and Gakko-bosatsu (Nara Period). To the side stand statues of Bonten and Taishakuten, also made by the dry-lacquer method. Next to the Bonten statue are the wooden statues of Fudomyoo (to the right) and Jizo-bosatsu (on the left). In the four corners of the room are the celestial guardians.

★★Hall of the Third Month

In the room at the back there are two processional shrines (Mikoshi) with pictures of Benzaiten, the goddess of love, and Kichijoten, the goddess of good fortune; there are also two guardian statues in dry-lacquer. Behind the Fukukenjaku Kannon is the clay figure of Shukongo-shin, a work by Roben, which can only be viewed on the anniversary of his death (December 16th).

Isuien Garden

The Isuien Garden extends to the west of the south gate leading into the Todaiji Temple area. To the left of the entrance stands the small Neiraku Museum, opened in 1969, with its exhibits of old Chinese and Korean arts and crafts. The Isuien Garden is a landscape garden in the Shakkei style (i.e. "borrowed scenery", with the surrounding landscape being incorporated into the total picture). Near the entrance stand the teahouses of Seishuan and Sanshutei and the waiting room, Teishuken. The rear part of the garden was laid in 1899 and has the south gate of the Todaiji Temple and Wakakusa Hill as a backdrop. On the island in the tiny lake there is a foundation stone from the Buddha Hall. The stepping-stones are old millstones used in the production of dyes. From time to time green tea is served in the thatched Hyoshintei teahouse.

Neiraku Museum

About 2km/1 mile outside the city centre lies the theme park Nara Dreamland (bus service from the centre). Conceived in the Disneyland mould, it offers an Adventureland, Fantasyland, World of Yesteryear and Tomorrow, as well as a 3km/2 mile long narrow-gauge railway.

Nara Dreamland

North-west Surroundings of Nara

North-west of the city lies the Heijo-kyuden Imperial Palace, which was uncovered during archaeological excavations (bus from Nara Main Railway Station, 15 mins, or from Yamato-Saidaiji Station, 5 mins). Occupying an area of 107ha/264 acres, it forms the political and cultural centre of the old capital city of Heijokyo. When the seat of government was transferred to Nagaoka in 784, the site fell into decay, so that today only the foundations are visible. The outline of the ceremonial hall, Daigokuden, is also discernible. To the south there were twelve other buildings, including the assembly hall, Choshuden. The whole complex was surrounded by a gallery with several gateways. During excavation work ditches, wells and paving have been uncovered, the finds being now on display in the Materials Hall.

Heijo-kyuden Imperial Palace

About 800m/½ mile east of the palace stands the Hokkeiji Temple, founded in the 8th c. by Empress Komyo. Its main hall was restored in 1601. The wooden statue of the Eleven-headed Kannon, which was apparently created by an Indian artist, is worth seeing.

★Hokkeiji Temple

★Kairyuoji
Temple

Close by is the Kairyuoji Temple, also founded by the Empress. Only the western main hall, the Sutra library (both partially restored in the 12th c.) and the five-storey pagoda have survived to the present day.

★★Akishino
Temple

North-west of Yamato-Saidaiji Station lies the Akishino Temple. Founded about 780 most of it was burnt down in 1135. The only building to be spared was the lecture-hall (Kodo), later converted into the Main Hall (Hondo). It is a good example of Nara Period architecture. The dry-lacquer statue of the deity Gigeiten dates in part from this era, but it is also partly attributed to the sculptor Unkei.

★★Saidaiji
Temple

A short distance to the west of the station lies another of the Seven Great Temples of Nara, the Saidaiji Temple ("Great West Temple"), built in 765 on the orders of Shotoku-tenno (the former Empress Koken). It is the main sanctuary of the Shingon-Ritsu sect. The buildings are chiefly of later date.

The Main Hall, Shakado, to the north of the ruins of the East Pagoda, dates from 1752. It contains a wooden statue of Shakyamuni, by the priest Eison (1201–90), and a statue of Monju-bosatsu of 1302.

To the south-west of the main hall is the Aizendo Hall with statues of Aisen-myoo (1247) and the priest Eizon (Kamakura Period).

Near the east gate is the Shido Hall with a number of statues of the late Nara Period (Tempyo Period), including one of the four celestial guardians (the Tamonten one of wood, the others of bronze). The figures of demons at the feet of the statues date from the time of the temple's foundation. The wooden statue of the Eleven-headed Kannon dates from the 12th c.

East of the Main Hall lies the temple treasury, Shuhokan, with sculptures, paintings and calligraphy. Twelve picture scrolls with illustrations of the guardians (Juni-shinsho) on silk also belong to the temple.

North-east of the temple is the tomb of the Emperor Seimu, a typical hill-grave of the Kofun Period.

Yamato-bunkakan
Museum

The Yamato-bunkakan Museum was opened in 1961 amid an upland landscape of woods and lakes to the west of the Saidaiji Temple (Gakuen-mae Station). Its art treasures come from the Asiatic countries (sculptures, paintings, ceramics, lacquerwork, etc.).

South-west Surroundings of Nara

The region to the south-west of Nara is today a peaceful agricultural area. In the 8th c. it was a spiritual centre for the whole region, evidence of which is still provided by a few temples which are among the oldest in the area and offer a delightful contrast with the green rice-fields and farms. Access to the region is from Nara (Kintetsu-Nara Station) on the Nara Line of the Kintetsu private railway as far as Yamato-Saidaiji, then southwards on the Kashihara Line.

Just to the west of Amagatsuji Station lies the tomb of Emperor Suinin, a tumulus with a keyhole-shaped outline lying in a lake. This tomb also dates back to the Kofun Period.

★★Toshodaiji
Temple

Nearly 600m/½ mile south of Amagatsuji Station stands the Toshodaiji Temple, founded in 759 by Ganjin – the oldest of some 30 temples of the Ritsu sect.

The only parts of the temple which have survived from the time of its foundation are the Main Hall and lecture-hall, the other buildings being of a later date. The visitor passes through the Great South Gate, Nandaimon (reconstruction 1960), to the Main Hall, Kondo, which with a surface area of 15×29m/49×95ft is the largest and most important example of Tempyo architecture. The pillared gallery attains a classical beauty. In the hall there is an 3.3m/11ft statue of the seated Rushana-butsu (dry-lacquer technique), designed by the Chinese pupils of Ganjin, T'an Ching and Szu T'o. Its magnificent aura was originally embellished by 1000 tiny Buddha figures,

Toshodaiji . . .   *. . . and Horyuji*

of which 864 have survived. Next to it on the left is a Thousand-handed Kannon (dry-lacquer, 5.5m/18ft high), on the right a statue of Yakushi-nyorai, also in dry-lacquer technique and attributed to the Ganjin pupils, Szu T'o and Ju Pao. There are also two 1.7m/5½ft wooden statues (Bonten and Taishakuten) by the master Chun Fa-li and one of the seated Dainichi-nyorai (3.7m/12ft high) from the early Heian Period.

Behind the Main Hall stands the lecture-hall, Kodo, originally the assembly hall of the Imperial palace, Heijo-kyuden, and brought here at the time of the temple's foundation. As a result of restoration work by Chun Fa-li (759) and later repairs, the original style of the hall has been compromised.

The most important sculpture in this hall is the 2.4m/8ft high Miroku-bosatsu, which is by Chun Fa-li. Also worth seeing are the statues of Jikokuten and Zochoten carved from a block of cypress wood.

To the right of the lecture hall there is a long building, which includes the priests' quarters, Higashimuro (to the north), and the sacred room, Raido (to the south). In front of it there is a drum-tower (Koro or Shariden), where the festival of Uchiwamaki takes place in May.

To the east of the priests' quarters are situated two buildings erected using Azekura-zukuri techniques: the Sutra library, Kyozo (to the south), and the Treasury, Hozo (to the north). The new Treasury, Shin-hozo (1970), contains paintings, documents and fragments of sculpture.

The portrait-gallery, Mieido, is to the north-west and is surrounded by a wall. It houses a dry-lacquer statue by Ganjin (80cm/31in. high), which was made in the year he died. The hall is only open to the public on June 6th. There is a path leading to Ganjin's tomb.

Yakushiji Temple can be reached from the next station to the south, Nishi-nokyo, on foot (750m/½ mile) from Toshodaiji. Founded in 680 under

★★Yakushiji Temple

Emperor Temmu, it is today the main temple of the Hosso sect (together with Kofukuji).

Emperor Temmu died during the temple's construction, which lasted until 698, and his consort ascended the throne in 687. After the transfer of the seat of government to Nara, the temple was brought from Asuka to its present site in 718. It was damaged on several occasions, notably in the Civil War of 1528.

The sanctuary at one time counted as one of the Seven Great Temples of Nara, but the only building to have survived from the original site is the East Pagoda. The other buildings all date from the Kamakura Period or later.

The Main Hall, Kondo, which was restored in 1600 and then rebuilt on the old foundations in 1976, contains the famous Yakushi Trinitas. Its central figure is the 2.6m/8½ft high Yakushi-nyorai (master of the eastern paradise), with the standing figures of Nikko-bosatsu and Gakko-bosatsu on either side. The statues, which were originally gold, were blackened during the fire of 1528; only the auras are still golden. The great bronze pedestal of the central figure displays Chinese and Indian influences. All three statues date from the year 697, as does the Yakushi-Trinitas in the lecture-hall, Kodo, behind the Main Hall.

Diagonally opposite stands the three-storey East Pagoda (37.9m/124ft high, thought to have been built in 698). Small false roofs have been added, with the result that the building appears six-storeyed. The metallic roof embellishments (Sorin) are also highly elaborate. The pagoda is the only extant example of Buddhistic architecture of the Hakuho Period.

Behind the pagoda stands the East Hall, Toin-do (1285). It contains the 1.9m/6ft high bronze Sho Kannon (also known as Kudara Kannon, dating from around 600), a gift from the King of Paeckche (Korea). On the other side of the pagoda is the Bussokudo Hall with a stone carrying a footprint of Buddha (Bussoku-seki).

Also of note is the Belltower, to the right of the Main Hall, with a Korean bell.

The contents of the Temple Treasury, Hozoden, include two fine paintings representing the goddess of beauty, Kichijo-ten, and a Chinese priest. The Treasury is only open from January 1st–15th and October 20th–November 10th.

Nara Basin

The Nara Basin, which extends to the south of the city, is also known as the Yamato Basin. It is watered by tributaries of the Yamato, which flows away from the plain to the west and empties into the sea south of Osaka. In this area the visitor will find yet more important temple sites dating back to the earliest periods of Japanese history.

From Nara (Kintetsu-Nara Station) the train goes via Yamato-Saidaiji and Tamagatsuji (see above) to Kintetsu-Koriyama (15 mins) and from there the journey continues by bus (20 mins) to the Hokkiji Temple. The temple was established in 638 and can be traced back to the priest Fukuryo, who by founding it fulfilled the last wish of Shotoku-taishi (574–622). As the temple was built on the site of the latter's palace, it is also called Okamoto Temple. The three-storey pagoda, erected in 685, displays the stylistic features of the early Nara Period.

Hokkiji Temple

◀ *Yakushiji Temple*

Nara

Horinji Temple

The Horinji Temple, situated to the south-west, can be reached on foot in 15 mins. It was built in 821 by a son of Shotoku-taishi. The dominant figure in the Main Hall, Kondo, is the wooden statue of the seated Yakushi-nyorai, created in the Tori-busshi style, which is based on Chinese and Korean models. Next to it are the sculptures of Kichijo-ten, Sho Kannon and Bishamonten, dating from the late Heian Period.

The lecture-hall, Kodo, contains coloured wooden statues of the Eleven-headed Kannon (4.8m/16ft high), Kokuzu-bosatsu and Jizo-bosatsu.

★★Horyuji Temple

About 1km/½ mile further south-west lies the oldest completely preserved temple site in Japan, the Horyuji Temple, a resplendent building of the Asuka Period (552–645), with superb works of art from all the cultural periods of Japanese history.

Yomei-tenno, the first Buddhist Emperor of Japan, was beset by a severe illness in 586. He gave orders for a statue of the Healing Buddha (Yakushi-nyorai) to be made, but died before its completion. In order to carry out his wish, Shotoku-taishi, the Emperor's son, had the Horyuji Temple built in 607. The temple became one of the Seven Great Temples of Nara and the centre for Buddhism in the whole country. It was from here that the new teaching was propagated to all corners of Japan. At that time the road linking the Imperial court with the coast passed this way.

The site of the Shotoku sect's main temple is in all made up of 45 buildings, which date from the Asuka through to the Momoyama Period. 17 of them are classified as "important national monuments". The temple is divided into the To-in complex (also Higashi-no-in, east part) with 14 buildings and Sai-in (also Nishi-no-in, west part) with 31 buildings.

The main entrance to Sai-in and to the whole temple area is the Great South Gate, Nandaimon, a building which has been restored on numerous occasions (the last during the Muromachi Period, 1438). From here one walks past the temple office to the Central Gate, Chumon, which dates back to the year of the temple's foundation. The gate, from which roofed corridors (Kairo) run on either side, is different from other gatehouses by the fact that it is supported by pillars. On either side of the entrance, which is divided by pillars, there are two guardian figures (Nio), the right-hand one in red as a

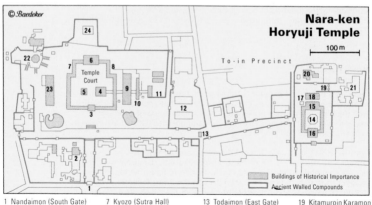

© Baedeker

Nara-ken
Horyuji Temple

100 m

To-in Precinct

Temple Court

Buildings of Historical Importance

Ancient Walled Compounds

1 Nandaimon (South Gate)	7 Kyozo (Sutra Hall)
2 Admin. Offices	8 Shoro (Bell-tower)
3 Chumon (Middle Gate)	9 Shoryoin
4 Kondo (Main Hall)	10 Tsumashitsu
5 5-Storeyed Pagoda	11 Kofuzo (Treasure Hall)
6 Daikodo (Lecture Hall)	12 Daihozoden (Treasury)

13 Todaimon (East Gate)	19 Kitamuroin Karamon
14 Yume-dono	20 Kitamuroin Hondo
15 E-den (Picture Hall)	21 Chuguji Temple
16 Raido	22 Saiendo
17 Shodo (Bell-tower)	23 Sangyoin
18 Dempodo	24 Kami-no-mido

symbol of light, the left-hand one in black as a symbol of darkness. Both were made in 711 and completely restored in 1964.

The corridors leading from the Central Gate enclose the inner temple area. Within this, on the right, stands the Main Hall, Kondo, a two-storey wooden building with an area of 9.1×7.3m/30×24ft and a height of 17.8m/58ft. It was put up in the Asuka Period and is supposedly the oldest surviving wooden building in the world. The inner walls of the hall used to bear famous frescoes, which in terms of style and execution were comparable with those in the Caves of Ajanta (India). They were, however, destroyed by fire in 1949. Photographs of the frescoes can be seen in the Great Treasure Chamber. In the hall stand several 7th c. statues, the most famous being the bronze Shaka Trinitas, which was cast by Tori-busshi in 623. The main figure, Shakyamuni, is flanked by Yakuo-bosatsu and Yakujo-bosatsu. To the right of the Trinitas is a statue of Yakushi-nyorai, commissioned by Yomei-tenno and cast in bronze in 607. To the left of the Trinitas stand a bronze statue of Amida-nyorai (1232) and the wooden statues of the goddess Kichijo-ten and the god of war Bishamonten, both dating from 1078. The wooden statues of the four celestial guardians, the oldest of this type to be preserved, date from the late Asuka Period.

The five-storey Pagoda, standing in the left-hand part of the temple courtyard, dates from the year of the temple's foundation and is 32m/105ft high. On the corners of the roofs there are talismans to protect against fire, while in the lower part of the pagoda a false roof (Mokoshi) has been inserted. On the ground floor there are four scenes from the life of Buddha, fashioned in clay; on the east side "Conversation between Yumia and Monju", on the south side "The Paradise of Miroku", on the west side "Buddha's Cremation" and on the north side "The Entry of Buddha into Nirvana".

On the north side of the temple courtyard is to be found the lecture-hall, Daikodo. The original building was destroyed by lightning in 925 and the hall was rebuilt in 990. Inside there is a gilded Yakushi-Trinitas made of wood (on either side of the main figure stand Nikko-bosatsu and Sakkobosatsu) and sculptures of the four celestial guardians.

To the west of the lecture-hall are the Sutra Hall, Kyozo, dating from the Tempyo Period, with a wooden statue of the Korean priest, Kanroku, who came to Nara in 607. The belltower, Shoro, was rebuilt in the Heian Period; the bell is supposed to date back to the 8th c.

In front of the gallery adjoining the courtyard to the east stands the Shoryoin Hall, dedicated to the soul of Shotoku-taishi. It was previously the priests' quarters, which were restored in 1121. It contains a statue of Shotoku-taishi, which shows the 45-year-old regent in T'ang Period ceremonial garb. Alongside are sculptures of dignitaries, including the priest Eji.

On the far side of the adjoining building, Tsumamuro, we come to the small Treasury, Kofuzo, with a few Buddhist sculptures, and then the twosectioned building of the Great Treasure Chamber, Daihozoden, which was built in 1941 on the occasion of the 1320th anniversary of the death of Shotoku-taishi. Inside there are outstanding works of art from several different periods. Of special mention is the Kudara Kannon, which comes from Korea and whose lines form a stark contrast to the stiff Japanese sculptures of that period. There is a Nine-headed Kannon made of wood and the Yumetagai Kannon, which turns bad dreams into good ones (both of these sculptures date from the Hakuho Period). In the south building there are pieces from the Main Hall, including the 2.4m/8ft high miniature shrine, Tamamushi-no-zushi, belonging to the Empress Suiko. It derives its name from the type of insect called "tamamushi" (*chrysochroa elegans*), because the shrine once had the many-coloured wings of the insect stuck on it. These are no longer visible. On every side of the shrine, which is decorated with openwork bronze mountings, there are paintings of Buddhist themes on black backgrounds. On the front doors are the celestial guardians, on the side-doors pictures of Bosatsu, on the back, pagodas, stars and a phoenix. The shrine is a good example of the ornamentation and painting of the Asuka Period, likewise the miniature shrine of Tachibana (mother of Komyo), which contains an Amida-Trinitas made of gilded bronze.

To the south-east of the Treasure Chamber, the Great East Gate, Todaimon, affords access to the To-in precinct, where the Ikaruga Palace of Shotoku-taishi stood until 622. After the death of the regent the palace fell into disrepair and in 739 on the orders of the Emperor was replaced by the East Temple, which was dedicated to Shotoku's family.

The Corridor (Kairo) leads to the Hall of Dreams, Yume-dono, with its elaborate bronze roof decorations. It is the oldest Japanese building with an octagonal groundplan. It is here that Shotoku-taishi is supposed to have meditated whenever he came up against concepts in his Sutra studies which were hard to understand. Then – according to legend – a wise man from the east would appear before him and explain the point of difficulty to him. The most important work of art in the hall is a gilded Guze Kannon (also called Nyoirin Kannon) made of wood, which resembles Shotoku and is reputed to have been made by him himself, although all that can be said with certainty is that it belongs to the Tori-busshi School. The statue can only be viewed from April 11th to May 5th and from October 22nd to November 3rd. Also worth seeing are a statue of the priest Gyoshin Sozu (dry-lacquer; Tempyo Period) and a clay figure of the priest Dosen (Heian Period).

On the north side of the enclosing wall lies the picture-hall, E-den, with paintings from the life of Shotoku; to the right is the Shariden Hall ("Hall of the Ashes of Buddha"). This building and the belltower visible to the left both date from the Kamakura Period.

To the north, on the far side of the picture-hall, is the prayer-hall, Dempodo, which used to be the residence of the Emperor's mother, Tachibana, and in 739 came into the possession of the temple. The hall contains sculptures dating from the late Nara Period. In the middle there is an Amida-Trinitas in dry-lacquer, while on either side there are two more Amida groups made of wood. There are also other wood sculptures from the Heian Period.

The north-eastern part of the To-in precinct is occupied by the Chuguji Temple, a convent for nuns, originally presided over by members of the Imperial family. Worth seeing is the richly expressive Nyoirin Kannon. 1.8m/6ft tall and of wood, it is thought to be by Shotoku. The Tenjukoku Mandara, a fragment of the oldest known embroidery in Japan (7th c.), is also on show. This work of art, originally 4.8m/15¾ft long, was created by the widow of Shotoku and her court ladies and depicts scenes from life during the Asuka Period.

The eastern part of the Nara Basin can best be reached on the JR Sakurai Line from Nara Main Railway Station.

Tenri

10km/6 miles to the south lies the town of Tenri (pop. 69,000), centre of the Tenri-kyo sect, founded in 1838, and home of a museum of folk art. 1.5km/ 1 mile east of the station stands the Isonokami Shrine with a two-storey gatehouse and an interesting hall of worship. A sword is kept here which, according to legend, was a gift from the deity Takemikazuchi-no-mikoto to the very first emperor, Jimmu, whose existence is also shrouded in legend.

Miwa
Omiya Shrine

Further south on the railway line lies Miwa (rail from Nara, 40 mins), a departure point for visits to the Omiya Shrine (also called Miwa Myojin) at the bottom of the 467m/1532ft high Mount Miwa. The shrine is dedicated to the deity Omonoushi and is thought to have been founded in the first century before Christ, making it one of the oldest in Japan. It is connected to the Isonokami Shrine to the north by an old road which goes past prehistoric burial mounds and old settlements.

The next railway station is Sakurai, from where there is a bus service serving the Hase-dera Temple to the east (25 mins).

Hase-dera Temple

The temple, which was founded in 686, is the centre of the Buzan School of the Shingon sect. In the Main Hall, which was founded by Emperor Shomu and restored in 1650, stands a 8m/26ft high wooden statue of the Eleven-headed Kannon. Standing apart from the temple are a No stage and the Treasury Museum. The temple site is popular with visitors, especially during the seasons of cherry-blossom (April/May) and peonies. There is a beautiful view of the surrounding slopes from the temple terrace.

From Sakurai the Osaka Line of the Kintetsu private railway continues eastwards to Muro-guchi-Ono Station. About 8km/5 miles south of this station is the Muroji Temple of the Shingon sect, built in 681 and restored by Kobo-daishi in 824. The attractive complex also includes a pagoda 16.2m/53ft high. The temple is supposed to have been built especially for women, as access to the holy mountain of Koya-san was for a long time denied them. For this reason Muroji was also known as the "Koya-san for women".

★★Muroji Temple

In the Main Hall, Kondo, there is a wooden Juichimen Kannon and statues of the seated Nyoirin Kannon and Shaka-nyorai, all three dating from the early Heian Period.

Sakurai is also the starting-point of a bus route which goes into the southern part of the Nara Basin. In 30 minutes one can reach the Tanzan Shrine at the foot of Mount Tonomine. It was founded in 701 by the priest Joe, the eldest son of Fujiwara no Kamatari, and was on restored on several occasions, most recently in 1850. Near the entrance to the shrine stands a thirteen-storey pagoda, probably the only one of its kind in Japan. The interior of the shrine itself (also known as the "Nikko Shrine of Kansai") is of the utmost simplicity.

Tanzan Shrine

Behind the pagoda a path leads to the summit of Tonomine, where the grave of Kamatari is to be found.

To the west of Sakurai lies the town of Kashihara (pop. 112,000; Sakurai railway line to Unebi Station) at the foot of Mount Unebi (199m/653ft), where the legendary Jimmu-tenno is supposed to have built his palace and where his tomb is also located. Close by is the Kashihara Shrine, dedicated to him and his wife Himetatara-Isuzu-hime. It was built in 1889 using pieces of wood from the Imperial palace of Kyoto. Behind the shrine is the tomb of the Empress.

Kashihara

Near the shrine to the north-east is the Archaeological Museum (Yamato-rekishikan) with finds from the Nara Basin dating from as far back as the late Stone Age.

A short distance south of the museum is Kashihara-jingu Station (Yoshino Line of the Kintetsu private railway). From here one can go by bus (20 mins) to the Tachibana Temple of the Tendai sect. The temple was built at the spot where it is believed Shotoku-taishi was born. Of the once extensive site only the Main Hall, Kondo, has survived. It was restored in 1864 and contains a wooden statue of Shotoku dating from the Muromachi Period.

★Tachibana Temple

Not far to the north stands the Asuka Temple (Angoin Temple; also buses from Sakurai, 15 mins). It used to be the priests' quarters of the Hokoji Monastery, which was founded in 596 and then transferred to Heijokyo (Nara) in 718. The temple contains a bronze statue of Shakyamuni, which was fashioned by Tori-busshi in 606.

Asuka Temple

Narita

Okadera Temple

From Kashihara-jingu there is another bus connection to the Okadera Temple (previously called Ryugaiji), which is situated about 1km/½ mile east of Tachibana. The temple was originally the palace of Emperor Tenchi and was handed over to the Hosso sect in 663. Inside there is a clay figure of the Nyoirin Kannon, dating from the Heian Period, as well as a wooden sculpture of the seated priest Gien (d. 728), dating from the Nara Period.

During excavations two burial mounds were uncovered to the south of Okadera (bus from Kashihara-jingu, 15 mins). The Ishibutai Tomb, thought to be that of Soga-no-Umako, dates from the 7th c. To the south-west is the Takamatsuzuka Tomb (also 7th c.), in which burial gifts displaying Chinese and Korean influences have been found (copies in the nearby Asuka-shiryokan Museum).

From Asuka Station it is possible to return to Nara on the Kintetsu private railway line (30km/19 miles).

Narita

Japanese equivalent

成 田

Location
60km/37 miles
east of Tokyo

Narita is famous for the nearby Shinshoji Temple, one of the most important places of pilgrimage in Japan, which is visited every year by over 7 million believers. The town has also gained in importance since the opening of the Tokyo International Airport.

Access

From Tokyo (Keisei-Ueno Station) Keisei Line (1¼ hrs).

From Tokyo International Airport, JR coach or Chiba Kotsu coach to Narita Station (30 mins).

Special train "Narita Express" (N'EX; from Yokohama) from Tokyo to Narita Airport.

Shinshoji
Temple

Leaving the railway station walk through the lively shopping district of Omote-sando to the Naritasan Shinshoji Temple, situated about 1km/½ mile to the north.

The sanctuary is dedicated to the god of light, Fudo, and dates back to the year 939, when Taira Masakado led a revolt in the area which today forms the prefectures of Chiba and Ibaraki. At the behest of Emperor Sujaku the statue of Fudo was moved from the Jingoii Temple at Kyoto to Kozugahara, to the west of the present-day Shinshoji Temple, in order to help mark the victory over the rebels. The uprising came to an end in 940 with the death of Masakado, and the temple was then erected in Kozugahara to house the statue. In 1705 it was moved to its present location.

The 20ha/49 acre temple site includes the Niomon Gate, the Hall of the Three Saints, the Buddha Hall and the Main Hall, Hondo, the latter having been built in 1963–68 in the traditional style. There is also a belltower and a three-storey pagoda. New Year and the festival of Setsubun (beginning of February) are occasions when the temple is visited by large numbers of faithful.

Naritasan Park

Adjoining the temple area is the 16.5ha/40 acre Naritasan Park, which is particularly delightful when the cherry and plum trees are in blossom.

Museum

In the park stands a Historical Museum with exhibits from the temple possessions and archaeological finds from the Boso Peninsula.

Cultural Centre

A short distance to the east is the International Cultural Centre, where once a month a special event is staged involving a tea ceremony, ikebana and calligraphy demonstrations, etc.

Sogo Reido

From the JR station there is a bus service to the Sogo Reido sanctuary (20 mins), the memorial for Kiuchi Sogo (also Sakura Sogo, 1612–53). Flouting the ban on having direct dealings with the shogun, Sogo delivered

Tokyo's International Airport at Narita

a petition to Tokugawa Ietsuna from the peasants who were suffering under the double burden of crop failure and high taxes. Although his mission was successful, he and the other five members of his family were sentenced to death and executed.

Scenes from the life of Sogo are depicted in the Remembrance Hall, Sogo Goichidai-Kinenkan. Nearby is a small museum.

To the east of the town lies Tokyo International Airport (Narita Airport). In addition to bus services to Tokyo, there is the Narita Express ("N'EX"), a special train which continues on to Yokohama, and the Keisei railway line. Nearby is the Aviation Museum (Koku Kagaku Hakubutsukan) with historical aircraft and a flight simulator.

Narita Airport

South of the airport lies the ancient town of Shibayama. As well as old graves, clay figures called "Haniwa" were uncovered here. They are now on show in the municipal museum.

Shibayama

In Sakura, south-west of Narita (rail, 15 mins, then bus, 15 mins), it is worth visiting the new National Historical Museum (Kokuritsu Rekishi Minzoku Hakubutsukan), built on the site of the former Sakura Castle.

★National Historical Museum

★★National Museum

F 2

国 立 博 物 館

Japanese equivalent

The National Museum in Ueno Park (see entry) is the largest museum in Japan. It houses more than 100,000 works of Japanese, Chinese and Indian art, including more than 100 of Japan's National Treasures. Its main

District
Taito-ku, in
Ueno Park

National Museum

Underground
Ueno-eki
(Ginza Line)

Railway station
Ueno
(Yamanote Line)

Opening times
Tue.–Sun.
9am–4.30pm

Closed
26.12.–3.1.

building comprises 25 exhibition galleries (of which 20 are normally open to the public).

The museum was built between 1932 and 1938 to replace the Imperial Museum, which was seriously damaged in the 1923 earthquake, and presented to the Imperial House. The latter ceded all proprietary rights over the building and its artistic treasures to the state in 1947.

Until 1868 the Kan-eiji Temple stood here; it was at the time the most important Buddhist temple in Edo. In 1875 the temple was rebuilt close by, just outside the park.

On the right-hand side of the main building lies the Museum for East Asiatic Art, with 15 exhibition galleries. It was opened in October 1968. The objects on display are changed periodically.

Rooms 1, 2 and 3 — Buddhist sculptures from the Asuka Period (552–645) to the present, as well as examples from China.

Room 4 — Old textiles, especially valuable examples from the Asuka Period.

Room 5 — Metalwork, especially Buddhist sacred vessels etc. (6th–16th c.)

Room 6 — Historical weapons and military equipment.

Room 7 — The swordsmith's art with examples from different centuries.

Room 8 — Historic Japanese clothing. Ceramics from Japan, China and Korea.

Rooms 9 and 10 — Japanese, Korean and Chinese pottery.

National Museum of Tokyo

Japanese painting from the Nara Period (645–794) to the Kamakura Period (1192–1333).	Room 11
Japanese painting from the Muromachi Period (1392–1573) including masterpieces by the monks, Josetsu, Shubun and Sesshu.	Room 12
Japanese painting from the Momoyama (1573–1603) and Tokugawa (1603–1868) periods, including works of the Kano, Tosa, Sumiyoshi, Korin and Maruyama schools.	Room 13
Coloured xylographs from the Tokugawa Period.	Room 14
Japanese and Chinese masterpieces of lacquerwork of various centuries, including examples of lacquer-carving, gold and silver lacquer, lacquer with mother-of-pearl, etc.	Rooms 15 and 16
Japanese painting of the Meiji Period.	Rooms 17 and 18
Japanese calligraphy from the Nara Period to the Tokugawa Period.	Rooms 19 and 20
Objects excavated from graves, settlements, etc. revealing the prehistory of Japan. The "Haniwa", clay figures which were buried with the dead, are especially worthy of note.	Hyokeikan
Sculptures, paintings, excavation finds from the East Asiatic area.	Toyokan
Objects from the old Horyuji Temple in Nara. The Treasure Chamber is open on Thursdays, but only in good weather.	Horyuji Homotsukan
Behind the main building there is a typical Japanese landscape garden. Three pavilions have been brought here, and they give it the character of an open-air museum.	Landscape Garden

The Tein Teahouse (Rokuso-an) dates from the 17th c. In the Okyo Pavilion (Okyo-kan) pictures with plant motives by the famous landscape artist Maruyama Okyo (1735–95) are on show, while pictures by painters of the Kano School are displayed in the Kujo Pavilion. There is also a storehouse from the Kamakura Period.

National Museum of Western Art

F 2

国 立 西 洋 美 術 館

Japanese equivalent

The National Museum of Western Art is situated in Ueno Park (see entry) just three minutes' walk from Ueno Station. It was built in 1959, to plans by the famous Swiss architect Le Corbusier. Most of the exhibits consist of Western sculpture and paintings which were collected by the industrialist Matsukata Kojiro at the beginning of the century during his stay in Europe.

District
Taito-ku, in
Ueno Park

Underground
Ueno-eki
(Ginza Line)

In the courtyard works by the French sculptor Auguste Rodin are on show, together with canvasses by the Impressionists Paul Cézanne, Claude Monet, Edouard Manet and Edgar Degas.

Railway station
Ueno
(Yamanote Line)

Opposite the museum to the south is the municipal Festival Hall (1961), where theatrical performances and concerts are staged.

Tue.–Sun. 9.30am–5pm.

Opening times

National Park for Natural History Studies C/D 7

Japanese
equivalent

国 立 自 然 教 育 園

District
Minato-ku

Underground
Maguro
(Yamanote Line)

The National Park for Natural History Studies is ten minutes' walk from Meguro Underground Station in a north-easterly direction. With its many sclerophyllous evergreens, it presents a rather gloomy aspect. It is certainly not a people's park, in the sense that Ueno Park is (see entry), nor is it a park devoted to traditional Japanese arts of horticulture, as, for example, Shinjuku Park (see entry). Rather it is intended to foster spiritual awareness. Groups of students with their teachers can frequently be seen walking here, seeking inner peace and wisdom in the surroundings and in their conversations.

There is an admission charge for entry to the park. Depending on the season, the park can close very early.

National Science Museum F 2

Japanese
equivalent

国 立 科 学 博 物 館

District
Taito-ku, in
Ueno Park

Underground
Ueno-eki
(Ginza Line)

Just a few minutes' walk from Ueno Station in the eastern part of Ueno Park (see entry) can be found the National Science Museum. There are departments for space research, atomic research, applied chemistry, architecture, electricity and transport, etc. as well as a laboratory and work room. In the courtyard there are a number of whale skeletons on display.

The visitor has a choice of various routes through the exhibits. The museum is open daily (except Mondays) from 9am to 4.30pm.

Outside the museum building stands the statue of the Japanese bacteriologist, Hideyo Noguchi (1876–1928), who from 1904 held a professorship at the New York Rockefeller Institute.

Nihonbashi

See entry for Ginza

★★Nikko

Japanese
equivalent

日 光

Location
about 150km/
90 miles north
of Tokyo

The little town of Nikko (pop. 25,000) lies some 150km/90 miles north of Tokyo. No one who has any interest in Japanese culture, however, should let this distance deter them from a visit. Nikko is famous for its shrines, its national park and its wonderful setting where lakes alternate with wooded hills, rivers and thermal springs. The highest waterfall in Japan is to be found here, too. Japan has some 60,000 wild monkeys and some of them can be seen here.

A day trip to Nikko can be arranged with the Japan Travel Bureau. Although this is fairly expensive, it does at least include an afternoon bus tour round Nikko National Park.

Access

By rail from Ueno Station (Tohoku-Shinkansen Line) in about 45 mins to Utsunomiya and from by JR in about 30 mins to Nikko. From Asakusa Station (Tobu Line) in about 1½ hrs to Nikko.

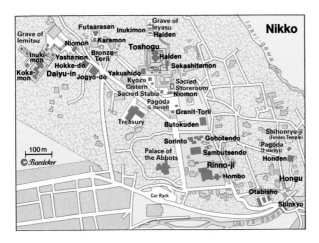

Temple and shrine sites

The railway stations of JR and the Tobu Line are close to one another and from them it is a 15-minute walk to the red-lacquered Holy Bridge of Shinkyo (also called Mihashi), which spans the River Daiya and leads across to the temple and shrine site with its profusion of cedar-trees.

★Shinkyo Bridge

The bushes and avenues bordering the roads leading to the shrine site were planted between 1625 and 1651 by Matsudaira Masatsuna. Although less prosperous than other daimios who paid their dues towards the building of the shrine, he was able, in this way, to make his contribution to the construction of the mausoleum for Ieyasu. Some 13,000 of these trees can still be seen.

The 28m/92ft long and 7.2m/24ft wide Holy Bridge, a reconstruction of the 1636 original, which was destroyed during a flood in 1902, marks the spot where, according to legend, the priest Shodo (735–817) crossed the river on the back of two giant snakes. Previously reserved for the use of the Shogun and his retinue, the bridge can now be crossed on payment of a toll.

Crossing the new bridge, which has been built directly alongside the old one, the visitor can reach the Hongu Shrine (also known as Futaarasan-Hongu), founded in 784 by Shodo and one of the oldest sanctuaries in Nikko. Nevertheless, the buildings visible today were not actually constructed until the end of the 17th c. This is also true of the Shihonryuji Temple, which stands behind the shrine. In the Main Hall of the temple can be seen statues of the Thousand-handed Kannon, Godaison and the temple's founder Shodo (the last reputedly a self-portrait).

Hongu Shrine
Shihonryuji
Temple

Taking the path continuing left from the bridge, the visitor will come to the Omotesando Pilgrim's Way, which leads to the Toshogu Shrine. The first building along the pilgrim's way is the Rinnoji Temple of the Tendai sect, which is thought to have been built in 848 by the priest Ennin (794–864, posthumously Jikaku-daishi) after the model of a temple situated on the holy mountain of Hiei. The abbatial residence (Hombo) and the garden which belongs to it are open to the public by prior arrangement. In the Main Hall, Sambutsu-do (Hall of the Three Buddhas; 1648) can be seen the 8m/26ft high gilded statue of Amida-nyorai, the Thousand-handed Kannon and the Bato Kannon (this last-named with a horse's head on the brow, a

★Rinnoji Temple

The Three Wise Monkeys in the Toshogu Shrine

symbol of the tutelary deity of animals). There are also portraits of the temple abbots, Tenkai (1536–1643, posthumously Jigen-daishi) and Ryogen (912–985, posthumously Gansan-daishi). To the north on an eminence stands the 13m/43ft high bronze column of Sorinto, which Tenkai had erected in 1643 as protection against evil spirits. To the right of the pillar is the hall, Gohotendo, which is dedicated to the deities, Daikokuten, Bishamonten and Benzaiten.

The pilgrim's way continues on to the Toshogu Shrine, the most important sanctuary in Nikko. The 22 buildings on the site date from a time when architecture and handicrafts were enjoying a golden period. Artists were brought in from all over the country to assist in creating a complex of buildings of unsurpassed magnificence. ★★Toshogu Shrine

A total of 15,000 craftsmen took part in the construction of the Toshogu Shrine, most of them from Kyoto and Nara, where architecture was enjoying its finest flowering. The result was a set of buildings almost over-endowed with opulent decorations, which managed to encapsulate the total splendour of the preceding Momoyama Period. The process of restoring and renovating shrines every twenty years or so has led to a state of affairs where the buildings are in an almost continuous state of repair.

Tokugawa Ieyasu died in 1616 and was initially buried on Mount Kunozan. In accordance with his last request he was brought to his final resting-place in Nikko a year later. In the same year he was posthumously granted the title of "Tosho-daigongen" ("incarnation of the Bodhisattva illuminating the east") by the Emperor. It was not until 1634 that his grandson Iemitsu began the construction of the mausoleum which was completed in the space of two years. Until the eclipse of the shogunate in 1868, the mausoleum was always under the supervision of an Imperial prince, who,

◀ *Nikko – a town in a beautiful setting*

The Sunlight Gate of the Toshogu Shrine

however, resided in Edo (Tokyo) and only travelled to Nikko three times a year.

The shrine only narrowly escaped destruction when a group of adherents of the Tokugawas entrenched themselves here during the Meiji Restoration. That the buildings were vacated without any fighting was due to the intervention of Itagaki Taisuke.

The first part of the building the visitor comes to is the Steps of the Thousand (Sennin-ishidan), which used to be the last place which was accessible to ordinary people on the way to the shrine. After that the visitor passes through a 8.4m/27½ft high torii made of granite with a plaque to the Emperor Go-Minuzoo (1596–1680). Next on the left is the five-storey pagoda of 1818. The stone steps lead on up to the Main Gate, Nio-mon (also called Omote-mon), which is the entrance to the courtyard with the three holy storehouses and the stable for the holy horses. The upper storehouse is decorated with a multicoloured carved relief on the side of the gable. It depicts two elephants and is thought to have been created by Kano Tanyu (1602–74) from a literary source, elephants being unknown in Japan at that time. The stable has carved representations of monkeys, including the famous group of three ("see no evil, hear no evil, speak no evil"). In the courtyard there is also the granite basin of the holy spring. To the northwest is the Sutra Library, Kyozo. Along the pathway stand numerous stone and bronze lanterns, which were installed by previous daimios.

A flight of steps leads on to the central courtyard with a belltower on the right and a drum-tower on the left. One of the bronze lanterns, which were made in Holland in 1636, carries the Tokugawa coat of arms. The bell is a gift from Korea. To the left of the drum-tower is the great hall, Yakushi-do, a reconstruction of the building which was burned down in 1961.

At the entrance to the inner courtyard is the magnificent Sunlight Gate, Yomei-mon, which only unarmed high-ranking samurai were allowed to pass through in the olden days. The gate is also known as "Higurashi-mon"

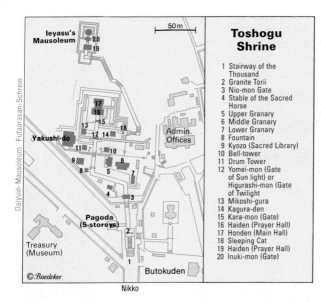

Toshogu Shrine

1 Stairway of the Thousand
2 Granite Torii
3 Nio-mon Gate
4 Stable of the Sacred Horse
5 Upper Granary
6 Middle Granary
7 Lower Granary
8 Fountain
9 Kyozo (Sacred Library)
10 Bell-tower
11 Drum Tower
12 Yomei-mon (Gate of Sun light) or Higurashi-mon (Gate of Twilight
13 Mikoshi-gura
14 Kagura-den
15 Kara-mon (Gate)
16 Haiden (Prayer Hall)
17 Honden (Main Hall)
18 Sleeping Cat
19 Haiden (Prayer Hall)
20 Inuki-mon (Gate)

Ieyasu's Mausoleum

Daiyuin-Mausoleum Futaarasan-Schrein

Yakushi-do

Admin. Offices

Pagoda (5-storeys)

Treasury (Museum)

© Baedeker

Butokuden

Nikko

("twilight gate"), the reason being, supposedly, that fascinated observers would linger here until twilight. The two-storey building is supported by twelve pillars and is extravagantly decorated with carvings, lacquerwork and gold-plating. On one tablet the name of the shrine is written in the hand of Emperor Go-Mizunoo. The two ceiling paintings, in which dragons are depicted, are by Kano Tanyu and Kano Yasunobu (17th c.). Inside there is a pillar with bas-reliefs which have deliberately been incorrectly applied, the intention, it is claimed, being to vitiate the perfection of the building and ward off the envy of evil spirits (Mayoke no hashira, "evil-repelling pillar").

Past the gate, on the left-hand side, lies the Mikoshi-gura Hall, where the processional shrines used for festivities are stored. To the right is the Hall of Devotional Dance, Kagura-den, and the shrine office. Access to the actual shrine is by Kara-mon Gate, in the Chinese style, predominantly in white and gold and embellished with beautiful carvings. The wall surrounding the shrine, Tamagaki, is made of stone at the bottom, but above boasts painted metal-covered carving.

Inside the shrine compound stands the Hall of Devotions, Haiden, with portraits of 36 poets painted by Tosa Mitsuoki (1617–91), whose works are included in the handwriting of Emperor Go-Minuzoo. The side chambers were once intended for the shogun and his followers and for the abbot of the Rinnoji Temple.

Passing through Ishi-no-ma ("stone room", so called because of its floor), we reach the Main Hall, Honden (16m/52ft long, 10m/32ft wide, 14m/46ft high), which consists of the Sacrifice Room, Heiden, the Inner Room, Naijin, and the Innermost Room, Nainaijin. In the last-named room, and surrounded by opulent decorations, stands the gilded shrine (Gokuden), in which Tokugawa Ieyasu was worshipped as a deity and Toyotomi Hideyoshi and Minamoto Yoritomo as secondary gods. In the gallery to the right of the Main Hall can be found the wooden sculpture of a sleeping cat (Nemuri-neko), which is attributed to the master Hidari Jingoro. We then

Figure of a guardian of the Toshogu Shrine

arrive at the ornate gate, Sakashita-mon. At one time even high-ranking samurai were forbidden to pass through this gate. A flight of 200 steps then leads to the Mausoleum of Ieyasu, situated behind the shrine, with the gate, Inuki-mon, in front of which two bronze Koma-inu sit (creatures resembling dogs and lions). Inside the gate is the tomb, in the shape of a small pagoda, restored in 1683 after an earthquake.

★Futaarasan Shrine

Between the five-storey pagoda at the entrance to the shrine and the Omotemon Gate, the path to the Futaarasan Shrine branches off to the left. The shrine was founded by Shodo in 784 and restored in 1619. It is dedicated to the husband-and-wife deities, Onamuchi and Tagorihime, and to their son, Ajisuki-takahikone, the deities of Mount Nantai (old name Futaarasan) to the west of Nikko. It comprises the main shrine, Honsha, the place of worship, Oku-miya, on the summit of the mountain, and the Middle Shrine, Chugushi, on Lake Chuzenji, which was built for pilgrims unable to climb Nantai.

The shrine includes a hall of worship, the Chinese gate, Kara-mon, and the Main Hall, Honden, where, on payment of an appropriate sum, the religious dance, Kagura, is performed by young dancers.

Hokke-do
Jogyo-do

South of the shrine stand the halls, Hokke-do and Jogyo-do, both belonging to the Rinnoji Temple, and also named Futatsu-do ("twin halls"). The halls were built in 848 and were modelled on a building on Mount Hiei. They house large numbers of Buddhist statues which were once kept in the Toshogu Shrine but were removed from there in the course of the Shinto renaissance during the Meiji Period. South from here, on the hill, Daikoku, stands the hall, Jigen-do, which also belongs to Rinno-ji and is dedicated to the close friend of Ieyasu and high priest of Nikko, Tenkai (1536–1643). On the way there the visitor will see the Amida Hall on the left, the Sutra Hall on the right and a belltower. Behind the Hall of Devotions, which is surrounded by a wall, lies the tomb of Tenkai.

A short distance to the west lies Daiyuinbyo, the Mausoleum of Iemitsu, the third Tokugawa shogun. Although this mausoleum was built only 16 years after the Tokugawa Shrine, it already shows recourse to the simpler style of the Edo Period. The colouring is limited to black and gold.

★★Daiyuinbyo

The first gate, Nio-mon, leads on to the second gate, Nitem-mon, a two-storey building with statues of the Buddhist gods Komoku-ten and Jikoku-ten (outer niches) and the gods of wind and thunder (inner niches).
In the central courtyard there are a belltower and a drum-tower. The path continues on through the third gate, Yasha-mon (also called Botam-mon, "peony gate"), with pictures of four Buddhist deities, and the fourth gate, Kara-mon (Chinese gate), into the inner courtyard. Here are to be found the Hall of Devotions and the Main Hall, Honden, linked with it by a connecting passageway, Ai-no-ma. In the Main Hall there is a statue of the seated Iemitsu. At the entrance to the innermost courtyard stands the Koka-mon Gate, built in the Ming Period style, followed by the Inuki-mon Gate, through which are to be found the inner hall of worship and, raised up, the bronze tomb of Iemitsu.

To the south-east of the mausoleum stands the shrine's Treasury with numerous works of art from the individual sanctuaries.

Treasury

The road leading west from Futaarasan goes past the Takino-o Shrine where the grave of the priest Shodo is to be found. Near the entrance is the Shiraito-no-taki waterfall.

★Takino-o

★Nikko National Park

Opening out to the west of the town is the 1407sq.km/543sq.mile Nikko National Park. With its mighty mountains, ancient forests, broad expanses of moorland, lakes and waterfalls, it counts as one of the most beautiful and most visited areas of the country.
The Nikko Museum is housed in a former Imperial villa (bus from Nikko Station, 15 mins). Its exhibits comprise flora and fauna from the national park and handicrafts of the region.

A number of waterfalls are to be found to the north and north-west of Nikko. Kirifuri-no-taki can be reached on foot in 1½ hrs (also buses in summer). The viewing platform provides an excellent panoramic view. Further north, on the slopes of Mount Maruyama, there is a winter-sports area with several ski-lifts.
To the west outside the town is the Jakko waterfall (also called Nunobiki Fall; bus to the Tanozawa stop, then 40 mins along a footpath).

There is a bus route serving the area of the park further to the west. It leads via Umagaeshi to Chuzenji Lake. On the eastern shores of the lake, near Chuzenji-onsen (50 mins from Nikko Station), the Kegon waterfall plunges down a drop of 100m/330ft (boat trips). The lake itself, which has Mount Nantai (2484m/8150ft) towering over it (lift to viewing platform), is a popular area with holidaymakers. The southern shore, with the towns of Teragasaki and Matsugasaki, is particularly attractive in its autumn colours. On the east shore stands the Chuzenji Temple (also Tachiki Kannon; second shrine of Rinno-ji in Nikko), which has a Thousand-handed Kannon by the priest Shodo.

★Chuzenji Lake
★Kegon Waterfall

The ascent of the extinct volcano of Nantai (beginning of May to mid-October) starts at the Middle Shrine (Chugushi), which belongs to the Futaarasan Shrine and has a hall of devotions (Haiden) and a main hall (Honden) which are worth seeing. The crater area (400m/440yds in diameter) takes about four hours to reach. A small charge is made for the ascent. Near the summit stands the Innermost Shrine (Okumiya).

Nantai

Lake Chuzenji with the Kegon Waterfall

Senjogahara Plateau

From Chuzenji-onse the bus route follows the north shore of the lake to Jigokuchaya. The Ryuzi waterfall is close by.

Lake Yunoko

Across the Senjogahara Plateau with its rich Alpine flora is Nikko-Yumoto-onsen, situated on Lake Yunoko, which is popular both with holidaymakers in summer and with winter-sports enthusiasts. The lake has rich stocks of fish and is therefore highly regarded by anglers.

★★Ozegahara

Crossing the Konsei Pass (2024m/6640ft) the moorland plateau of Ozegahara and Lake Ozenuma in the extreme west of the national park are reached.

Shiobara-onsen

Even the most north-easterly section of Nikko National Park is not difficult to get to. The starting-point is the spa, Shiobara-onsen, about 25km/16 miles to the north, which is overshadowed by Takahara in the south and the Nasu Ridge in the north.

Takahara

From Oku-Shiobara a 8km/5 mile path makes the ascent of the two peaks of Takahara: Keicho (1766m/5794ft) and Shaka (1795m/5889ft). These summits offer wonderful views of the surrounding mountain area.

Nasu Volcano

The spa region of Nasu-onsenkyo is situated at the foot of Nasu Volcano. The spa towns are Nasu-Yumoto, Kita, Benten, Omaru, Sandogoya, Takao and Itamuro.

The Nasu Plateau Toll Road goes through the volcano area. Kakkodaira is the start of the relatively gentle ascent route up to Chausu (also Nasu; 1917m/6289ft). From this peak it is possible to reach Asahi (1903m/6243ft).

Oshima

See Izu

★Paper Museum

紙の博物館

Japanese
equivalent

In Japan paper is rated as an art form, and out in the country it is still possible to see it being made by hand.

Address
1-1-8. Horifune, Kita-ku

The Tokyo Paper Museum is the only one of its kind in the world. It has a rich display of various types of paper and, above all, prints. Also on show is the equipment needed for making and processing paper by hand. The museum is open from 9.30am to 4.30pm every day except Monday.

Railway station
Oji

Parliament Building

E 5

国 会 議 事 堂

Japanese
equivalent

The Parliament Building, situated in the government area of Marunouchi, is called Kokkai-gijido in Japanese. On seeing the building, it is impossible to not to form the conclusion that, just as the country's machinery of government has more or less totally adopted the procedures and values of the West, so this new style of administration can only be accommodated in a

District
Marunouchi

Parliament Building

Underground
Kokkai-gijido
-mae (Chiyoda-,
Marunouchi
Line)

building which has no connection with native Japanese architectural styles.

The massive grey-granite building is modelled on the American Congress. It has a portico supported on columns and a central tower 65m/200ft high which is colonnaded and surmounted by a stepped pyramid. Just as the Japanese gave democracy a typical Japanese stamp, so, too, they have tried to link Western architectural styles with the Japanese character.

The right-hand wing of the building belongs to the Upper House, while the Lower House meets in the left-hand wing. In the entrance hall stand bronzes of the "fathers of Japanese parliamentarianism": Prince Ito, Okuma and Itagaki.

★Rikugi-en Park   E 1

Japanese
equivalent

六義園

District
Bunkyo-ku

Railway station
Komagome
(Yamanote Line)

Opening times
Tue.–Sun.
9am–4pm

The magnificent Rikugi-en Park is just eight minutes' walk from Komagome Station in a southerly direction. It is a characteristic example of 17th/18th c. landscape gardening, with a knoll, called Tsukiyama, a lake and an island. The park was originally established on the orders of Yanagisawa Yoshiyasu (1658–1714), but was then presented as a gift to the city of Tokyo in 1938 and made accessible to the general public. The unusual thing about the park is that the various landscape features are all connected with literary themes.

Nearby is the Gokokuji Temple (see entry).

Rikugi-en Park

Roppongi

六本木

Most of the night-life of Tokyo takes place in the district of Roppongi.

District
Minato-ku

There is a large and varied range of entertainments: inexpensive Yakitori bars (generally recognisable by the red lantern at the entrance), luxury restaurants with international cuisine, exorbitantly priced "hostess bars", but also plenty of discothèques, night-clubs and live music to set the atmosphere.

Underground
Roppongi
(Hibiya Line)

The Roppongi quarter is also the location of a number of foreign embassies.

Sea Life Park

beyond the limits of the city plan

東京都葛西臨海水族園

Japanese
equivalent

The Kasai Rinkai Koen Park is situated in the district of Edogawa-ku to the east of the city centre.

Address
6-2-3, Rinkai-cho,
Edogawa-ku

The Tokyo Sea Life Park was opened there in 1989. Its attractions include the largest aquarium in Japan, an enclosure with penguins, as well as many different species of sea-birds.

Sea Life Park

Sengakuji Temple – graves of the 47 Ronin

★★Sengakuji Temple

D 7

Japanese
equivalent

泉 岳 寺

District
Takanawa

Underground
Sengakuji
(Toei-Asakusa
Line)

Railway station
Shinagawa
(Yamanote Line)

The Sengakuji Temple was founded in 1612 by the Soto sect of Zen Buddhism. The present-day temple building is a reconstruction carried out in 1953; its main gate (Sammon) dates from the 19th c.

Even today the fate of the 47 samurai who avenged the death of their master is still lamented, especially by women, while in the 18th c. their unhappy end moved the minds of all Japanese. The samurai all lie buried in the Sengakuji Temple and the faithful still come every day to light joss sticks to their memory on their stone memorials in the beautiful temple gardens.

The lord and master of the Forty-seven, Asano Naganoni, Lord of Ako (1665–1701), drew his sword to defend his honour when the court chamberlain, Kira Yoshinaka, insulted him. The use of armed force on Imperial soil was considered a heinous crime, which could only be expiated by death. The daimio was accordingly sentenced to commit "seppuku" (ritual suicide).

His samurai, who now no longer had any master and were deprived of his protection, became "ronin" ("men of the waves"): they no longer had a home and their lives were purposeless. Moreover they had no desire to enter the service of any other daimio. Instead their desire was to avenge the

View of Shinjuku with the New City Hall (See page 138) ▶

death of their master – an action which, according to the code of honour of the samurai, would demonstrate the noblest sort of devotion.

For months on end they adopted an air of indifference, made a show of being reconciled to events and secretly prepared for the day of reckoning: Kira was to be slain and, as a sign of propitiation and satisfaction, his head was to be placed on the grave of their master in the Sengakuji Temple.

And so it came to pass: led by Oishi Yoshio Kuranosuke, they burst into Kira's home, struck off his head, cleaned it and placed it on the gravestone.

This act of loyalty earned widespread approbation, but, nevertheless, like their master, the samurai had to pay the price for it by dying by their own hand. With the satisfaction of having served their master loyally, even after his death, and of having restored his honour, they carried out the sentence which had been imposed on them, not far from Asano's grave.

Their heroic deeds live on as a symbol of loyalty in the Kabuki play, "Chushingura".

The graves of the 47 "ronin" are to be found in the temple cemetery, while the temple museum contains wooden portraits of them and other mementoes.

Senso-ji

See entry for Asakusa Kannon Temple

Shinjuku (City district)   B/C 3/4

Japanese
equivalent

新宿

District
Shinjuku-ku

Underground
Shinjuku
(Marunouchi Line)

Railway station
Shinjuku
(Chuo, Yamanote
Lines)

Shinjuku forms the western part of Tokyo and is a secondary centre of population and trade situated some 10km/6 miles from the city centre. During the Edo Period (1603–1867) it was a posting station (Naito-Shinjuku) on the Kashu Road and today it is one of the busiest traffic intersections in Tokyo. Shinjuku Station, with rail and underground connections, serves over 1½ million commuters every day.

East of the railway station lies the second largest shopping centre in Tokyo with department stores and an underground mall. Even more importantly, this district also boasts the well-known entertainment district of Kabuki-cho with gaming dens, bars, cafés, jazz cellars, discothèques, cinemas, theatres and art galleries.

There are also many skyscrapers, which at one time were something of a rarity in Japan. These include the New City Hall (1991; 243m/797ft; see entry), the Keio Plaza Intercontinental Hotel (169m/558ft, 47 storeys), the Shinjuku Sumitomo Building (200m/660ft, 52 storeys) and the Shinjuku Mitsui Building (212m/695ft, 55 storeys). The viewing platforms of these skyscrapers offer superb panoramas of the city.

The extensive Shinjuku Park (see entry) and the Waseda University with the Tsubouchi Theatre Museum (see entry) are also located in Shinjuku.

Shinjuku Park   C 4

Japanese
equivalent

新宿御苑

District
Shinjuku-ku

Japanese garden design, with what strikes foreigners as a completely different style of artistic arrangement, is an unfailing source of delight. The

Shinjuku-Gyoen National Garden is a park that combines everything which is expected of Japanese gardening. It is situated only five minutes' walk from Shinjuku Railway Station.

The grounds of the park covers some 58.5ha/145 acres, most of it formerly belonging to the Naito daimio family. Towards the end of the 19th c. it came into the possession of the Imperial house, which transferred ownership to the state after the Second World War. As the park is also a botanical garden, with botanical specimens from all over the world, it is divided into two main sections, one European and the other Japanese. The models for the European section were the French parks and the English landscaped garden. The Japanese section, with its pretty pavilion in the Chinese style, attracts crowds of visitors, particularly in April when the cherry trees are covered in blossom. At that time of year 1100 trees comprising 34 different varieties may be seen in all their glory. Those who prefer chrysanthemums wait for November when shows of the flower are held in the park.

Underground
Shinjuku-gyoen-mae (Marunouchi Line)

Opening times
Tue.–Sun.
9am–4pm

Closed
29.12–3.1.

★★Sword Museum
B 4

刀 剣 博 物 館

Japanese equivalent

The reverence accorded the sword in Japan is well illustrated by the richly-stocked Sword Museum. It displays masterpieces of Japanese swordsmiths' craft from every period in the country's history.

The "way of the sword" (Ken-do), has its origins, along with the traditional tea ceremony, in Zen Buddhism. Mastering this particular art was supposed to help body relaxation and control and to assist in overcoming an arrogant ego.

Address
4-25-10, Yoyogi, Shibuya-ku

Railway station
Sangubashi (Odakyu Line)

Sword Museum

Tokyo Disneyland

Swordfighting was originally practised by the samurai with proper swords (in contrast to today). Protected by light armour in only those parts of the body which were particularly vulnerable, the combatants attempted to strike one another with the sword wielded in both hands. About 1750 the use of the sword was replaced by safe weapons (bamboo canes), and from the old swordsman's art (kenjut-su) the "way of the sword" developed.

Naturally it was not just a question of the swordsman being initiated, but also his instrument, the sword. The swordmaker was not, therefore, just any smith, but rather a kind of master of ceremonies. Since the beginnings of the Japanese art of swordmaking – and it dates back to the 10th c. when the samurai were emerging as a distinct group – the swordsmith has enjoyed the highest public regard. The sword which was to aid the Emperor or the samurai in achieving victory must on no account be infected with evil spirits. But as the master swordsmith was the only person in possession of the requisite knowledge and skill, he was a highly respected man.

The act of forging the sword was from very early on a kind of ritual. The swordsmith would avoid any contact with the unclean outside world, donned special garments purely for the forging ceremony, while over his hearth hung a Shinto cord of straw to ward off evil spirits.

★★Tokyo Disneyland (Theme park)

Japanese
equivalent

東京ディズニーランド

Location
15km/9 miles
south-east of
Tokyo;
1 Maihama
Urayasu-shi
Chiba-ken 272-01

The Tokyo Disneyland theme park was opened in 1983 and covers an area of 46ha/114 acres. It was conceived along the tried and tested lines of its American model: with a "Main Street", which the theme areas, such as "Adventureland", "Fantasyland", "Westernland" and "Tomorrowland" adjoin. Tokyo Disneyland has the added attraction of its very own theme area, "3000 Years of Japanese History".

The visitor has some 30 restaurants and snack-bars to choose from. The open-air theatre hold 15,000 spectators. There are approaching 40 attractions in the park and the intention is that year by year a further one or two are added.

By underground (Tozai Line) to Urayasu Station and then on by shuttle bus service; by bus direct from Tokyo Main Railway Station and from Narita International Airport; by car along the No. 9 expressway.

Access

The main central area of the park is the "World Bazaar", which is completely under cover and recalls the type of "main street" which existed in American frontier towns around the turn of the last century. The visitor will find many restaurants, shops, boutiques and amusement facilities here.

World Bazaar

Adventureland offers a boat trip on a winding jungle river with African, South American and Asian symbols and features along the bank. One can also take a ride in a wild west steam train through a primeval dinosaur-inhabited environment.
   "Pirates of the Caribbean" re-enacts a 20-minute pirate attack on a harbour in the Caribbean, including cannon-shots.

Adventureland

Westernland simulates the American wild west at the time of the pioneers. The paddle-steamer "Mark Twain" and Indian canoes travel up and down the "Rivers of America". They circle round "Tom Sawyer Island" with Joe's cave, Tom Sawyer's wooden shack and Fort Sam Clements.
   The "Golden Horseshoe Revue" holds the record of being the longest show of its kind in the world to have been staged continuously without a break (since 1955).

Westernland

Fantasyland takes visitors through the fairy-tale world of Walt Disney. They will meet Cinderella, Snow White, Peter Pan and Pinocchio. The climax of a visit is the "Mickey Mouse Revue".
   "It's a Small World" presents costumed dolls and folk songs from 100 countries. "Haunted Mansion" is a haunted house inhabited by 999 ghosts and creatures of fable.
   Outside Fantasyland there is a Swiss cable-car railway which offers a fine view of the park as it proceeds to . . .

Fantasyland

Tomorrowland, where the visitor meets the world of the future and technological progress in all its many shapes and forms.
   A "Space Mountain" provides the opportunity to fly in space and the "Magic Carpet Round the World" affords a 360° panoramic view of the most famous places in the world.

Tomorrowland

Tokyo National Museum

See National Museum

Tokyo Tower (Telecommunications Tower)   E 6

東 京 タ ワ ー

Japanese equivalent

On a hill in Shiba Park, where the Zojoji Temple (see entry) is also situated, stands Tokyo's tallest building, Tokyo Tower, which dates from 1958 and is modelled on the Eiffel Tower in Paris. It is 333m/1098ft high, 13m/43ft higher than its Parisian predecessor. When visibility is good, visitors can even make out Fuji-san and there is always a good view over the vast

District
Minato-ku, in
Shiba Park

Tokyo Tower

Tokyo Tower in Shiba Park

cityscape of Tokyo. There are viewing platforms at heights of 150m/490ft and 250m/795ft.

Every year four million visitors climb or are conveyed to the top of this tower, which weighs some 4000 tonnes. The tower is both a symbol of Japanese post-war reconstruction and also a city landmark. It houses an aquarium with over 8000 species of fish, as well as the first waxworks in Asia. At its base stands the Museum of Modern Science.

Seven television stations and a host of radio transmitters make use of the tower, which is also the transmission mast for radio communications between large companies.

A battery of instruments constantly measures the amount of pollution over Tokyo, while seismatic indicators monitor the faintest earth tremors.

Underground
Kamiyacho
(Hibiya Line)

Railway station
Hamamatsucho
(Keihin-Tohoku
Line;
Yamanote Line)

Tsubouchi Theatre Museum   C 3

坪 内 博 士 記 念 演 劇 博 物 館

Japanese
equivalent

The grounds of Waseda University are five minutes' walk from Waseda Underground Station. The university was founded in 1882 by the politician Okuma Shigenobu (1838–1922). It is one of the largest private higher education establishments in the country, with seven faculties in all.

Location
1-chome,
Nishi-Waseda,
Shinjuku-ku

The Tsubouchi Memorial Theatre Museum is situated on the university campus. It was established in 1928 as a memorial to Tsubouchi Shoyo (1859–1935), a famous dramatist and translator of Shakespeare. It is the only museum of its kind in Japan with objects and documents on show which illustrate the history and the nature of Far Eastern theatre. For those who are going to see Noh and Kabuki theatre, this is a very good source of additional information about a quite alien theatrical world.

Underground
Waseda
(Tozai Line)

Opening times
Mon.–Fri.
9am–4pm.
Sat. 9am–2pm
Sun. closed

★Tsukiji Fishmarket   F 6

築 地 中 央 卸 売 市 場

Japanese
equivalent

The Tsukiji Market is the largest trading-place in Tokyo for vegetables, fruit, meat, poultry and fish.

A lot of fish is eaten in Japan and, regardless of whether it is imported goods or domestic catches, whether it is to be sold deep-frozen or fresh, almost all the fish which the city consumes finds its way through the famous Tsukiji Fishmarket, where, together with oysters, crayfish, ink-fish and crabs, the whole mouth-watering display is set out.

The market covers an area of 20ha/50 acres and lies 200m/220yds south of the Tsukiji Honganji Temple (see entry). Selling at this wholesale market commences every day at four o'clock in the morning. It is therefore best to visit the market between 4.30am and 8am. Waterproof shoes and a spare film for the camera are to be recommended. The fishmarket is closed on Sundays and on one Wednesday in every month.

District
Chuo-ku, on the
River Sumida

Underground
Tsukiji
(Hibiya Line)

Railway station
Shinbashi
(Yamanote Line)

Tsukiji Honganji Temple   F 5

築 地 本 願 寺

South-east of the shopping street of Ginza (see entry) (300m/330yds east of the Kabukiza Theatre) lies the Tsukiji Honganji Temple of the Jodo Shinshu

Tsukiji Honganji Temple

Tsukiji Fishmarket (See page 143)

Location
Shin-ohashi-dori,
Ginza, district
of Chou-ku

Underground
Tsukojo
(Hibiya Line)

Railway station
Yurakucho
(Yamanote Line)

sect. The temple, which is a subsidiary temple of the Nishi-Honganji Temple in Kyoto (see entry), is built in the Hindu style.

It was founded in 1630, but was subsequently destroyed by fire on several occasions, most recently in the earthquake of 1923, after which it was rebuilt in 1935 using new earthquake-proof technology.

The temple is noteworthy because weddings take place following Buddhist rites, in contrast to the practice in other Buddhist sects. There are also Buddhist services in English here on Sundays.

★Tsukuba Science City

**Japanese
equivalent**

筑波研究学園郡市

Location
60km/37 miles
north-east of
Tokyo

The newly-opened Tsukuba Science City, one of the largest and most up-to-date scientific centres in the world, lies at the foot of the 876m/2874ft high Mount Tsukuba.

Access

By rail from Ueno Station (JR) in about 45 mins to Tsuchiura and from there (Kanto-Tsukuba Line) to Tsukuba Station.

This "test-tube" town was designed by the architect Fumihiko Maki and has been growing in size over the past few years (at the latest count over 25,000 inhabitants). Built on a site of some 270ha/600 acres in open countryside, it consists of over 1650 buildings (including futuristic high-rise ones), a central area and extensive pedestrianised zones.
The town is the home of about a third of all Japanese national research

institutes as well as a university, a "glass artificial mountain" with 26 faculty areas for research and six for academic teaching accommodating more than 3000 scientists and about 10,000 students. There are also residential areas, shopping centres, schools, leisure facilities and entertainment centres.

The technological and scientific installations of this "thought factory", which is not expected to be finally completed until the end of this century, include state-of-the-art laboratories (wind-tunnels, electronic microscopes, laser and radar instruments, etc.), a seven-storey reinforced concrete building with an earthquake simulator, a road-traffic testing road more than 6km/4 miles long and a 380m/415yd long tunnel for experiments in noise reduction, ventilation and illumination. Besides many other research projects it is intended in the future to study the possibilities of increasing factory automation through industrial robots.

★Ueno Park

F 2

上 野 公 園

	Japanese equivalent
	District Taito-ku
	Underground Ueno (Ginza Line)
	Railway station Ueno (Yamanote Line)

The 84ha/208 acre large Ueno Park is one of the most popular places to go to in the whole of the inner-city area of Tokyo. It is criss-crossed by gravel paths; hot-dog sellers advertise their wares with loudspeakers, and there are many cinemas and amusement centres in the vicinity. Tokyo's largest park is, with its zoo and aquarium, a real people's park, but also a cultural centre with a number of museums, many temples, shrines and pagodas, as well as some important official buildings. The main entrance lies at the south-eastern edge of the park, near Ueno Station.

Memorial to Saigo Takamori

Once part of a daimio's residence, the park came into the possession of the Tokugawa shoguns in the early 17th c. In 1873 it passed into public ownership.

In 1868 Kaneiji, which had been built by the Tokugawas as a domestic temple, was the last stronghold of the troops remaining loyal to the Shogun. In the course of the fighting everything was destroyed except for a five-storey pagoda. There is a memorial to the fallen who fought for the Emperor and a bronze statue of Saigo Takamori (1827–77), one of the leaders of the Meiji Restoration. As a general of Emperor Meiji's troops he conducted the war against Korea, but came into conflict with the central government. Consequently he became a leader of the Kagoshima Rebellion. When it was put down he committed "seppuku" (ritual suicide) in accordance with the samurai code of honour. Nowadays, however, he is revered as a national hero. A flight of stone steps with many cherry trees on either side leads up to the memorial and the inscriptions. (The cherry trees are in blossom in early April.)

Takamori Memorial

145

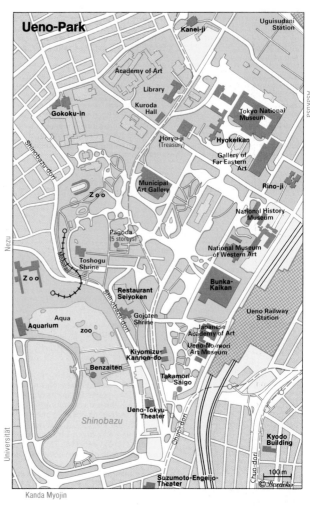

Kanda Myojin

Kiyomizu Temple	On the left-hand side lies the Kiyomizu Temple, modelled on the temple of the same name in Kyoto (see entry). Inside there is a statue of the Thousand-handed Kannon.
Art Museum	North-east of the memorial stands the Ueno-no-Mori Art Museum, established in 1887, where frequently changing exhibitions are on view. Immediately adjoining are the buildings of the Japanese Academy of Art.
Concert Hall	The Tokyo Bunko Kaikan Concert Hall was built in 1961, on the occasion of the city's five-hundredth jubilee. It contains both a larger and smaller auditorium (2230 and 611 seats), in which concerts and opera performances take place.

Ueno Park

The southern section of the park is occupied by Shinobazu Lake (2km/1 mile in circumference; boat hire). The Benzaiten Temple stands on a strip of land protruding into the lake. The lake itself is famous for its lotus blossom in August.

Shinobazu

At the north-west end of the lake stands the Aquarium, one of the largest of its kind in the Far East. Here are to be found amphibians and reptiles.

Aquarium

The Zoo extends along the northern edge of the lake, its two sections being connected with one another by a monorail. Opened in 1882, it is the oldest zoological garden in Japan. It has around 850 animals, mainly in open-air enclosures.

Zoo

The Toshogu Shrine is situated by the monorail and has a pathway with 256 stone and bronze lanterns on either side leading up to it. It was built in memory of Tokugawa Ieyasu in 1627 and restored in 1651. Of particular interest here are the Main Shrine, built in the Gongen-zukuri style, and the five-storey pagoda (1639), which was originally part of the Kaneiji Temple (see above). The pagoda was transferred here, being the only part of the destroyed temple to survive the fighting mentioned above. The Kara-mon Gate in front of the Main Shrine has carvings which are said to be by the sculptor Hidari Jingoro (17th c.).

Toshogu Shrine

Just to the east of the zoo stands the building housing the Tokyo Metropolitan Art Gallery (1926), which regularly has temporary exhibitions.

Tokyo Metropolitan Art Gallery

To the north of the Bunka Kaikan Concert Hall is the National Museum of Western Art (see entry).

National Museum of Western Art

Immediately to the north-east of the National Museum of Western Art are the buildings of National Science Museum (see entry).

National Science Museum

National Museum

In the northern part of Ueno Park stands the large building of the National Museum (see entry).

Horyuji

Some distance to the west of the National Museum is the Treasury of the Horyuji Temple (Horyuji Homotsukan), which is of considerable interest with its collection of weapons, furniture, etc. Behind it there is a pretty garden with three old pavilions.

To the west just beyond the park limits are the Tokyo Arts Academy and the Ueno Library, part of the parliament library and with one of the largest stocks of books in the country.

Kaneiji Temple

Right in the north of the park and to the east of the Tokyo Arts Academy can be found the new Kaneiji. As the Chorakuji Temple it stood in Serada, in the prefecture of Gumma. After the destruction of the original Kaneiji (see above, Takamori Memorial), it was transferred to Ueno Park in 1875 as a replacement.

Yasukuni Shrine   E 4

Japanese equivalent

靖 国 神 社

Location
Kudan Kita,
3-chome,
Chiyoda-ku

The Yasukini Shrine is in the district of Kudan Kita, to the north-west of Mizugami Park. It was built in the Shinto style in 1869 and is dedicated to Japan's war-dead.

Underground
Kudanshita
(Tozai Line)

The entry to the outer precinct is through two immense torii: at the south entrance stands a 12m/39ft high granite torii, and at the entry to the inner precinct there is a bronze torii 22m/74ft high. Both of these were put up in 1933.

Along the path to the shrine stands a bronze statue of Omura Masujiro (1825–69), a leading political figure from the early Meiji Period.

The grounds of the temple are beautiful with ginkgo trees and ornamental cherries. This gave rise to the customary farewell of soldiers departing for the war: "We'll meet again under the cherry trees on Kudan Hill".

The spring festival at the shrine takes place between April 21st and 23rd, the autumn festival from October 17th and 19th.

Yasukini Shrine, in as much as it is a sanctuary for state Shintoism, still gives rise to political contention. It was here that with great secrecy the urns containing the remains of the men condemned to death by the International Military Court in 1948 as war criminals were laid to rest. By this act of burial they acquired the status of "kami", i.e. beings who were godlike and deserving of reverence.

Yokohama

Japanese equivalent

横 浜

Location
30km/19 miles
south of Tokyo

Yokohama, the second largest city in Japan, lies in eastern Central Honshu, a short distance to the south of Tokyo, and with its larger neighbour forms the industrial conurbation of Keihin (Tokyo–Kawasaki–Yokohama). Yokohama is the capital of the prefecture of Kanagawa, the largest trading port in the country and for sea passengers the most important gateway to

The port of Yokohama

Japan. The city's important industrial base comprises shipping wharves, machine and automobile engineering, petro-chemicals, etc.

Rail from Tokyo Main Railway Station (Tokaido; Yokosuka Line) to Yokohama Station; by urban railway from Tokyo Main Railway Station (Keihin-Tohoku Line) to Sakuragi-cho Station or Kannai Station.

Access

Yokohama is a new city. In 1854, after the Black Ships of Commodore Perry forced their way into the Bay of Tokyo, the opening of Japan to the Western world was secured in the Treaty of Kanagawa. The tiny fishing village then rapidly developed into a thriving port and trading town. In 1859 the first foreigners settled here, including the first Consul General of the United States in Japan, Townsend Harris. By 1889 the population of the town had risen to over 120,000. Parts of the city were destroyed in the earthquake of 1923 and in the Second World War. In 1989 Yokohama celebrated its centenary and the 130th anniversary of the opening of the harbour.

History

Places of Interest

Sakuragicho Station lies south-east of the Main Railway Station, close to the city centre. It is from here that the most important places of interest can be most easily reached.

To the west of the Station (10 mins, on foot), in the north of the Naka-ku district, stands the Iseyama Shrine. Built in 1870, it belongs to the Ise group of shrines and is dedicated to the tutelary god of the city. The shrine possesses a 10m/33ft high torii made of cypress wood.

Iseyama Shrine

Just to the north is Kamon-yama Park, famous for its cherry blossom in the middle of April. It contains a statue of the politician Ii Naosuke (1815–60), who played a key role in opening Japan to the outside world.

Kamon-yama Park

149

Yokohama

Nogeyama Park

South-west of the Iseyama Shrine (about 7 mins, on foot) lies Nogeyama Park with its zoo and swimming pool. The park is situated on a hill, from which there are fine views. To the south-east is Isezaki-cho, a shopping street, which leads from Naka-ku back into the city centre.

Prefectural Museum

South-east of Sakuragicho Station (5 mins, on foot) lies the Prefectural Museum. The prestigious building in which it is housed dates from 1904. The museum includes both scientific and historical collections. Further south-east is a brick building dating from 1917 with a belltower, which today serves as a remembrance hall for the opening of the harbour. Next to it is a monument to Okakura Tenshin, the city's most famous sculptor.

Port

Going north-eastwards from Yokohama Park we come to the port area (harbour trips several times a day). Next to Osambashi Pier stands the nine-storey Silk Center which includes the Yokohama International Tourist Association, the post office, the offices of the aircraft companies, the Silk Hotel and the silk museum. To the right, extending along the harbour basin, is Yamashita Park (boat service from the quay to the east of Yokohama Station, 15 mins; view over the harbour). In the harbour the former trans-oceanic ship "Hikawa Maru" is anchored. It is now used as a museum and also contains an aquarium with tropical fish. To the south-west stands the 108m/354ft Marine Tower, built to commemorate the centenary of the opening of the harbour and offering yet another view of the city (particularly impressive at night).

Chinese Quarter

500m/550yds west of here is the Chinese Quarter (Chuka-gai) with numerous restaurants, shops and places of entertainment.

Yamate-machi

To the south, on the other side of the River Nakamura, will be found the shopping street, Motomachi. This is where Yamate-machi (also called Bluff), the foreigners' quarter, begins. The foreigners' cemetery, for

In the Chinese Quarter

Old buildings in Sankei-en

example, is situated here. To the east is Minato-no-mieru-oka Park with rewarding views of the port area.

On the south-eastern edge of the city lies the beautiful Sankei-en Garden (bus from east exit of the station, 35 mins, then 10 mins on foot). Several historic buildings originating in other parts of the country are located here. These include the 500-year-old three-storey pagoda from the Tomyoji Temple in Kamo (Kyoto), the Rinshun-kaku (former villa of the Tokugawa line, which used to live on the Kii Peninsula; 1649), the tea pavilion, Choshu-kaku, of Tokugawa Iemitsu, the Yanohara-ke farmhouse (18th c.) and the Tenzuiji Juto Sayado Temple (from Daitoku-ji in Kyoto; 1592). In the southern part of the park is the building, Hasseiden, erected in 1933, which contains the statues of the eight wise men of the world: Shakyamuni, Confucius, Socrates, Christ, Shotoku-taishi, Kobo-daishi, Shinran and Nichiren.

★Sankei-en

From the Main Railway Station it is possible to travel south-west on the Keihin Kyuko private railway line, or the underground, to the Gumyo-ji Temple of the Shingon sect, the oldest temple in the city, which contains a 9th c. wooden statue of the Eleven-headed Kannon.

Gumyo-ji Temple

To the east of the Temple (20 mins on foot from the Makita underground station) is the Archaeological Museum, Santondai, with excavation finds from the surrounding area.

Archaeological Museum

To the north-east of Sakuragicho Station lies the Nippon-maru Memorial Park with the sailing instruction ship "Nippon-maru", now no longer in service, and a maritime museum.

Maritime Museum

Not far to the north-east of the Main Railway Station in the district of Kanagawa-ku stands the Hongakuji Temple of the Soto sect. In 1858 the

Hongakuji Temple

building was temporarily the residence of the Consul General of the United States and it was here that the signing of the Japanese-American trading agreement took place.

Sojiji Temple

To visit the Sojiji Temple of the Soto sect take the JR Tohoku Line from the Main Railway Station in a north-easterly direction to Tsurumi Station. The temple was built in 1321 in the prefecture of Ishikawa and after a fire in 1898 was rebuilt on its present site. It is one of the most important Zen temples in Japan and has authority over 15,000 other temples.

There are several educational establishments located on the temple site.

Yokohama Dreamland

South-west of the city limits, near Matanocho, is the 66ha/163 acre amusement park, Yokohama Dreamland, in the style of Disneyland (JR Odakyu Line to Ofuna, Fujisawa, Totsuka or Chogo, then by bus). The park was opened in 1963 and possesses a large number of amusements and facilities, including an open-air theatre, an ice-rink and a hotel.

Yumenoshima Park   outside the area covered by the city plan

Japanese equivalent

夢の島公園

District
Koto-ku

Underground
Minami-Suna-machi
(Tozai Line)

Yumenoshima Park is situated in the south-east of the city, between the Rivers Sumida and Arakawa, in the middle of a large commercial area, criss-crossed by canals. The park contains a number of sports grounds and a swimming pool.

The park is also home to the restored fishing-boat "The Lucky Dragon", whose crew was severely affected by radioactive fall-out while sailing in the waters around the Bikini Atoll in the 1950s. Today the boat is a memorial symbolising opposition to the USA's atomic weapon tests.

Yumenoshima Park – tropical plant dome

The main attraction of the park is the Tropical Plant Dome, which is a tropical-plant hothouse composed of several spheres.

Yushima Seido (Shrine) F 3

Japanese equivalent

The Confucian shrine of Yushima Seido is situated on a hill not far from the railway station. It was founded in 1690 by the fifth shogun Tsunayoshi and under the auspices of the Tokugawas developed into a centre of Confucianism. The shrine has been destroyed on numerous occasions (the last time in the earthquake catastrophe of 1923). The present buildings date from 1935. The bronze sculptures of Confucius and other Chinese sages in the Main Hall are particularly impressive.

District
Bunkyo-ku

Underground
Ochanomizu
(Marunouchi Line)

Railway station
Ochanomizu
(Chuo and Sobu Lines)

Every year on the last Sunday in April there is a ceremony in honour of Confucius.

★Zojoji Temple E 6

Japanese equivalent

A pleasant footpath leads from the Shiba-koen Underground Station through Shiba Park to the Zojoji Temple. This former family temple of the Tokugawas was founded in 1393 by the priest Shoso. It belongs to the Jodo sect, which helped the Tokugawa clan build up the power of the shogunate. Under their despotic rule Japan cut itself off from the outside world for three centuries.

The temple and surrounding parkland were badly destroyed in the 1923 earthquake and in the Second World War. The Sammon entrance gate is the only part of the complex which still dates back to 1605. The 48m/157ft long and 35m/115ft high Main Hall, Hondo, is a 1974 reconstruction.

District
Minato-ku, in Shiba Park

Underground
Shiba-koen
(Hibiya Line)

Among the temple treasures are pictures from the life of the priest Honen, a black Buddha statue and the Great Temple Bell. In an enclosure behind the temple there is a tomb belonging to the Tokugawa shoguns, but this is not open to the public; the second one is in Nikko (see entry).

Practical Information

Addresses

The following announcement from a hospital was inserted in the *Asahi Evening News*:

"Use the west exit from Ikebukuro Station. Keep to the main street for 500m/540yds, that is, for six minutes' walk. Then when you come to a filling station, turn right into a little side street with a grocer's shop on one side and a postbox on the other". It is more or less like this that Japanese tell their acquaintances the way to a temple or a shop. If possible they also provide a sketch-map. In Japan there are no addresses of the sort used in Europe.

12–8-A Shiroganedai 5-chrome Minato-ku is, for instance, a house or dwelling in the administrative district of Minato in Tokyo. This district is divided into sub-districts which have distinctive names which it is possible, with some effort, to make out on a good English-language plan of the city. Shiroganedai is one of them. Each sub-district is then further split up into blocks (chrome). Then within the blocks the visitor must try to find the plot designated as 12–8, for there are, as may have been guessed, no house numbers either. On this plot stand several houses and you have to look for the one that has the letter A. Accordingly you have to go round looking for a door with the nameplate of your acquaintance on it. It is a difficult business even for local postmen and taxi-drivers.

Example

Visitors are best advised to get every address written down for them on a card before setting out. Hotel receptionists are quite used to requests for this particular service. Also write the telephone number as well so that the taxi-driver can call the number for directions if he gets lost. Often signs are put up near to particular blocks which give the names of all the people living there, although these are, of course, in Japanese script. Allowances are made for foreign guests who arrive late, as they are bound to encounter more difficulties than the Japanese; even for them Tokyo is a jungle.

Advice

Help can also be sought at the "koban", the local police station (see Police), where they will know the area well and be willing to help. If there are language problems they can telephone police headquarters where an interpreter is always available

Air Travel

Narita (Tokyo International Airport)

Narita, Tokyo's ultramodern new international airport lies 65km/40 miles east of the city centre.

Narita flight information: tel. 3423–01 11

Information

◀ *Eye appeal of Japanese food*

A Jumbo Jet (Boeing 747) of Japan Air Lines

Arrival	From the airport into Tokyo:
Shuttle service by train	Keisei Railway Skyliner Line: Narita–Ueno Central Station Journey time: about 1 hour Trains every 30 minutes; seat tickets compulsory. There are shuttle buses between the air terminal and Keisei station in Narita (additional ½ hour journey).
	Japan Rail Line: Narita–Tokyo Journey time: about 1¼ hours Trains operate 16 times a day between Narita City Station and Tokyo. Shuttle buses from Narita airport to the JR station take about ½ an hour.
	Narita Express (N'EX) Line: Narita–Tokyo–Yokohama Journey time: about 1 hour to Tokyo (an additional 30 minutes to Yokohama). About 23 trains per day.
Shuttle service by airport bus	These buses travel between Narita Airport and the Tokyo City Air Terminal approximately every 5 to 20 minutes. Journey times is usually 1½ hours but can take up to 2½ hours depending on the traffic.
By taxi	Taxis can be the most comfortable way of getting from the airport into Tokyo but they are also the most expensive; the journey normally takes about an hour but when traffic is at its height it can take considerably longer.

Narita Airport terminal

Haneda National Airport

Haneda National Airport in Tokyo's southern outskirts handles domestic flights only.

It has good public transport connections with the rest of Tokyo, including the monorail to Hamatsucho Station. Allow about two hours for transfers by bus to Narita airport; helicopter transfer takes about 30 minutes.

Haneda flight information: tel. (0476) 32–28 00   Information

Tokyo City Air Terminal

Tokyo City Air Terminal (TCAT) is at Nihombashi, Hakozaki-cho, Chuo-ku.

Facilities include enquiry desks for flight information, bookings, etc.

Tel. 36 65–7156   Information

Allow about three hours for the process of getting to the airports on   Departure
departure. Check in luggage at the City Air Terminal as early as possible,
and make sure you know the correct terminal to go to. When making
last-minute purchases and changing back currency remember that all
departing passengers have to pay a "Passenger Facility Service Charge"
(2,000 yen for adults).

Airlines

Daini Tekko Building   Japan Air Lines
2–7–3 Marunouchi, Chiyoda-ku, J-100 Tokyo   (JAL)
tel. 52 59–37 77 (international flights)
tel. 54 89–21 11 (domestic flights)

Antiques

All Nippon Airways (ANA)	Kasumigaseki Building 3–2–5 Kasumigaseki, Chiyoda-ku, J-100 Tokyo tel. 32 72–12 12
Other airlines	The following airlines are located in Narita Airport's Terminal 1:

American Airlines: tel. 3285–02 02
British Airways: tel. 3593–88 11
Canadian Airlines: tel. 3281–74 26
Northwest Airlines: tel. 533–60 00
United Airlines: tel. 3817–44 11

The following airlines are in Terminal 2:
Air New Zealand: tel. 3213–09 68
All Nippon Airways: tel. 3272–12 12
Continental Airlines: tel. 3592–16 31
Japan Airlines; tel. 5489–11 11
Qantas Airways: tel. 3593–70 00

Antiques

The Japanese are keen collectors themselves and this has forced up prices. Bargaining is virtually impossible and care must be taken to avoid fakes.

In Japan age is not necessarily consonant with value, and pieces which may be newer but are by a well-known master or from a famous school are often much more expensive. Between 50,000 and 100,000 yen is a reasonable price for a Samurai sword. Cast-iron vessels, wooden cabinets with metal fastenings, table-type ovens with a hollow for the charcoal, or painted scrolls can also cost thousands. Genuine netsuke (ebony figurines formerly used as toggles) are now virtually unobtainable. The best things to look out for are 18th and 19th c. woodcuts.

Antique shops

The antiques trade is not centred on anywhere particular in Tokyo and the best places to go are the big department stores which have permanent art displays. Others worth recommending include:

Art Plaza Magatani
5–10–13 Toranomon, Minato-ku; tel. 3433–63 21

Oriental Bazaar
9–13 Jingumae 5–chome
Shibuya-ku (Omotesando); tel. 3400–39 33

Asahi Art Center
Hibiya Park Building
1–8–1 Yuraku-cho, Chiyoda-ku; tel. 3271–62 60

Baths

Bathhouses

The Japanese bathhouse is a social institution where people meet after a hard day's work to relax and talk politics or catch up on the latest gossip.

The very hot water of the communal bath is for soaking, not washing. This must be done first and every trace of soap then rinsed away so that the bathwater stays clean for everyone else.

Anyone not used to a very hot bath should only venture in with great care, and sufferers with cardiac problems should avoid Japanese baths altogether. It is unwise to tax the system by staying in for longer than 20 minutes in any event.

Bathing in one of Japan's many hot springs (onsen) is a favourite holiday pastime, at its most romantic of an evening under a starry sky. Onsen are usually in natural settings, complete with rocks and ferns, and the atmosphere is so relaxed that bathers are free to go window-shopping before and after or even dine in the light robes provided. Although there are no onsen in the Greater Tokyo area they are within easy reach as part of a day out to the Hakone area (see A–Z).

Hot springs

Korakuen Pool; tel. 3811–21 11
Train: Suidobashi. Open: 31.5.–31.8.

Outdoor pools

Tokyo Kosei Nenkin Sports Centre Pool; tel. 3416–26 11
Train: Odakyu line, Seijogakuenmae. Open: 1.7.–mid-September.

Toshimaen Pool; tel. 3952–22 26
Train: Seibu line, Toshimaen. Open: 1.6.–mid-September.

Yoyogi Stadium Pool (heated); tel. 3468–11 71
Train: Harajuku. Open all year round.

Indoor pools

Meiji Jingu Pool; tel. 3403–34 56
Train: Sendagaya. Open: June–mid-September.

Buses

See Public Transport

Car Rental

Tokyo City Air Terminal,
42–1, Hakozaki Nihombashi, Chou-ku; tel. 3561–05 43

Budget

1–7–8 Moto Akasaka, Minato-ku; tel. 3796–80 02

Hertz

Toyota Rent-a-Lease,
2–3–18 Kudan Minami, Chiyoda-ku; tel. 3263–63 21

Toyota

Chemists

See Health Care

Cinema

Japan has an important film industry and the Japanese are great cinema-goers. Fortunately for tourists most foreign films are not dubbed and only have Japanese subtitles. Most cinema-going is during the day, with the last showing at 7pm. Tickets are quite expensive and often cost 2000 to 2500 yen.

Even visitors with no knowledge of the language can gain a useful insight into Japanese daily life by watching Japanese films, and a good way of doing this is to visit the Film Service Center (3–7–6 Kyobashi 3–chome, Chuo-ku; tel. 3561–08 23) which screens many Japanese classics at modest prices.

Film Service
Center

Information about programmes for all the city centre cinemas can be found in the English-language newspapers (see Newspapers and Periodicals).

Clothing

Rainwear

Rainwear is in order in every season apart from winter. Since Tokyo shares the same latitude as Las Vegas, Crete and Teheran it has a relatively warm climate. However, it also has over twice the average precipitation rate of most parts of Europe. The weather is at its worst during the typhoon season, which is roughly August and September, when there are very bad storms and the humidity is also unpleasantly high. This, combined with high temperatures, makes summer the worst time of year for a visit.

Warm clothing is called for only during the brief and none too cold winter, which, with its clear skies, is also one of the best seasons for a visit.

Footwear

Shoes are removed when visiting people's homes and entering temples. This is for religious rather than hygienic reasons since footwear is usually made from the skins of dead animals and therefore deemed unclean in the spiritual sense. Consequently it is a good idea to take casual shoes without laces in order to save time for everyone when entering temples, etc. If your shoe size is anything above 9/43 your are unlikely to find new shoes to fit you in Japan.

Sizes

Women's dresses and suits

Japanese	9	11	13	15	17	19	21
American	10	12	14	16	18	20	22
English	32	34	36	38	40	42	44
Continental	38	40	42	44	46	48	50

Men's coats, overcoats and sweaters

Japanese		S		M		L	LL
American	34	36	38	40	42	44	46
English	34	36	38	40	42	44	46
Continental	44	46	48	50	52	54	56

Shirts and collars

Japanese	36	37	38	39	40	41	42
American	14	14½	15	15½	16	16½	17
English	14	14½	15	15½	16	16½	17
Continental	36	37	38	39	40	41	42

Women's shoes

Japanese	23	23½	24	24½	25	25½	26
American	6	6½	7	7½	8½	9	
English	4½	5	5½	6	6½	7	7½
Continental	36	37	38	38	38	39	40

Men's shoes

Japanese	24½	25	26	27	27½	28	29
American	5½	6½	7½	8½	10½	11½	
English	5	6	7	8	9	10	11
Continental	39	40	41	42	43	44	45

Crime

See Police

Currency

Tokyo is by far the most expensive of the world's capital cities, with prices almost double those of Western Europe.

The unit of currency is the yen (¥). Banknotes are in denominations of 1000, 5000 and 10,000 yen. Coins are 1 yen (aluminium), 5 yen (copper with a hole), 10 yen (bronze), 50 yen (cupro-nickel with a hole), 100 yen (cupro-nickel) and 500 yen (cupro-nickel).

Currency

There is no limit on currency imports, but no more than 3 million yen may be exported.

Import/Export

Foreign currency can be changed in many of the hotels and in foreign-exchange banks.

Changing money

Bank opening hours are weekdays 9am to 3pm and Saturdays 9am to noon.

Banks

The following list is just a selection of Tokyo's foreign-exchange banks.

Foreign-exchange banks

American Express, Toranomon Mitsui Building,
3–8–1 Kasumigaseki, Chiyoda-ku; tel. 3504–33 41

Bank of America, Tokyo Kaijo Building,
2–1 Marunouchi 1–chome, Chiyoda-ku; tel. 3214–02 41

Commercial Bank of Australia Ltd., Shin Tokyo Building,
3–3–1 Marunouchi, Chiyoda-ku; tel. 3214–24 56

First National City Bank, Time-Life Building,
2–3–6 Otemachi 2–chome, Chiyoda-ku; tel. 3279–54 11

Lloyds Bank International Ltd., Yurakucho Denki Building,
1–7–1 Yuraku-cho, Chiyoda-ku; tel. 3212–09 58/9

Thomas Cook Bankers Ltd., No. 24 Mori Building,
2–23–5 Nishi Shimbashi, Minato-ku; tel. 3436–49 46

Credit cards (American Express, Diner's Club, Visa, Mastercard, etc.) are only accepted in leading hotels and the big stores and restaurants.

Credit cards

The best way to carry money is as traveller's cheques, especially those in American dollars.
   Eurocheques are virtually unknown in Japan and can only be cashed in branches of European banks.

Traveller's cheques

Customs Regulations

The duty-free allowance for persons over 19 is 400 cigarettes, 500 gr. tobacco or 100 cigars and 3 760ml. bottles of alcoholic beverages, plus gifts and souvenirs up to the value of 200,000 yen.
   The importation of drugs and pornographic books and magazines is prohibited.
   Permits are required for certain kinds of plants, weapons, swords and explosives, and pet animals require official authorisation.
   On arrival travellers must hand in a customs declaration. These can be completed on the plane or at the airport, and should include details of currency in cash and unaccompanied luggage.

Entry

Diplomatic Representation (embassies)

2–1–14 Mita, Minato-ku; tel. 3453–02 51

Australia

7–3–38, Akasaka, Minato-ku; tel. 3408–21 01

Canada

New Zealand	20–40 Kamiyamacho, Shibuya-ku; tel. 3467–22 71
United Kingdom	1 Ichiban-cho, Chiyoda-ku; tel. 3265–55 11
United States	1–10–5 Akasaka, Minato-ku; tel. 3224–50 00

Earthquakes

Tokyo is in a zone of very frequent tremors from earthquakes both out to sea and inland, so special safety precautions must be observed in all buildings. There are emergency shelters throughout the city and an earthquake early warning system.

Electricity

Electric current is 100–110 volts AC at 50 cycles in eastern Japan, and that includes Tokyo. Leading hotels have sockets for both 110 and 220 volts but these will usually only take two-pin plugs. Consequently most European electrical appliances will require an adapter, although room service may well be able to supply hair dryers, etc.

Emergency Numbers

Police	Tel. 110
Fire, Ambulance	Tel. 119
Police infoline in English	Tel. 3501–01 10

Events and Festivals

January

January 1st–3rd: New Year Celebrations. Businesses and public buildings are closed and air pollution is noticeably reduced, with unusually blue skies over Tokyo when the weather is fine. People visit their families and make pilgrimages to the temples and shrines, all specially decorated for the festive season. The Meiji Shrine and Asakusa Kannon Temple are particularly popular, and the Yasukuni Shrine in Kuda, Chiyoda-ku, also has performances of Koto music and dance and Noh theatre.

January 2nd: New Year visit to the Imperial Palace, when the public can visit the Palace Garden between 9am–3pm and pay their respects to the Emperor when he appears on the balcony.

January 6th: Dezome-shiki, when the Tokyo Fire Brigade hold their New Year parade along Chuodori Street in the Harumi district of the city and perform breathtaking acrobatics perched on their bamboo ladders.

Mid-January: antiques market on the streets of Setagaya-ku; first Sumo tournament of the year in Kokugikan Hall, Ryoguku.

February

February 3rd/4th: Setsubun. This ancient folk festival marking the end of the lunar year and the casting out of bad luck is celebrated at many of Tokyo's temples and shrines as priests and others throw dried beans, symbolising good luck, at the assembled parishioners. The best places to see the festivities include the Asakusa Kannon Temple, the Zojoji Temple in Shiba (near Tokyo Tower) and the Hie Shrine in Akasaka (Underground: Akasaka).

February 25th: start of Ume Matsuri, the plum festival, which continues, with its truly lovely blossom, until March 15th at the Yushima Tenjin Shrine in Bunkyo-ku (underground: Yushima). The tea ceremony is held in the open air on Saturdays and Sundays.

March 3rd: Girls' Day. Since the war girls as well as boys have been deemed worthy of having their own festival, and there are displays of beautifully dressed dolls.

March

March 3rd, 4th: Daruma Ichi. This daruma fair is held in Chofu's Jindaiji Temple (train: Chofu), and there are thousands of these little tumbler-type figures on show, to the accompaniment of Japanese dance and music.

2nd Sunday in March: Hi Watari. The festival is celebrated in Kotsu Anzen Kito-cho on Mount Takao. Priests from the hill monastery walk barefoot over the glowing embers of a fire lit for the souls of the departed.

March 18th: Kinryu-no-mai. Dragon dances at 2 and 4pm, and parade, in the Asakusa Kannon Temple (underground: Asakusa).

March 26th: Sakura Matsuri: Start of the cherry blossom festival in Ueno Park which continues until about April 15th.

April 8th: Hana Matsuri. Temple flower festivals to mark the Buddha's birthday. A white papier mâché elephant is carried in procession, and all the Buddha's statues are decked with flowers, an occasion when the Asakusa Kannon Temple is particularly worth visiting.

April

April 9th–16th: Kamakura Matsuri. Festival at the Tsurugaoka Hachiman Shrine in Kamakura with a parade in historical costume, a Mikoshi parade of portable shrines and a Yabusame, an archery competition on the last day with the bowmen mounted on horseback.

April 12th: Shirasagi-no-mai. Dance of the white heron at Asakusa Kannon Temple, 11am and 1pm.

April 23rd/24th: Yasukuni Shrine Matsuri, spring festival.

April 29th: Greenery Day, marking the start of Tokyo's Golden Week when public buildings and many businesses close for the week and the city is quieter than at any other time as people take their holidays.

International Trade Fair. This is hosted by Tokyo for the whole month of April in odd-numbered years.

May 3rd–5th: Meiji Shrine Festival. Spring festival with performance of classical Japanese dance, Bugaku and Noh and a Kyudo archery contest on the last day.

May

May 3rd: Yokohama Minato Matsuri. Festival to celebrate the opening of the port of Yokohama to foreign shipping. An international parade sets out from Yamashita-koen park at about 11am, ending up at Maita-koen park at around 2pm.

May 5th: Boys' Day when parents of sons rejoice by hanging out brightly coloured cloth carp to flutter in the breeze.

Weekend closest to May 15th: Kanda Festival at the Myojin Shrine in Kanda, Tokyo's university and bookshop district when shrines and litters are paraded through the streets.

Events and Festivals

May 17th–19th: Sanja Matsuri, one of Tokyo's greatest and most magnificent popular festivals featuring lion dances and grand Mikoshi processions of floats and portable shrines in and around the Asakusa temple precincts (Asakusa Station on the Ginza underground line), and also involving Geishas and Binzasaramai dancers.

May 20th, 21st: Minato Matsuri. Grand parade with bands, folk dances and portable shrines at Yokosuka on the Kiura peninsula.

June

June 10th–16th: Sanno Matsuri. Biennial festival involving a procession around the Sanno Hie Jinja shrine in Akasaka Mitsuke near the Hilton Hotel, with Shinto music and rituals and open-air tea ceremonies.

July

July 13th–16th: Mitama Matsuri. Festival of Remembrance for the Souls of the Dead. This is the time when Buddhists believe the souls of the dead visit the earth, and little lights burn in their honour in graveyards and people's homes. There are performances of Bon-odori and classical dance and some 6000 lanterns festoon the Yasukuni Shrine.

Varying dates in July: Hozuk-ichi. Cherry fair at Asakusa Kannon Temple when plants are put on show and they sell cherry branches decorated with fruit and windmills.

July 17th: Edo-shumi Horyo Taikai. Start of the summer evening festival which continues until August 15th, in Ueno Park on the edge of Shinobazu pool and in the grounds of the pagoda.

Last Saturday in July: Hanabi Matsuri. Spectacular evening firework display over Asakusa's Sumida-gawa River.

August

Early August: Fireworks in Keio Tamagawa on the River Tamagawa, also viewable from boats.

August 13th–15th: Festival of portable shrines in Fukagawa.

September

September 16th: Yabusame. Japanese archery festival at the Tsurugaoka-Hachiman Shrine in Kamakura, when bowmen in historical costume compete on horse-back.

October

October 1st–10th: Festival commemorating the founding of Tokyo first held in 1956 when the city was 500 years old. Events include the Harbour Festival, Miss Tokyo Contest, procession of decorated floats, parade of lanterns and various displays and exhibitions.

October 12th: Ikegami Honmon-ji Temple Oeshiki Festival, commemorating the Buddhist saint Nichiren with the carrying of large lanterns, decorated with paper flowers, into the temple.

October 17th–19th: Autumn Festival at the Yasukuni Shrine with performances of classical dance, Noh plays and an archery competition.

October 18th: Kiryu-no-mai. A dragon dance at Asakusa Kannon Temple.

October/
November

Meiji Shrine Autumn Festival, a harvest festival with performances of classical music and dance, Noh and Bugaku plays, Japanese archery and aikido displays.

November

November 3rd: Daimyo Gyoretsu. Procession in costumes of the Edo Period in the Hakone-Yumoto district.
  Shirasagi-no-mai. Dance of the white heron at the Asakusa Kannon Temple.
  Festival commemorating Emperor Meiji at the Meiji Shrine.

164

November 15th: Shichi-go-san. Day of special blessings for children aged three, five and seven and their parents, who all visit the shrines dressed in their magnificent best. The ceremonies are particularly worth seeing at the Meiji, Kanda and Hie shrines.

Various dates in November: Tori-no Ichi. Rooster Fair at Otori Shrine in Asakusa, held on the appropriate day in the Eastern calendar, when people buy "kumade", ornamental bamboo "bear's paw" rakes.

December 14th: Gishi Sai. Festival of the 47 Ronin at the Sengakuji Temple in Manato-ku.

December

December 17th–19th: Hagoita Ichi. Fair at the Asakusa Kannon Temple where people buy their New Year's decorations.

December 23rd: Birthday of the Emperor.

December 31st: Omisoka. The great Old Year's Day Festival when the temple bells toll 108 times – 107 for the sins of the Old Year and once for the New, an occasion when Shiba's Zojoji Temple and the Asakusa Kannon Temple are particularly worth visiting.

See entry

Public holidays

Festivals

See Events and Festivals

Fleamarkets

The Tourist Information Centres (see Information) can supply up-to-date lists of the fleamarkets which particularly warrant a visit. Much of what is on offer comes from the shrine and temple areas, sufficient in itself to make them worth a look.

Food and Drink

The Japanese eat with chopsticks ("o-hashi") but if as a foreigner you cannot manage them no-one will take offence. If necessary you can always ask for European cutlery. This is quite easy since the Japanese is based on English – naifu is knife, spun is spoon and foku is fork. In any case most restaurants are none too fussy about people's eating habits, especially since soup, for example, which is served during or even at the end of the meal rather than at the beginning, is supposed to be slurped audibly as a gesture of appreciation.

Eating with
chopsticks

Flea market (See page 165)

Eating with chopsticks is in fact a lot less complicated than it appears. Japanese chopsticks are almost invariably made of wood and still joined at one end to show they have not been used before. Separate them and then hold them in the right hand as shown below, with the lower one acting as a support, lying in the hollow between the thumb and the forefinger and resting on the tip of the "ring" finger, and the upper one, held between the thumb, forefinger and middle finger, acting as a guide.

Chopsticks can be used to stir sauces and soups and pick up morsels of food, but must not be used for rice as this only happens with ceremonial meals for the dead.

Food

It will soon become apparent that Japanese food is also a feast for the eye. Colours are planned to go with one another and everything is meticulously prepared and presented. The following dishes are among the best of many:

Shabu Shabu — Wafer-thin slices of beef simmered with bean curd, vermicelli and assorted vegetables and then dipped in sauce.

Soba — Noodles with various additional ingredients plus dips and garnishes. Like spaghetti but eaten cold.

Sukiyaki — Thin slices of meat cooked fondu-style in stock at the table with mushrooms, onions, and other vegetables.

Sushi — Balls of vinegared rice with toppings of raw fish and seafood which you dip in soya sauce. Best eaten with the fingers.

Deep-fried morsels of meat, fish or vegetables in an egg and flour batter, as introduced to Japan in the 16th c. by the Portuguese. — Tempura

Sliced raw fish and seafood which are then dipped in a sauce of your own making. — Sashimi

Noodles served in a broth, usually along with meat, fish and other ingredients. — Udon

Breaded and fried pork cutlet served with shredded raw cabbage. — Tonkatsu

Small chunks of chicken, liver and vegetables on bamboo skewers grilled over charcoal. Excellent as a snack. — Yakitori

All these dishes lean towards Western tastes; Tokyo also has innumerable Western restaurants run by and for the Japanese who have long been familiar with all kinds of food from the West. — Hint

If you want to try truly original Japanese food it is best to go with someone local who knows their way around. If on your own, choose places which have their dishes on display in the windows.

Drink

Tokyo tapwater is clean and drinkable but tastes of chlorine. If worried about drinking the local water on a trip out of town you can always ask for tea.

When it comes to social drinking and alcohol you do need to take care but for a different reason. Too many convivial rounds of sake (rice wine) can soon bring on a hangover, especially since the measures seem to get more generous by the round.

The Japanese love whisky, largely because of what to them are its "exotic", i.e. American, connotations. Usually, however, they take it with plenty of water.

The local spirits include shochu, usually distilled from the lees of sake and not particularly pleasant to the Western palate, and awamori, also distilled from sake but more acceptable in taste.

Japanese wine is not something for the connoisseur. This is due not so much to the expense as to the chemically induced flavour.

Japanese beer is good almost without exception, especially the Krin, Sapporo and Suntory brands.

Visitors who like an alcoholic drink need to know that "kampai" means "cheers"!

Take care as a foreigner not to get drunk in public since in Eastern eyes this entails considerable "loss of face".

See entry — Restaurants

Fortune-tellers

Fortune-tellers are a Tokyo institution, appearing usually in the evening and setting up their tables in the shopping centres where having your hand read or your horoscope cast is a very popular pastime.

Fortune-tellers rule Japan's everyday life. They are brought into many private and professional issues, and in particularly difficult cases will also come to the house and hang up spells which, for example, should charm wayward offspring back onto the straight and narrow.

Astrology and soothsaying also play a part in official life as for example when the government of the day paid out large sums to be told when it would be propitious to hold the 1980 general election. Sure enough, they were rewarded with a landslide victory.

Galleries

Travellers bemused by this strange new world will be reassured in their search for Japanese art by the realm opened up to them by most of the private galleries. Not only is the choice they offer much broader than in many so-called museums, constrained as these are by political parsimony, but there are also English-speaking staff on hand to give advice.

Idemitsu Gallery: 1–1, 3–chome, Marunouchi, Chiyoda-ku, Namiki-dori

Natenshi Gallery: 3–6–5 Kyobashi, Chuo-ku
Supplier to American and European museums and galleries. Specialises in contemporary art; sculptures and oil paintings on 3rd floor.

Yoseido Gallery: 5–15 Ginza, 5–chome
Yoseido is the only Tokyo gallery which deals in modern Japanese lithographs, engravings and prints. It has about 130 artists on its books, and charges accordingly.

Geishas

See Facts and Figures, Customs.

Getting to Tokyo

By air
Most visitors to Tokyo arrive by air at Narita International Airport (see Air Travel). From Europe the main air-routes are via Greenland and Alaska (Anchorage), or Moscow and Siberia, or the South-East Asia route, including several stopovers, via Rome and the Middle East.

By sea
There are no passenger liners direct from Europe to Japan. Visitors arriving by sea usually dock at Yokohama as part of a Far Eastern cruise or at other ports on ferries from South Korea, Taiwan or China. There is also a steamship service to Nakhodka (see below).

By rail and air/sea
One very interesting way of travelling to Japan for those who have time to spare is to combine the journey by Trans-Siberian Railway across Russia from Moscow to Vladivostock or Nakhodka and then continue by air or by steamship.

Guides

Information about English-speaking guides is available from the Japan Guide Association (Shinkokusai Building, 3–4–1 Marunouchi, Chiyoda-ku; tel. 3213–27 06).

Rates
The charge is around 15,000 yen for half a day, 20,000 yen for the whole day.

Hotels and travel agencies can assist with information about licensed professional tour guides as well, and Tourist Information Centres (see Information) can also provide details of the Goodwill Guides service, operated by the Japan National Tourist Organisation, which supplies volunteer guides free of charge for foreign visitors.

Health Care

Medical treatment in Japan is very expensive, so be sure to have adequate insurance cover for your visit. For information on English-speaking doctors and dentists contact one of the Tourist Information Centres (see Information). These can also supply you with the free "Tourist's Handbook" which contains pictures and phrases in English and Japanese that help to explain the nature of your problem.

Some useful phrases:

chemist	yakyoku, kusuriya
clinic, doctor's surgery	clinic
dentist	shi-ka, ha-isha
doctor	isha
hospital	byoin
I am ill	byo-ki desu
come quickly please	hayaku kite kudasai
get a doctor for me	isha o yonde kudasai
take me to a doctor	isha ni tsurete itte kudasai

Chemists (yakyoku, kusuriya)

Many medicines are available in Japan without a prescription but if you are on regular medication take enough to last the trip as well as clearly-written prescription forms if necessary.

Most chemists are open during the week from 9am to 6pm.
Chemists used to dealing with foreigners include:

The American Pharmacy, Hibiya Park Building,
1–8–1, Yurakucho, Chiyoda-ku; tel. 3271–40 34

Hill Pharmacy, 4–1–6, Roppongi, Minao-ku; tel. 3583–50 44

Hospitals (byoin)

For hospital information: tel. 3212–23 23

Information

Hospitals and dental clinics where English is understood include:

International Catholic Hospital (Seibo Byoin)
2–5–1 Naka-Ochiai, Shinjuky-ku; tel. 3951–11 11

Saint Luke's International Hospital (Seiroka Byoin)
9–1 Akashicho, Chuo-ku; tel. 3541–51 51

Tokyo Sanitarum Hospital (Eisei Byoin)
3–17–3 Amanuma, Suginami-ku; tel. 3392–61 51

Empire Dental Clinic
28 Daikyo-cho, Shinjuku-ku; tel. 3356–29 10

Royal Dental Clinic, Komuro Building, 2nd floor,
4–10–11 Roppongi, Minato-ku; tel. 3404–08 19

As a general rule no vaccinations are required for a visit to Japan. If, however, you decide while in Japan you need vaccinations for elsewhere you can get them at the Hibiya Clinic (Mitsui Building, 1st Floor, 1–1–2 Yurakucho, Chiyoda-ku; tel. 3501–63 77). Surgery hours are Mon.–Fri. 9.30am–noon, 1–4.45pm, Sat. 9.30am–noon. See also Travel Documents.

Vaccinations

See entry

Massage

169

Hotels

Western-style Hotels

Western-style hotels providing first-class service and accommodation up to top international standards are to be found in all the major cities and resorts. Many of them have their own speciality restaurants and shopping arcades and often carefully landscaped grounds as well.

Rooms usually have their own television facilities and full air-conditioning. Prices are on a par with international levels.

Business Hotels

Business hotels are comparatively less expensive, especially for the single traveller. Usually located near railway stations they have many more single rooms than doubles and although the services are much more limited (no room service, for example) almost all of them have a restaurant with Japanese and Western food on the menu.

Since they were originally aimed at Japanese business travellers there is unlikely to be anyone on the staff who speaks English.

Capsule Hotels

Capsule hotels are a Japanese invention, consisting of pre-fabricated sleeping quarters in units about 7¼ft long and 3½ft wide by 3½ft high (certainly not for the claustrophobic!) with just the bedding, light, TV, stereo and air-conditioning.

They also tend to be located around the railway stations.

Ryokan

Ryokan are traditional Japanese inns and differ fundamentally from Western-style hotels. The atmosphere is much more like a Japanese home, with tatami (straw mats) on the floor and walls of sliding paper screens. Meals, usually included in the price, are served in your room.

All guests are expected to observe the traditional Japanese customs and before entering the ryokan exchange their shoes for slippers which in turn must be removed before stepping on the tatami. Special slippers are also required for a visit to the toilet.

The maid will show you to your room, welcome you by serving tea and ask when you want to have your bath and take dinner. You will be provided with a yukata, a kimono-type house robe, to wear in and around the ryokan, including the garden and the pool if there is one.

The bath (o-furo), which though communal nowadays tends to be used by men and women at different times, is for relaxation, not washing.

This is done beforehand so that you are clean by the time you plunge into the very hot water of the communal tub – and make sure you leave the hot water in after you for others to use.

Capsule hotel

The maid will serve dinner following the bath and then when you have finished will clear it away before transforming your room into a bedroom by making up your bed on the floor with a comfortable soft futon.

Be sure to take a turn in the ryokan garden, since this will usually be a lovingly landscaped work of art however minute the setting.

Ryokan owners can be reluctant to take bookings from foreigners because of the language difficulties and lack of experience with foreign guests so it is advisable to reserve through a Japanese travel agency. The 2000–plus members of the Japan Ryokan Association (1–8–3 Marunouchi, Chiyoda-ku, Tokyo; tel. 231–53 10) take great pains to meet the requirements of foreign guests, although this can be at the expense of the traditional Japanese style. A Ryokan Guide is also available from Tourist Information Centres (see Information).

In terms of comfort (and price) a first-class ryokan easily bears comparison with the best of Western-style hotels.

Welcome Inns

Welcome Inns are not part of a hotel chain as the name suggests but budget accommodation of all kinds, including ryokan and business hotels, which appear in the "Directory of Welcome Inns" (available from JNTO offices) and can be booked through TICs (see Information) and the Welcome Inn Reservation Centre, an organisation supported by the JNTO.

Several of the larger Welcome Inns (WI) are included in the following selection of hotels.

Young People's Accommodation	See entry

Hotels in Tokyo (selection)

Western style:
Akasaka Prince Hotel, 1–2 Kio-cho, Chiyoda-ku, 761 r.
Akasaka Tokyu Hotel, 2–14–3 Nagata-cho, Chiyoda-ku, 535 r.
ANA Hotel Tokyo, 1–12–33 Akasaka, Minato-ku, 903 r.
Asakusa View Hotel, 3–17–1 Nishi-Asakusa, Taito-ku, 324 r.
The Capitol Tokyu Hotel, 2–10–3 Nagata-cho, Chiyoda-ku, 459 r.
Century Hyatt Tokyo, 2–7–2 Nishi-Shinjuku, Shinjuku-ku, 757 r.
Hotel Daiei, 1–15–8, Koishikawa, Bunkyo-ku, 82 r.
Diamond Hotel, 25 Ichiban-cho, Chiyoda-ku, 159 r.
Fairmont Hotel, 2–1–17 Kudan-Minami, Chiyoda-ku, 208 r.
Gajoen Kanko Hotel, 1–8–1 Shimo-Meguro, Meguor-ku, 98 r.
Ginza Dai-ichi Hotel, 8–13–1 Ginza, Chuo-ku, 793 r.
Ginza Nikko Hotel, 8–4–21 Ginza, Chuo-ku, 112 r.
Ginza Tokyu Hotel, 5–15–9 Ginza, Chuo-ku, 440 r.
Hotel Grand Palace, 1–1–1 Iidabashi, Chiyoda-ku, 467 r.
Haneda Tokyu Hotel, 2–8–6 Haneda-kuko, Ota-ku, 306 r.
Hilltop Hotel 1–1 Kanda Surugadai, Chiyoda-ku, 75 r.
Holiday Inn Metropolitan Tokyo, 1–6–1 Nishi-Ikebukuro, Toshima-ku, 818 r.
Holiday Inn Tokyo, 1–13–7 Hatchobori, Chuo-ku, 119 r.
Imperial Hotel, 1–1–1 Uchisaiwai-cho, Chiyoda-ku, 1059 r.
Keio Plaza InterContinental Hotel, 2–2–1 Nishi-Shinjuku, Shinjuku-ku, 1462 r.
Hotel Kokusai Kanko, 1–8–3 Marunouchi, Chiyoda-ku, 95 r.
Miyako Hotel Tokyo, 1–1–50, Shirokanedai, Minato-ku, 498 r.
Hotel New Meguro, 1–3–18 Chuo-cho, Meguro-ku, 31 r.
The New Otani, 4–1 Kioi-cho, Chiyoda-ku 1722 r.
Hotel Okura Tokyo, 2–10–4 Toranomon, Minato-ku, 885 r.
Hotel Pacific Meridien Tokyo, 3–13–3 Takanawa, Minato-ku, 954 r.
Palace Hotel, 1–1–1 Marunouchi, Chiyoda-ku, 404 r.
Royal Park Hotel, 2–1–1 Kakigara-cho, Nihombashi, 450 r.
Shiba Park Hotel, 1–5–10 Shiba-koen, Minato-ku, 399 r.
Hotel Sunroute Tokyo, 2–3–1, Shibuya-ku, 542 r.
Hotel Takanawa, 2–1–17 Takanawa, Minato-ku, 132 r.
Takanawa Prince Hotel, 3–13–1 Takanawa, Minato-ku, 416 r.
Takanawa Tobu Hotel, 4–7–6 Takanawa, Minato-ku, 197 r.
Hotel Tokyo, 2–17–8 Takanawa, Minato-ku, 48 r.
Tokyo Hilton, 6–6–2 Nishi-Shinjuku, Shinjuku-ku, 807 r.
Tokyo Hotel Urashima, 2–5–23 Harumi, Chuo-ku, 982 r.
Tokyo Marunouchi Hotel, 1–6–3 Marunouchi, Chiyoda-ku, 210 r.
Tokyo Prince Hotel, 3–3–1 Shiba-koen, Minato-ku, 484 r.
Tokyo Station Hotel, 1–9–1 Marunoughi, Chiyoda-ku, 62 r.
Hotel Tokyukanko, 2–21–6 Akasaka, Minato-ku, 373 r.
Yaesu Fujiya Hotel, 2–9–1 Yaesu, Chuo-ku, 373 r.
Hotel Suehiro (WI), 8–1–5 Nishi-Kamata, Ota-ku, 46 r.
Asia Center of Japan (WI), 8–10–32 Akasaka, Minato-ku, 172 r.
Sky Court Koiwa (WI), 6–11–4 Kita Koiwa, Edogawa-ku, 105 r.
Resort Hotel Yushima (WI), 2–15–3 Yushima, Bunkyo-ku, 70 r.
Hotel Asakusa Mikawaya (WI), 2–7–11 Hanakawado, Taito-ku, 22 r.
Ginza Capital Hotel (WI), 3–1–5 Tsukuji, Chuo-ku, 572 r.
Hotel Gimmond Tokyo (WI), 1–6 Odenmacho, Nihombashi, Chuo-ku, 220 r.
Aoyama Shanpia Hotel (WI), 2–14–15 Shibuya, Shibuya-ku, 135 r.
Akasaka Shanpia Hotel (WI), 7–6–13 Akasaka, Minato-ku, 232 r.
Hotel I.B.A. Ikebukuro (WI), 3–10–7 Higashi-Ikebukuro, Toshima-ku, 60 r.
Suigetsu Hotel (WI), 3–3–21 Ikenohata, Taito-ku, 139 r.
Dai-ichi Inn Ikebukuro (WI), 1–42–8 Higashi-Ikebukuro, Toshima-ku, 139 r.
Tsukuba Hotel (WI), 2–7–8 Moto-Asakusa, Taito-ku, 93 r.

New Otani Hotel

Ryokan:
Hotel Atamiso, 4–14–3 Ginza, Chuo-ku, 76 r.
Fukudaya, 6 Kioicho, Chiyoda-ku, 11 r.
Tokiwa Ryokan Shinkan, 7–27–9 Shinjuku, Shinjuku-ku, 50 r.
Hotel Yaesu Rumeikan, 1–3–22 Yaesu, Chuo-ku, 21 r.
Shimuzu Bekkan (WI), 1–30–29 Hongo, Bunkyo-ku, 18 r.
Ryokan Mikawaya Bekkan (WI), 1–31–11 Asakusa, Taito-ku, 12 r.
Ryokan Seifuso (WI), 1–12–15 Fujimi, Chiyoda-ku, 16 r.
Kikuya Ryokan (WI), 2–18–9, Nishi-Asakusa, Taito-ku, 9r.
Ryokan Sansuiso (WI), 2–9–5 Higashi Gotanda, Shinagawa-ku,
    10 r.
Sawanoya Ryokan (WI), 2–3–11 Yanaka, Taito-ku, 12 r.
Ryokan Katsutaro (WI), 4–16–8 Ikenohata, Taito-ku, 7 r.
Ryokan Kaneda (WI), 5–21–1 Minami-Koiwa, Edogawa-ku, 17 r.
Sakura Ryokan (WI), 2–6–2 Iriya Taito-ku, 18 r.
Ryokan Fuji (WI), 6–8–3 Higashi-Koiwa, Edogawa-ku, 10 r.
Suzuki Ryokan (WI), 7–15–23, Yanaka, Taito-ku, 15 r.
Ryokan Kangetsu (WI), 1–2–20 Chidori, Ota-ku, 58 r.

Hotels in excursion destinations (selection)

Western style: Hakone
Fujiya Hotel, 359 Miyanoshita, 146 r.
Hakone Kanko Hotel, 1245 Sengokuhara, 111 r.
Hakone Prince Hotel, 144 Moto-Hakone, 96 r.
Hotel Kagetsuen 1244 Itari, Sengokuhara, 70 r.
Hakone Highland Hotel, 940 Shinanoki, Sengokuhara, 60 r.
Hotel de Yama, 80 Moto-Hakone, 93 r.
Yumot Fujiya Hotel, 256 Yumoto, 94 r.

Hotels

Ryokan:
Hakone Hotel Kowaki-en, 1297 Ninotaira, 1237 r.
Hakone Suimeiso, 702 Yumoto, 41 r.
Ichinoyu, 90 Tonosawa, 22 r.
Mikawaya Ryokan, 503 Kowakidani, 41 r.
Naraya Ryokan, 162 Miyanoshita, 20 r.
Hotel Okuyumoto, 211 Yumotochaya, 50 r.
Senkyoro, 1284 Sengokubara, 41 r.
Suizanso, 694 Yumoto, 25 r.
Tenseien, 682 Yumoto, 105 r.
Yoshiike Ryokan, 597 Yumoto, 67 r.

Kamakura
Western style:
Kamakura Park Hotel, 33–6 Sakanoshita, 41 r.

Ryokan:
BB House Lady's Inn (WI; women only), 2–22–31 Hase, 5 r.

Kyoto
Western style:
Hotel Fujita Kyoto, Nishizume, Nijo-Ohashi, Kamogawa, Nakagyo-ku, 189 r.
Hotel Gimmond, Takakura Oike-dori, Nakagyo-ku, 142 r.
Holiday Inn Kyoto, 36 Nishihiraki-cho, Takano Sakyo-ku, 270 r.
International Hotel Kyoto, 284 Nijo-Aburanokoji, Nakagyo-ku, 286 r.
Hotel Keihan Kyoto, 31 Nishi-Sannocho. Higashi-Kujo, Minami-ku, 308 r.
Kyoto Brighton Hotel, 330 Shitei-cho, Nakadachiuri-sagaru, Shinmachi-
    dori, Kamigyo-ku, 183 r.
Kyoto Century Hotel, 680 Higashi-shiokoji, Shichijo-sagaru, Shimogyo-ku,
    243 r.
Kyoto Dai-ni Tower Hotel, 570–1 Higashi-shiokoji, Shichijo-sagaru,
    Shimogyo-ku, 306 r.
Kyoto Grand Hotel, Shiokoji-horikawa, k Shimogyo-ku, 506 r.
Kyoto Palaceside Hotel, Shimodachiuri-agaru, Karasuma-dori
    Kamigyo-ku, 120 r.
Kyoto Park Hotel, 644–2 Sanjusangendo Mawari-mchi, Higashiyama-ku,
    268 r.
Kyoto Royal Hotel, Sanjo-agaru, Kawaramachi, Nakagyo-ku, 331 r.
Kyoto Tokyu Hotel, 580 Kakimoto-cho, Gojo-sangaru, Horikawadori,
    Shimogyo-ku, 433 r.
Kyoto Tower Hotel, 721–1 Higashi-shiokoji, Karasumadori, Shichijo-
    sagaru, Shimogyo-ku, 158 r.
Miyako Hotel, Sanjo Keage, Higshiyama-ku, 364 r.
The Mount Hiei Hotel, Ipponsugi, Hieizan, Sakyo-ku, 74 r.
Hotel New Hankyu Kyoto, 579 Higashi-shiokoji, Higashi-iru,
    Shimogyo-ku, 319 r.
Hotel New Kyoto, Horikawa-Marutamachi, Kamigyo-ku, 301 r.
New Miyako Hotel, 17 Nishi-Kujoincho, Minami-ku, 710 r.
Hotel Sunflower Kyoto, 51 Higashi-Tennocho, Okazaki, Sakyo-ku, 77 r.
Kyoto Traveller's Inn (WI), 91 Ensyoji-chi, Okazaki, Sakyo-ku, 8 r.
Kyoto Daisan Tower Hotel (WI), Shichijosagaru, Shinmachi-dori,
    Shimogyo-ku, 118 r.
Hotel Sunroute Kyoto (WI), Matsubarasagaru, Kawaramachi-dori,
    Shimogyo-ku, 145 r.
Hotel Hokke Club Kyoto (WI), Karasuma-chuoguchi Shomen, Kyoto-eki,
    Shimogyo-ku, 134 r.
Hotel Gimmond Kyoto (WI), Nishiru, Takakura, Oikedori, Nakagyo-ku, 140 r.
Sanjo Karasuma Hotel Kyoto (WI), 80 Mikuracho, Sanjo-Karasuma-nishi-
    iru, Nakagyo-ku, 154 r.
Hotel Oaks Kyoto -shijo (WI), Nishinotoin-nishiiru, Shijo, Shimogyo-ku,
    138 r.
Maruko Inn Kyoto (WI), Shijo-sagaru, Nishinotoin-dori, Shimogyo-ku,
    108 r.
Kyoto City Hotel (WI), 857 Kitafunabashi-cho, Imadegawa-agaru,
    Horikawa-dori, Kamigyo-ku, 80 r.

Kyoto Tower Restel (WI), 579–27 Higashi-shikojicho, Karasuma-nishi-iru,
Kizuyabashi-dori, Shimogyo-ku, 46 r.
Hotel Palace-side Kyoto (WI), Karasuma-dori-shimodachiuriagaru,
Kamigyo-ku, 120 r.
Kyoto Gion Hotel (WI), 555 Minamigawa, Gion-cho, Higashiyama-ku, 135 r.
Kyoto Daigo Plaza Hotel (WI), 74–1 Naramachi, Rokuzijo, Uji-shi, 68 r.

Ryokan:
Chikiriua, Takoyakushi-dori, Tominokoji-nishi-iru, Nakagyo-ku, 45 r.
Gion Fukuzumi, Shinbashi-dori Yamato oji, Higashi-iru, Higashiyama-ku,
22 r.
Gion Yoshiima, Shinmonzen, Hanamikoji, Nishi-iru, Higashiyama-ku,
15 r.
Hatoya Zuihokaku, Nishinotoin-dori, Shiokojokado, Shimogyo-ku, 51 r.
Hiragiya Ryokan, Fuyacho-Aneyakoji-agaru, Nakagyo-ku, 33 r.
Ikumatsu, Kiyamachi-dori, Oike-agaru, Nakagyo-ku, 24 r.
Kaneiwaro Bekkan, Kiyamachi-dori, Matsubara-sagaru, Shimogyo-ku,
23 r.
Hotel Rantei, 12 Usukinobamba-cho, Tenryuji Saga, Ukyo-ku, 21 r.
Momijiya, 2 Umenohata-cho, Umegahata, Ukyou-ku, 16 r.
Ryokan Nakahara, Sanjo Minami-iru, Higashinotoin-dori, Nakagyo-ku, 30 r.
Hotel Sanoya, Higashinotoin-dori, Shichijosaxaru, Shimogyo-ku, 43 r.
Seikoro, Tonyamachi Gojo-sagaru, Higishiyama-ku, 23 r.
Shokaro, Kiyamachi-dori, Shijo-sagaru, Shimogyo-ku, 24 r.
Sumiya, Fuyacho-dori, Sanjo-sagaru, Nakagyo-ku, 19 r.
Tawaraya Ryokan, Fuyacho-Aneyakoji-agaru, Nakagyo-ku, 19 r.
Hotel Tozankaku, 431 Myohoin-Maekawa-cho
Tsuruki, Kiyamachi-Gojo-agaru, Shimogyo-ku, 16 r.
Yachiyo, 34 Nanzenji-Fukuchi-cho, Sakyo-ku, 22 r.
Ryokan Hiraiwa (WI), 314 Hayao-cho, Kaminoguchi-agaru, Ninomiyama-
chi-dori, Shimogyo-ku, 21 r.
Ryokan Rakucho (WI), 67 Hangi-cho, Shimogamohigashi, Sakyo-ku, 8 r.
Matsubaya Ryokan (WI), Higashinotoin Nishi, Kamijuzuyamachi-dori,
Shimogyo-ku, 11 r.
Ryokan Hinomoto (WI), 375 Kotake-cho, Matsubara-agaru, Kawaramachi,
Shimogyo-ku,, 6 r.
Kyoka Ryokan (WI), Higashi-iru, Higashinotoin, Shimoyuzuyamachi-dorit,
Shimogyo-ku, 10 r.
Ryokan Yuhara (WI), 188 Kagiyacho, Shomen-agaru, Kiyamachi-dori,
Shimogyo-ku, 8 r.
Murakamiya Ryokan (WI), 270 Sasayacho, Shichijo-agaru, Higashinotoin-
dori, Shimogyo-ku, 8 r.
Ryokan Mishima (WI), 3–Chome, Kamiumamachi, Higashijori Higashiru,
Shibutani-dori, Higashiyama-ku, 9 r.
Nashinoki Inn (WI), Futasujime Aguru, Imadegawateramachi Nishir,
Kamigyo-ku, 7 r.
Izumiya Ryokan (WI), Nishi-Honganijimae Shichijo Aguru, Horikawa-dori,
Shimogyo-ku, 18 r.
Ryokan Oto (WI), Hitosujime-minamisaguru, Kamogawa-higashi, Shichijo,
Higashiyama-ku, 12 r.
Kitanoya Ryokan (WI), 524 Futasujigaru-higashiiru, Higashiyama-sanjo,
Sakyo-ku, 8 r.
Matsui Inn (WI), Rokkakusaguru, Yanaginobanba, Nakagyo-ku, 35 r.
Hotel Matsui (WI), Takakurahigashiiru, Rokkakudori, Nakagyo-ku, 40 r.
Ryokan Rikiya (WI), 462–23 Shimogawara-cho, Kodaiji, Higashiyama-ku,
10 r.
Yukiyoshi Ryokan (WI), Higashijori-matsubara-nishiiru, Higashiyama-ku,
10 r.
Heianbo (WI), 725 Nishiiru-Higashishikojicho, Shichijo-sagaru, Karasuma-
dori, Shimogyo-ku, 20 r.
Hatoya Zuihokaku (WI), Shikoji-sagaru, Nishinotoin-dori, Shimogyo-ku,
51 r.

Ikebana

Nara

Western style:
Hotel Fujita Nara, 46–1 Shimo Sanjo-cho, 118 r.
Nara Hotel, 1096 Takabatake-cho, 132 r.
Nara Royal Hotel, 254 Hokkeji-cho, 127 r.
Hotel Sunroute Nara, 1110 Bodai-cho, Takabatake, 95 r.
Hotel Yamatosanso, 27 Kawakami-cho, 51 r.
Business Tourist Hotel Rakuyho (WI), 908–5 Higashi-jurincho, 10 r.
Hotel Sunroute Nara (WI), 1110 Takabate-cho, 95 r.

Ryokan:
Heijo, 728 Kawakami-cho, 24 r.
Kasuga Hotel, 40 Noborioji-cho, 42 r.
Nara Park Hotel, 4–18–1, Horaicho, 35 r.
Hotel New Iroha, 500 Sanjo-machi, 35 r.
Uosa Ryokan, 15 Imamikado-cho, 63 r.
Yoshidaya Bekkan Hotel Yamatoji, 1118 Bodai-cho, Takabatake, 41 r.
Matsumae Ryokan (WI), 28 Higashiterabayashicho, 13 r.
Ryokan Seikanso (WI), 29 Higashikitsujicho, 13 r.
Tsubame Ryokan (WI), 243 Jogonji, Nishikitsujicho, 5 r.
Ryokan Koto (WI), 28 Higashi-terabayashicho, 19 r.
Nara Miyako Hotel (WI), 1–1 Aburasaka-chihocho, 10 r.

Narita

Western style:
Holiday Inn Tobu Narita, 320–1 Tokko, 250 r.
Narita View Hotel, 700 Kosuge, 504 r.
Hotel Nikko Narita, 500 Tokko, 528 r.
Business Hotel Sky Court Narita (WI), 161 Shinden, Daeimachi, 100 r.

Ryokan:
Ogiya Ryokan (WI), 474 Saiwai-cho, 21 r.

Nikko

Western style:
Nikko Kanaya Hotel, 1300 Kami-Hatsuichi-machi, 81 r.
Nikko Lakeside Hotel, 2482 Chugushi, 100 b.
Nikko Prince Hotel, 2485 Shobugahama, Chugushi, 92 r.

Ryokan:
Chuzenji Hotel, 2478 Chugushi, 115 r.
Hotel Harumoto, 5–13 Yasukawacho, 22 r.
Itaya Ryokan, 2549 Yumoto, 24 r.
Kamaya Ryokan, 2548 Yumoto, 18 r.
Konishi Ryokan Bekkan, 1115 Kami-hatsuishi-machi, 24 r.
Namma Hotel, 2519 Yumoto, 88 r.
Nikko Grand Hotel, 2549–7 Yumoto, 37 r.
Nikko Green Hotel, 9–19 Honcho, 43 r.
Aizuya Ryokan (WI), 928 Nakahatsuichimachi, 15 r.
Taigetsu Kan (WI), 2478 Chugushi, 15 r.

Yokohama

Western style:
Hotel Aster, 87 Yamashita-cho, 72 r.
Bund Hotel, 1–2–14 Shin-Yamashita, Naka-ku, 50 r.
Hotel Empire, 700 Matano-cho, Totsuka-ku, 58 r.
Hotel New Grand, 10 Yamashita-cho, Naka-ku, 202 r.
Satellite Hotel Yokohama, 76 Yamashita-cho, Naka-ku, 102 r.
Shin Yokohama Hotel, 3–8–17, Shin-Yokohama, Kohoku-ku, 50 r.
The Hotel Yokohama, 6–1 Yamashita-cho, Naka-ku, 50 r.
Hotel Yokohama Garden, 254 Yamashita-cho, Naka-ku, 50 r.
Yokohama Tokyu Hotel, 1–1–12 Minami-Saiwai, Nishi-ku, 212 r.

Ikebana

Ikebana schools

Ikebana, the Japanese art of flower-arranging so much admired by Europeans, is taught in a number of schools which tourists can also attend by

prior appointment. This can be arranged either with the school itself or through the hotel front desk. For further information contact a Tourist Information Centre or Ikebana International (tel. 3293–81 88). Schools in Tokyo include:

Ikenoo Ochanomizu School; tel. 3292–30 71
Courses: Mon., Wed., Fri. 2–4pm. Station: Ochanomizu

Sogetsu School; tel. 3408–11 26
Courses: Tue. 10am–noon and 1.30–3pm. Station: Aoyama-Ichome

Ohara School; tel. 3499–12 00
Courses: Mon.–Fri. 10am–noon. Station: Omotesando

See also Facts and Figures, Art

Information

Japan National Tourist Organisation (JNTO)

Japan's semi-governmental National Tourist Organisation runs the country's tourist offices at home and abroad as well as publishing a number of useful brochures, leaflets, etc. for visitors.

Kotsu Kaikan Building, 10th Floor, 10–1–2 Yurakucho, Chiyoda-ku; tel. 3216–19 01	JNTO head office in Tokyo
115 Pitt St., Sydney, NSW 2000; tel. (02) 232–45 22	Australia
165 University Ave., Toronto, Ontario M5H 3B8; tel. (416) 366 71 40	Canada
167 Regent Street, London W1; tel. (0171) 734 96 38	United Kingdom
Rockefeller Plaza, 630 Fifth Avenue, New York, NY 10111; tel. (212) 757 56 40	United States

401 N. Michigan Avenue, Chicago IL 60601; tel. (312) 222 08 74
624 S. Grand Avenue, Los Angeles, CA 90017; tel. (213) 623 19 52

Tourist Information Centres (TIC)

JNTO Tourist Information Centres provide information and assistance to foreign visitors but usually do not take bookings for accommodation or excursions.

Kotani Building, 6–6–1 Yurakucho, Chiyoda-ku; tel. 3502–14 61/2 Open: Mon.–Fri. 9am–5pm, Sat. 9am–noon.	Tokyo TIC
Narita International Airport, Terminal 2; tel. (0476) 34–62 51 Open: daily 9am–8pm.	Narita TIC

Because of the language difficulties it may also be necessary to seek advice from the hotel or local friends and acquaintants. For problems with visas the office to contact is:

Tokyo Immigration Office
3–20, Konan 3–chome, Minato-ku; tel. 3471–51 11

See entry	Guides
See entry	Travel agencies

Japan Travel Phone

Japan Travel Phone is a telephone information service in English for foreign tourists. Outside Tokyo and Kyoto the numbers to ring are:

01 20–222 800 for information about eastern Japan
01 20–444 800 for information about western Japan

These calls are free. If using a public phone you get your 10 yen coin back after the call ends.

In Tokyo and Kyoto calls cost 10 yen, and the numbers to ring are:

3503–44 00 in Tokyo
371–56 49 in Kyoto

Teletourist
Service

Teletourist Service is a tape-recorded listing in English of what's on in Tokyo and Kyoto. The number to ring is: 3503–29 11.

See also Programme of Events

Interpreters

Agencies

Japan Convention Services
Nippon Press Center Building
2–2–1 Uchisaiwai-cho, Chiyoda-ku; tel. 3508–12 11

Japan Guide Association
Shin Kokusan Building
4–1 Marunouchi 3–chome, Chiyota-ku; tel. 3213–27 06

Japan Lingua Service
2–9–13, Ginza, Chuo-ku; tel. 3567–38 14

Rates

The standard day rate for business interpreting is about 25,000 yen, and about 18,000 yen for half a day.

Japanese Society and the Visitor

For centuries Japan was highly xenophobic. Fishermen kept too long at sea by bad weather were quickly suspected of having had contact with other seafarers and expected to be punished accordingly. For this reason even nowadays children of fishing communities have difficulty marrying into families further inland.

Today's traveller will find little trace of this xenophobia since the Japanese have come to respect the "foreign devils" and treat them with utmost courtesy. But behind the good manners many Japanese still harbour enough suspicion – or possibly insecurity – to prevent them from entirely dropping their guard, and anyone who gets invited to a Japanese home can account it a major achievement.

Remember in your dealings with the Japanese that although Western ways have made great advances considerable importance is still attached to the rules of conduct and etiquette which have evolved over many centuries.

Politeness

The politeness of the Japanese is legendary. For example, they will never contradict you directly and will try to find a conciliatory way round of saying things instead. Impatience and shows of anger or disapproval are considered a loss of face; communication is much more through smiles and unfailing evenness of temper.

When meeting or greeting someone it is customary not to shake hands but to bow instead.

People love presents in Japan but unlike the West here gifts must never be unwrapped in the presence of the giver. Anything too valuable can embarrass the host or oblige them perform great favours. Souvenirs from back home make the most acceptable presents, and that includes whisky, wine and good food. Great importance is also attached to the way presents are wrapped.

Presents

Great store is set on being properly dressed, even though Western influences are steadily on the increase, and shorts or garish shirts are not generally acceptable.

Dress

On entering a Japanese home or temple shoes must be exchanged for slippers, and tatami, the straw mats, may only be walked on in socks.

Chairs are relatively new to Japan and on many occasions – at home, in a restaurant or ryokan – people still sit on the floor. The typical sitting position (suwaru) is calculated to stop the circulation of most foreigners (gajin), who can often been seen hobbling through the streets of Tokyo, trying to get their limbs going again after venturing out to eat in a restaurant. The small cushions provided for guests are not much help either.

Indoor behaviour

The ability to hold your drink is much admired in Japan but foreigners should be wary about going too far since getting drunk means you lose face.

Social drinking

Karaoke

Karaoke, literally "empty orchestra", is of course a Japanese invention which has since swept through the bars and pubs of the West. Here the pop songs to a recorded accompaniment are in Japanese, as are the words flashed up on the screen. Foreign visitors will be urged to join in for hours on end; fortunately there are also usually some familiar Western hits in the repertoire.

Language

Although nowadays English is taught in Japanese schools communication can still be a problem, especially since written Japanese presents a barrier which should not be underestimated. Apart from tourist guides and hotel staff relatively few Japanese can speak eigo-no (English) fluently, especially among the older generation, including taxi-drivers and public transport employees, since they have little opportunity to practise, and they generally understand better if any questions are written down. In any event, keep to sentences that are simple and to the point, speak clearly, and make allowances for the Japanese pronunciation of English. For instance, because Japanese is a polysyllabic language, they often put u or o on the end of English words and change r into an l. Thus "the cat has four legs" might be pronounced "the catsu hasu folu legsu".

In syllables transcribed according to Hebonshiki the consonants are pronounced as in English and the vowels as in Italian. Vowels are always short, unless marked with an accent and double consonants are pronounced twice. The e is always spoken, whereas i and u between consonants and at the end of words are often almost inaudible ("miruku" sounds almost like

Pronunciation of Japanese

179

"milk"). The r is an intermediate sound between r and l; ng is pronounced as two separate letters.

See also Facts and Figures: Language

Useful phrases

It is worth knowing a few words and phrases, especially since this will be much appreciated by the Japanese.

English	Japanese
Good morning	ohayo gazaimasu
Good day	konnichiwa
Good evening	kombanwa
Good night	oyasuminasai
I am American	watakushiwa amerikajin desu
I am British	watakushiwa igirisujin desu
I am Canadian	watakushiwa kanadajin desu
Pleased to meet you	hajime mashite
What is your name?	onamae wa nanto osshaimasuka?
My name is . . .	. . . to moshimasu
Thank you very much	arigato gozaimasu
Don't mention it	do itashi mashite
Excuse me	shitsurei
Yes	hai
No	iie
Goodbye	sayonara
Yesterday	kino
Today	kyo
This morning	kesa
This evening	komban
Tomorrow	asa
Where is . . . ?	. . . wa dokodesuka?
Where is the post office?	yubinkyoku wa dokodesuka?
Where is the bank?	ginko wa dokodesuka?
Where is the station?	eki wa dokodesuka?
Where is the department store	depato wa dokodesuka?
Where is the taxi rank?	takushi noriba wa dokodesuka?
Where is the left luggage office?	nimotsu azukarijo wa dokodesuka?
Where is the youth hostel?	yusy hosuteru wa dokodesuka?
Where is the toilet?	toire wa dokodesuka?
Please show me this	kore wo misete kudasai
How much is this?	ikura desuka?
That's too much	takasugimasu
Please show me something cheaper	mo sukoshi yasui no wo
I'll take this	kore wo kudasai
Film for colour prints	purinto yo kara firumu
Film for colour slides	suraido you kara firumu
Tape recorder	tepu-rekoda
Camera	kamera
Watch	tokei
Folk art	mingeihin
Souvenir	miyagehin
Doll	ningyo
Toy	omocha
Cigarettes	tabako
Restaurant	resutoran
Clear soup	konsome
Thick soup	potaju

English	Japanese
Salt	shio
Pepper	kosho
Cake	keki
Coffee	kohi
Tea	kocha
Beer	biru
Milk	miruku
Bread	pan
Menu	menyu

Beautician	bi-yoin
Hairdresser	rihatsuten
Tourist Office	kanko annaijo
Hotel	hoteru
Bill	kanjo
Doctor	isha
Airport	hikojo
Underground railway	chikatetsu
Porter	akabo
Ticket office	kippu-uriba
North	kita
East	higashi
South	minami
West	nishi
Left	hidari
Right	migi

Block	cho, chome
District	machi
Ward	ku
Town	shi
Village	mura
Province	gun
Prefecture	ken

0	zero	8	hachi	Numerals
1	ichi	9	kyu	
2	ni	10	ju	
3	san	100	hyaku	
4	shi, yon	1000	sen	
5	go	10000	ichi-man	
6	roku	31520	san-man ni-sen	
7	nana, shichi		go-hyajy-ni-ju	

See also Health Care

Lost Property

Experience shows that retrieving lost property in a cosmopolitan city like Tokyo is no easy matter, particularly since few of the staff concerned speak English.

Metropolitan Police Board Central Lost & Found Office   Police
1–9–11 Koraku, Bunkyo-ku; tel. 3814–41 51

Tokyo Metropolitan Government Lost & Found Section   Local Authority
Tokyo Kotsu Kaikan Building
2–10–1 Yurakucho; tel. 3216–29 53

Central Sation (Tokyo eki); tel. 3231–1880   JR Rail

Underground	Ueno Underground Station; tel. 3834–55 77
Private rail & bus companies	Anything found will first be taken to the terminus for that particular line. Central Lost Property Office; tel. 3216–29 53
Taxis	Tokyo Taxi Kindaikan Center Shinsei Kaikan Building Shinanoma-chi, Shinjuku-ku; tel. 3648–03 00

Massage

Tokyo is ideal for anyone in search of a really good massage. Hotels will make appointments for qualified masseurs and provide you with the cotton kimono to be worn during the massage. A full massage will leave you feeling every bone in your body the next day, but you can also ask for a gentler treatment (karuku). Check on the price beforehand.

Motoring

The rule of the road in Japan is drive on the left and pass on the right. Foreigners can drive in Japan provided they hold an international driving licence, but driving a car in Tokyo, with its permanent traffic chaos, narrow streets, and parking problems, is something of an adventure to say the least, and if you are only there for a short time it is better to go by public transport or taxi.

Speed limits

The speed limits are 60–80kph/37–50mph on expressways, depending on the signs, 40kph/25mph in built-up areas and in some places only 25kph/15½mph.

Parking

Make sure you never park in a no-parking or no-waiting area, since as many as 60,000 cars a day get towed away in Tokyo for doing just that. It can take half a day simply to find out where your car has been taken, and recovering it will prove expensive.

Department stores have car parking, but these are often full.

Information

Motoring information, including "Rules of the Road" in English, is available from the International Affairs Department of the Japan Automobile Federation (3–5–8 Shiba Park, Minato-ku; tel. 3436–28 11).

Car Rental

See entry

Museums

Tokyo museums

Bridgestone Museum of Art
Bridgestone Building, 2nd Floor,
1–1 Kyobashi, Chuo-ku (near Central Station)
Open: daily (except Mon.) 10am–5pm
Founded by tyre manufacturer Ishibashi, whose name translates into English as "Bridgestone", the museum's collection of 18th and 19th c. Japanese and Western art includes works by the French Impressionists.

Communications Museum, see A–Z, Museum of Communications Technology.

Crafts Gallery of National Museum of Art
Takebashi
Open: daily (except Mon.) 10am–5pm
Japanese art and crafts in a restored building from the Meiji period.

Furniture Museum
3–10 Harumi, JFC Building, Chuo-ku
Open: daily (except Wed.) 10am–4.30pm

Goto Art Museum
3–9–25 Kaminoge, Setagaya-ku
Open: daily (except Mon.) 9.30am–4.30pm
Art and crafts from Japan, China, India, etc.

Hara Museum of Contemporary Art
4–7–24 Kita-Shinagawa, Shinagawa-ku
Open: daily (except Mon.) 11am–5pm
Contemporary art (post 1950) from Japan and the West

Hatakeyama Collection
2–20–12 Shiroganadai, Minato-ku
Open: Apr. 1–June 15; July 1–Sep. 15; Oct. 1–Dec. 15; Jan. 8–Mar. 15 daily
(except Mon.) 10am–4.30pm
Sumie pictures, art and craftwork connected with the tea ceremony; temporary exhibitions

Idemitsu Art Gallery
1–1, 3–chome, Marunouchi, Chiyoda-ku
Open: daily (except Mon.) 10am–5pm
Arts and crafts of ancient Japan and elsewhere in the Far East

Japan Folk Crafts Museum
3–30, 4–chome, Komaba, Meguro-ku
Open: daily (except Mon.) 10am–5pm
Folk crafts, including early and primitive art, from Japan and Korea

Japanese Sword Museum, see A–Z, Sword Museum

Kite Museum
Taimeiken Building (5th floor) 1–12–10 Nihombashi, Chuo-ku
Open: Mon.–Sat. 11am–5pm
Collection of kites from Japan and elsewhere

Kurita Museum
2–17–9 Nihombashi, Hama-cho, Chuo-ku
Open: daily 10am–5pm
Imari and Nabeshima porcelain

Maritime Science Museum
3–1 Higashi Yashio, Shinagawa-ku
Open: daily 10am–5pm

Matsuoka Museum of Art
Matsuoka-Tamuracho Building (8th floor), 5–22–10 Shinbashi, Minato-ku
Open: daily (except Mon.) 10am–5pm
Japanese paintings, Egyptian, Greek, Roman and Indian sculpture

Meiji Shrine and Treasure House, see A–Z, Meiji Shrine

National Museum of Modern Art
Tokyo 3, Kitanomaru-Park, Chiyoda-ku
Open: daily 10am–5pm
Arts and crafts since 1907

National Museum of Western Art, see A–Z

National Science Museum, see A–Z

Museums

Nezu Institute of Fine Arts
6–5–36 Minami-Aoyama, Minato-ku (Underground: Omotesando)
Open: daily (except Mon.) 9.30am–4.30pm
Over 8000 ancient Oriental fine arts and crafts exhibits

Okura Shukokan Museum
3, Aoi-cho, Akasaka, Minato-ku (Underground: Toranomon)
Open: daily (except Mon.) 10am–4pm
Pictures, ceramics, swords, Buddhist art

Ota Memorial Museum of Art
1–10–10 Jingu-mae, Shibuya-ku
Open: daily (except Mon.) 10.30am–5.30pm; closed from the 25th to the
end of each month
Extensive collection of Ukiyo-e woodcuts

Paper Museum, see A–Z

Pentax Gallery
Kasumicho Corp., 3–21–20 Nishi-Azabu, Minato-ku
Open: daily (except Sun. and public holidays) 10am–5pm

Riccar Art Museum (Ukiyo-e-Museum)
6–2–3, Ginza, Chuo-ku
Open: daily (except Mon.) 11am–6pm
Old Japanese art and woodcuts

Sumo Museum
Kuramae Kokugikan, 1–3–28 Yokoami, Sumida-ku
Open: Mon.–Fri. 9.30am–4.30pm
Gallery of 5000 famous Sumo wrestlers

Suntory Museum of Art
Suntory Building, 2–3 Moto Akasaka 1–chome, Chiyoda-ku
Open: daily (except Mon.) 10am–5pm
Art and crafts from the feudal period

Tobacco and Salt Museum
1–16–8 Jinnan, Shibuya-ku
Open: daily (except Mon.) 10am–6pm

Tenri Museum
Tenrikyo-Kaikan Building, 1–9 Nishiko-cho
Open: daily 9am–5pm

Tokyo Central Museum of Arts
Ginza-Boeki Bldg. (5th floor), 2–17–18 Ginza, Chuo-ku
Open: daily (except Mon.) 10am–6pm
Japanese and Western art

Tokyo Metropolitan Art Gallery
Ueno Koen, Taito-ku
Open: daily 9am–4pm
Contemporary Japanese art

Tokyo National Museum, see A–Z, National Museum

Transport Museum
1–25 Kanda Sudacho, Chiyoda-ku
Open: daily (except Mon.) 9.30am–5pm

Tsubouchi Theatre Museum, see A–Z

Yamatane Museum of Art
7–12 Kabuto-cho, Nihombashi, Chuo-ku
Open: daily (except Mon.) 10.30am–5pm
Japanese painting from 1868 to the present

Music

Tokyo is full of enthusiastic concert goers. Guest performances by foreign orchestras are extremely popular and almost always sell out. Touring ballet and opera companies are also consistently a resounding success.

See also Facts and Figures: Music

NHK Hall, 2–2–1 Jinnan, Shibuya-ku; tel. 3465–11 11   Concert halls

Metropolitan Festival Hall
5–45 Ueno Park, Taito-ku; tel. 3828–21 11

Hibiya Hall, 1–3 Hibiya Park, Chiyoda-ku; tel. 3591–63 88

Yamaha Hall, 7–9–14 Ginza, Chuo-ku; tel. 3572–31 11

See entry   Ticket agencies

See Programme of Events   What's On

Newspapers and Periodicals

Japan's daily English-language newspaper is "The Japan Times". This includes what's on listings as well as national and international news coverage. The "Tokyo Journal" has monthly listings particularly for Tokyo. There is also a free weekly paper in English, "The Tour Companion", which is available in hotels and the big supermarkets and has comprehensive cover of what's on in Tokyo.   Japanese publications

Foreign papers are on sale by the South Exit of Marunouchi Station and in some hotels, together with periodicals and magazines, some of which can also be bought in Western supermarkets.   Foreign papers and periodicals

Nightlife

Tokyo has an extremely lively nightlife although in some parts of town it comes to an abrupt end at midnight when the bars close and Japanese night owls head for home, packing the trains and making it very difficult to get a taxi. With over 300,000 restaurants and countless bars there is plenty of choice, but most Western visitors would do well to concentrate on the more cosmopolitan entertainment scene in the districts of Akasaka, Ginza (expensive) and Roppongi (fashionable).

Blue Note Tokyo, 5–13–3 Minami-Aoyama, Minato-ku (jazz)   Live music

Body and Soul, Senme Building, 1F, 3–12–3 Kita-Aoyama, Minato-ku (jazz)

Independent House, 6th floor Toa Kaikan, Kabukicho 12, Shinjuku-ku

Gin Paris, 9–11, Ginza 7–chome (French chansons)

Club Casanova, Roppongi. Open from 7pm, closed Sun., rock & roll.   Nightspots

Club Charon, Social Akasaka Bldg. 5th floor, Akasaka. Open from 7pm, closed Sun. Small club with English-speaking hostesses, piano music.

Club Morena, Roppongi. Open from 7.30pm, closed Sun. Three nightclubs in one building, with Club Morena the best value for money.

Cordon Bleu, Akasaka. Open from 7pm, closed Sun. Dinner theatre with French food, singers and topless dancers.

Crown, Ginza. Open from 6pm, closed Sun. English-speaking hostesses.

International Club 88, Unakami Bldg. 3rd floor, 3–11–6 Roppongi. Open from 6pm, closed Sun., striptease.

L'Osier, Shiseido Parlor Bldg., 7th floor, Ginza. Open from 6pm, closed Sun., Italian decor.

People, Roppongi Square Bldg. Open from 6pm, closed Sun., with drag-shows, hostesses until midnight when the gay scene takes over.

Opening Times

Banks	Mon.–Fri. 9am–3pm
Businesses	Mon.–Fri. 9am–5pm, Sat. 9.30am–noon
Chemists	Mon.–Sat. 9am–6pm
Department stores	10am–6pm (also 7pm in Ginza district); usually closed one day a week but this varies from store to store

A Pachinko Hall

10/11am–7/8pm, no fixed day of closing

Other stores

Mon.–Fri. 9am–5pm, Sat. 9am–12.30pm

Post offices

Mon.–Fri. 9am–5pm, Sat. 9am–noon

Public offices

Most restaurants are open until 10pm, but traditional Japanese ones close at around 9pm.

Restaurants

Pachinko

Anyone who fancies themselves as a pinball wizard should try their hand in Tokyo's pachinko, the Japanese amusement arcades, where pinballs dance and a win brings flashing lights and yet more pinballs. One in three Japanese spends several hours a week on their favourite gambling game where the winnings can be exchanged against olive oil, cigarettes or hosiery. Anyone who tries their luck in the amusement arcades where hundreds of pachinko freaks spend hours on end chancing their arm will be welcomed with open arms and initiated into the beginner's tricks of the trade – language is no barrier, the foreign guest has proved a true friend in a strange country, and the fun to be had is cheap at the price.

Photography and Film

You can photograph almost anything in Japan without giving offence. However, when the Japanese present themselves in truly exotic costumes you should still ask permission, unless it is a really impossible throng, by making the appropriate gesture or saying "sumimasen" – "please may I". Your request will usually be granted since the Japanese are keen photographers themselves, especially of one another.

Needless to say, Japanese camera shops can supply equipment of every conceivable kind.

Police

Tel. 110

Emergency calls

Tokyo is one city where unlike, say, New York, foreigners need have no fear about going out alone by day or by night. Contrary to what is happening elsewhere crime is on the decline and the clear-up rate is on the increase.

Street crime

Kobans are the little police stations located at every major road junction which serve as the local beat base from which the police go out on regular round-the-clock patrols, usually in twos. Since most of them have been patrolling the same beat for years they know every family and every address on their patch, and this can prove very helpful for visitors. If you get lost you need have no qualms about turning to the nearest koban for advice. Even if they cannot speak English the local police will put you in touch with police headquarters where there is always an interpreter on standby.

Kobans

Police information line in English: tel. 3501–01 10

Information

Pornography

The Japanese are traditionally broad-minded about eroticism. Much of Japanese literature and art contains representations which would be considered pornographic by Western standards, and this is often true, in unimaginably brutal forms, of the comics that school children can be seen reading on the train. Despite this fact officials are very strict about the importation of anything which in their eyes could prove offensive, such as, for example, a volume of drawings by Rubens, intended by the unwitting visitor as a present, and they are not above deleting what they consider objectionable. It would seem that, as a country, Japan is not without its double standards!

Post

Central Post Office	Tokyo Central Post Office (Tokyo Chuo Yubinkyoku), 7–2 Marunouchi, 2–chome, Chiyoda-ku). Near Tokyo Station (Marunouchi exit) and open round the clock.
International Post Office	Tokyo also has its own International Post Office (Kokusai Yubinkyoku, 2–3–3 Otemachi, Chiyoda-ku). This is in Otemachi on the Imperial Palace side of Tokyo Station.
Post offices	Japanese post offices are recognisable by their red T symbol topped by two parallel bars. Local post offices are open Mon.–Fri. 8am–5pm, Sat. 8am–noon. Because of the language problem foreign visitors to Tokyo would be well advised to use either the Central or International Post Office.
Stamps and postboxes	Stamps can be bought in most hotels as well as at all post offices. Red postboxes are only for internal mail. Any international mail should be posted in the blue postboxes.
Telephone, telegrams	See Telecommunications

Programme of Events

Musical events	Early information about cultural events such as concerts and guest performances by foreign exponents can be obtained from the International Musical Arts Service (2–21–2 Nishi-Asabu, Minato-ku; tel. 3400–33 86).
Tokyo as listings	Most hotels provide the free weekly "Tour Companion" and "Weekender" which give full listings of what's on in Tokyo as well as guides to shops and how to find them. Events listings can also be found in the monthly and quarterly periodicals "Tokyo Journal", "Tokyo Today", and "Joyful Tokyo" (see Newspapers and Periodicals).
Kyoto, Osaka	Other monthly publications include the Kyotot Visitor's Guide and the Osaka Visitor's Guide.
Teletourist Service	See Information

Public Holidays

January 1st	New Year's Day
January 15th	Coming-of-Age Day
February 11th	National Foundation Day

Spring Equinox Day	March 20th/21st
Greenery Day	April 29th
Constitution Memorial Day	May 3rd
Children's Day	May 5th
Respect-for-the Aged Day	September 15th
Autumn Equinox Day	September 23rd/24th
Health and Sport Day	October 10th
Culture Day	November 3rd
Thanksgiving Day	November 23rd
Emperor's Birthday	December 23rd

If a public holiday falls on a Sunday it is celebrated on the following Monday, and when a day other than Sunday comes between two public holidays it is also a holiday (e.g. May 4th). Although May Day (May 1st) is not a national holiday the marches which set out from Harakuju Station can cause considerable disruption to Tokyo's traffic.

Public Transport

Underground/Subway

Tokyo's fastest and cheapest form of public transport is its Underground system. This has twelve lines and runs from 5am until midnight.

The entrances to subway stations are marked by a stylised wheel if it is a public line and an S if it is a private line. The larger stations have several entrances and these can be quite far apart. Some entrances can be for only one particular direction on a line, so it is best to check beforehand whether this is the case.

    The names of stations are given in Roman script as well as Japanese, with two other names underneath or beside it. The one on the right is the previous station and the one on the left is the next station.

Subway stations

All the lines and trains are colour-coded to match, which makes it easy to follow the route you need when changing at different stations.

Colour-coding

Tickets can be bought at the ticket window or from vending machines. These usually give change and take coins and 1000 yen notes. If there is no fare chart in English buy the cheapest ticket shown on the vending machine and pay the difference at the fare adjustment office at the other end. It is also possible to save time by buying orange cards from special vending machines. These are for 1000, 3000 and 5000 yen and can be used on JR trains and subways, as can the Japan Rail Pass (see Rail Travel). It is also possible to buy day passes for combined travel by underground, tram, bus and inner-city trains.

Tickets

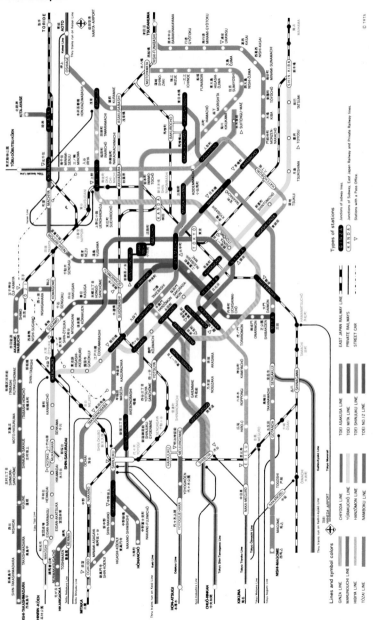

© TRTA

Types of stations

○ ① ② ③ ④   Junctions of subway lines

(K A N D A)   Junctions of Subway, East Japan Railway and Private Railway lines.

▽   Stations with a Pass Office.

EAST JAPAN RAILWAY LINE

PRIVATE RAILWAYS

STREET CAR

TOEI ASAKUSA LINE

TOEI MITA LINE

TOEI SHINJUKU LINE

TOEI NO.12 LINE

Lines and symbol colors

GINZA LINE

MARUNOUCHI LINE

HIBIYA LINE

TŌZAI LINE

CHIYODA LINE

YŪRAKUCHŌ LINE

HANZŌMON LINE

NAMBOKU LINE

Buses

Tokyo has a dense network of bus lines but finding the way around them can be very confusing for a foreigner, especially since none of the signs are in English. Tickets are dispensed by vending machines and have to be handed in as you leave, which is when any excess fare will be collected.

See entry

Taxis

Radio and Television

Most of Japan's VHF stations cannot be picked up by non-Japanese radios because of the different frequencies. The American Forces' Far East Network broadcasts news bulletins on medium wave every hour on the hour.

Radio

Japanese State television, funded by a mixture of taxes and commercials, broadcasts on two channels, one for general entertainment and information, the other more of an education channel.

Television

There are also five commercial stations, all funded by advertising.

Rail Travel

Japan Rail (JR)

The best line for visitors to get around on is Japan Rail's Yamanote line. This loops round Tokyo, its green trains leaving at five minute intervals in both directions from the central station, Tokyo Eki, from early morning until late at night, as well as calling at Yurakucho, the other city centre station in the Ginza district. In all it stops at 29 stations, including Ueno and Shinjuku which are not only in interesting parts of town but also the departure points for various lines out of the city.

Yamanote line

Tickets can be bought from vending machines or ticket offices, and any excess fares can be paid at the other end.

Tickets

Many of the places for excursions from Tokyo can be reached by train, and you can find out which is the appropriate station to leave from by asking at any station, tourist information centre, or travel agent, or at the hotel desk.

Japan Rail Pass

The Japan Rail Pass, valid for 7, 14, or 21 days' travel by JR anywhere in the country, is worth having if you plan to make a number of trips by train, especially since a 7–day pass costs less than the round-trip fare from Narita Airport to Kyoto via Tokyo. The pass is for tourists with the status of "temporary visitor" and will only be issued against a voucher bought outside Japan. These vouchers ("exchange orders") are obtainable from the overseas offices of Japan Travel Bureau International, Nippon Travel Agency, Kinki Nippon Tourist, Tokyu Tourist Corporation and other associated local travel agents, or from overseas Japan Airlines offices if travelling by JAL.

Stations

Tokyo Eki, 9–1 Marunouchi, 1–chome, Chiyoda-ku
The Daimaru department store has been built over the station and the shopping arcades below, with their stores and restaurants, extend almost into Ginza.

Tokyo Main Station

Trains to Kamakura and the Shinkansen also leave from Tokyo Station.

191

Rail Travel

Shinjuku   Shinjuku Station, 38–1 Shinjuku, 3–chome, Shinjuku-ku
The station is under the Odakyu department store and serves as an inter-change for several of the main train and underground lines.

Ueno   Ueno Station, Chuo-dori, Taito-ku
JR trains leave from here for North Honshu.

Ikebukuro   Ikebukuro Station, 28 Ikebukuro, 1–chome, Toshima-ku
This is a major interchange for the commuter lines from the suburbs, and has many shops and restaurants as well.

Shinkansen

Anyone with long legs going on a journey of any length by Japan's super express, the bullet train, should travel First Class and book a seat in one of the Green Cars, since even the Shinkansen expects passengers to be of Japanese dimensions. One of the fastest trains in the world, the Shinkansen speeds along at up to 275kph/170 miles an hour, and the service on board is outstanding, with a non-stop flow of snacks and o-bento lunch boxes. It also runs so smoothly you can safely sleep as you go, with the added security of knowing that if there is an earthquake or a typhoon threatens an automatic warning system will either stop the train or divert it into a specially built shelter.

The Shinkansen is Japan's most important means of transport since the north–south axis only has one motorway-type expressway, and that is usually packed solid with traffic. Tickets, which also serve as seat reservations, should be bought as early as possible, especially on public holidays when millions of people are travelling as few Japanese take regular vacations as such.

The super express train Shinkansen

The Shinkansen line links Tokyo to Nagoya, Kyoto, Osaka, Kobe, Okayama, Hiroshima, Kitakyushu and Fukuoka. There are two types of train, the "Hikari" (i.e. lightning), which only stops in the main cities, and the "Kodama" (i.e. echo) which takes much longer because it stops at the smaller stations as well.

Tickets are best booked via the hotel or through the Japan Travel Bureau (see Travel Agencies) where the computerised ticketing system will mean a virtually immediate response.

Restaurants

Just about every country in the world is represented among Tokyo's restaurants. French, Italian, German, Chinese, Russian, Indian, Thai, they are all here, at subway, street and highrise level, along with the many typically Japanese types of eating places. Hotel restaurants tend to be more expensive.

A welcome feature of eating out in Japan is the oshibori, a hot damp cloth for wiping your hands. Chopsticks (ohashi, see Food and Drink) can prove more difficult to handle, but it is quite in order to bring the bowl or dish right up to your mouth and shovel the food in with chopsticks; slurping is acceptable too, and with noodle soup it is actually unavoidable. Different kinds of food are served in different dishes – rice in a porcelain bowl, soup in a lacquer or plastic bowl with a lid, fish and meat on porcelain or ceramic plates.

Western restaurants will have menus in English and European-type cutlery; you usually pay as you leave but in many fast-food places and department store cafeterias you pay as you enter.

Menus

Plastic imitations assist in selecting food

193

Restaurants

To help you choose most restaurants have plastic versions of the day's dishes on display so you only need to point to what you want.

Tipping · It is not usual to tip; in the better restaurants a 10–15% service charge is added to the bill. If this is over 7500 yen it is subject to a 6% tax.

Japanese Specialities

Sushi · In sushi bars you sit at a counter behind which the many varieties of rice-cakes are prepared to order, or you can just ask for a selection.

Tempura · Tempura restaurants are similar places, where the freshly prepared food is served straight from the pan.

Yaki · Yaki (grill) restaurants have tables with their own grills or hotplates for cooking sukiyaki and similar dishes. Some of them have charcoal grills near the entrance for preparing dishes such as yakitori.

Many of these unusually small restaurants are great fun for tourists, despite the often uncomfortable seating arrangements, and worth trying just for the experience. And noodle soup is a passing snack not to be missed, be it on the street, in a department store or at a station.

Department store restaurants · The department store restaurants (see Shopping, Department Stores), have very good food which is brought to the table. They are usually open from 11am to 9pm and located either on the top floor or in the basement. The top floors of highrise buildings often have beer gardens as well.

Getting a meal is relatively simple. You choose what you want from the glass display case at the entrance, take down the number of the dish, tell the cashier and then pay for it. Find a seat then give the waiter your receipt with the number, and the meal of your choice will be brought to the table.

Shopping centre restaurants · The enormous shopping centres around the train and underground stations all have restaurants which are open daily from 11am to 9pm.

Restaurants in Tokyo (selection)

Akatomba
1–15–12 Toranomon, Minato-ku;
tel. 3501–04 16: Western

Benihana of New York
6–3–7 Ginza, Chuo-ku;
tel. 3571–90 60: speciality teppanyaki

Chinzanso
2–10–8 Segiguchi, Bunkyo-ku;
tel. 3943–11 11: Japanese and Western

Clark-Tei
Toho Seimei Building
2–15–1 Shibuya, Shibuya-ku;
tel. 3406–41 88: speciality tonkatsu

Furusato
3–4–1 Aobadei, Meguro-ku;
tel. 3463–23 10: Japanese

Ginza Happo-en
6–4–7 Ginza, Chuo-ku;
tel. 3571–40 13: Japanese

Happo-en
1–1–1 Shiroganedai, Minato-ku;
tel. 3443–31 11: Japanese

Hasejin Azabu-ten
3–3 Azabudai, Minato-ku;
tel. 3582–78 11: speciality sukiyaki

Ima-Asa
Shimbashi-ekimae Building
2–20–15 Shimbashi, Minato-ku;
tel. 3572–52 86: speciality sukiyaki

Inagiku
2–6 Kayabacho, Nihombashi, Chuo-ku;
tel. 3669–55 01: speciality tempura

Isolde
3–2–1 Nishi-azabu, Minatoku;
tel. 3478–10 55: French

Isshin
4–21–29 Minami Aoyama, Minato-ku;
tel. 3401–46 11: Japanese

Kinsen
Kintetsu Building (5th floor)
4–4–10 Ginza, Chuo-ku;
tel. 3561–87 08: Japanese

Kokeshiya
3–14–6 Nishi-Ogi-Minami, Suginami-ku;
tel. 3334–51 11: Western

Kurawanka
Daian Building
3–36–6 Shinjuku, Shinjuku-ku;
tel. 3352–51 11: Japanese

Mikasa Kaikan
5–5–17 Ginza, Chuo-ku;
tel. 3571–81 81: Japanese, Chinese, Western

Restaurant Stockholm
Sweden Center Building
6–11–9 Roppongi, Minato-ku;
tel. 3403–90 46: Swedish

Seryna Honten
3–12–2 Roppongi, Minato-ku;
tel. 3402–10 51: Japanese

Suehiro
Ginza 4–chome Store
Kintetsu Building, 7th and 8th floors
4–4–10 Ginza, Chuo-ku;
tel. 3562–05 91: speciality steaks

Ten-ichi
6–6–5 Ginza, Chuo-ku;
tel. 3571–19 49: speciality tempura

Totenko
1–4–33 Ikenohata, Taito-ku;
tel. 3828–51 11: Chinese

Ueno Seiyoken
4–58 Ueno Park, Taito-ku;
tel. 3821–21 81: Western

Yaesu-Chinzanso
1–8–3 Marunouchi, Chiyoda-ku;
tel. 3215–21 31: Japanese and Western

Shopping

Souvenirs

Kimonos, pearls, fabrics	A shopping expedition normally begins at Ginza which has nearly all the big department stores and where someone who can speak English is usually on hand to help. Keep a look out for kimonos, fabrics, handmade paper and of course the pearls and ceramics for which Japan is famous.
Woodcuts	Woodcuts make another good buy. These are still being printed from the great Japanese masters' original blocks, and are of an excellent quality and reasonably priced at around 5000 yen and above. This is an area where you will be well served by the department stores which also function as galleries (see entry) and hold regular exhibitions, but check first when they are open since although they open at weekends they also close for one day during the week.
Books	See A–Z, Kanda
Electronics	The place to go for Japan's world-famous high-tech electronic goods such as mini-TV sets, CD players and the like is Akihabara (see A–Z), but check first that they can be used on the voltage at home.
Tax-free shops	You can save as much as 40% of the purchase price on goods bought in the "tax-free shops" found in hotels and the main shopping areas such as Ginza, Shibuya and Shinjuku. This involves filling out a "Record of Purchase Commodities Tax Free Form" which is then attached to your passport and is proof on departure that the item has not been passed on to someone in Japan.
Shopping arcades	The top hotels have their own exclusive shopping arcades.

Specialist Shops

Antiques	See entry
Crafts	Komingu Kottokan (Tokyo Folk Craft & Antique Hall) 9–5, Minami Ikebukuro 3–chome, Toshima-ku; tel. 3980–82 28 Craft centre with about 30 shops
	Oriental Bazaar 5–9–13 Jingu-mae, Shibuya-ku; tel. 3400–39 33 Antiques, porcelain, textiles, lacquerware, etc.
	Japan Traditional Craft Center Plaza 246, 3–1–1 Minami Aoyama, Minato-ku; tel. 3403–24 60 Arts and crafts
	Tokyu Hands 12–18 Udagawa-cho, Shibuya-ku; tel. 5489–51 11 Traditional handicrafts

Kinokuniya
Shinjuku-ku, near Tokyo Station
Open: daily 10am–7pm except 1st and 3rd Wed. in the month

English books

Large department stores (see below)

Kimonos

All large department stores (see below)

Maps, newspapers

Washington Shoe Store
5–7–7 Ginza, Chuo-ku
Men's shoes

Shoes

Kawamura Silk
8–9–17 Ginza, Chuo-ku; tel. 3572–01 81

Silk

Hanae Mori Boutique
Arcades at the Imperial and Okura Hotels
Carries some clothing for export, so larger sizes; elegant and expensive

Women's wear

Department Stores (depato)

Tokyo's department stores are a sight in themselves and well worth a visit, with their breathtaking range of goods, and service to match. They are used to foreigners, and English is spoken and understood so there are none of the usual language problems.
   Everything is here under one roof, from souvenirs to ancient art (see Antiques, Galleries), and between purchases – there are Western as well as Japanese consumer goods – you can eat, relax, or visit an art exhibition.
   Many of the department stores are in Shinjuku and Ginza, where the obligatory walkabout in this most famous district can be combined with a visit to one of these giant stores.

Department stores always stay open at weekends but close one day during the week instead. If in doubt as to which one check in an English-language newspaper or ask at the hotel.

Mitukoshi; tel. 3562–11 11. Closed Mon.

Ginza

Hankyu; tel. 3575–22 31. Closed Thu.

Matsuya; tel. 3567–12 11. Closed Thu.

Mitsukoshi; tel. 3354–11 11. Closed Mon.

Shinjuku

Keio; tel. 3342–21 11. Closed Thu.

Odakyu; tel. 3342–11 11. Closed Tue.

Daimaru, Tokyo Station; tel. 3218–80 11. Closed Wed.

Elsewhere

Mitsukoshi, Nihombashi; tel. 3241–33 11. Closed Mon.

Takashimaya, Nihombashi; tel. 3211–41 11. Closed Wed.

Shopping Areas

See A–Z

Akihabara

District: Taito-ku. Station: Okachimachi or Ueno (Keihin-Tohoku line, Yamanote line). One of Tokyo's busiest market streets, between Ueno and Okachimachi stations.
   Foodstuffs, sporting and imported goods, clothing, leather goods.

Ameya-Yokocho

Sightseeing

Ginza	See A–Z
Harajuku	District: Shibuya-ku. Stations: Harajuku (Yamanote line), Meiji-Jingu-Mae Underground (Chiyoda line).
	Jeans, leather goods, accessories, Parisian haute couture.
Ikebukuro	See A–Z
Kanda	See A–Z
Shinjuku	See A–Z

Sightseeing

Guided Tours

Coach tours

Guided coach tours operated by Japan Travel Bureau's Sunrise Tours (tel. 3276–77 77) and Japan Gray Line (tel. 3436–68 81) include shorter 4-hour morning and afternoon city tours, and a number of all-day tours such as Dynamic Tokyo (with visits to Asakusa Kannon Temple and Meiji Shrine, pearl cultivation), Shogun's Choice (with tea ceremony, Kabuki drama, a stop in Ginza), Country & Crafts (bonsai-cultivation, doll factory), and Tokyo by Night (Japanese dinner, kabuki, nightclub and geisha show, depending on which tour).

Japan Guide Association

Personal guided tours can be arranged through the Japan Guide Association (tel. 3213–27 06) who also provide interpreters (see entry). These are for groups of up to four persons and cost around 20,000 to 30,000 yen for an eight-hour day.

Sumida river tours

Although Tokyo's largest river, the Sumida, can no longer be said to rival the charms of the Seine, the daily riverboat trips do provide an interesting opportunity to see much more of the city than can be glimpsed from any subway line.

It is worth making a point of going as far as Asakusa (see A–Z) since this is a quarter of Tokyo that should on no account be missed. Hotels will have information about where boats leave from and when.

Home Visit System

The Home Visit System is a scheme whereby foreign visitors can gain a greater insight into Japanese life during a one or two-hour visit to local families who have volunteered to welcome foreigners into their home. These visits are free apart from any transport and interpreting costs and, say, a small present (see Japanese Society and the Visitor).

Remember to exchange shoes for slippers on entering your host's home, and then remove the slippers before stepping onto the tatami (straw matting). Usually you will just be offered tea and cakes.

Applications need to be made in writing at least a day beforehand. For information contact a Tourist Information Centre (see Information).

Industrial tours

Japan owes its more recent fame not so much to tea, temples and samurai as to its high-tech industry, supplying state-of-the-art consumer goods throughout the world.

Consequently Sunrise Tours offers a couple of Industrial Tours on Tuesdays and Thursdays, costing between 9500 and 13,500 yen, and including a visit to a car plant and either the Tokyo Stock Exchange or a monorail trip to the JAL facilities, ending up with lunch and talks with management.

Sightseeing Programme

Some parts of Tokyo are particularly important for visitors on account of their concentration of particular sectors, such as Ikebukuro, Shinjuku and Shibuya for shopping, entertainment and nightlife, Akasaka for the big western-style hotels, Marunouchi for banks and business, and Ginza for shopping.

The following itineraries are for the first-time visitor to Tokyo with only a short time available and are intended as a guide to the main sights. Places in **bold** are featured in the A–Z section.

Anyone with limited time on their first visit to Tokyo should take part in one of the guided tours referred to earlier. These include both the main city sights and also give an insight into Japan's traditional crafts and industries. Tours of Tokyo by night usually include a traditional Japanese meal, kabuki drama and other typical entertainment.

Anyone with more time to spend on sightseeing in Tokyo should start with the **Imperial Palace** in the centre. The best way to get a view of the palace grounds, which are only open to the public twice a year, is to visit the roof of the Palace Hotel. It is worth making a tour on foot around the palace grounds and venturing out briefly into the neighbouring parts of town.

City tour

From the northern gate of the eastern garden you can turn north and get to **Kanda**, about 800m/875yds further on, with its interesting bookstores and Meiji University. Proceeding anti-clockwise from the eastern garden you reach Kitonamaru, the delightful park north of the palace, which contains the National Museum of Modern Art, the Science Museum and the Nippon Budokan sports hall (see Sport), a remarkable example of modern Japanese architecture.

About 800m/875yds further on north of the Imperial Palace you arrive at **Korakuen Park**, one of the city's few classic gardens. Near the park is the Kodokan Judo Hall (see Sport).

Just north-west of the Imperial Palce is the **Yasukuni Shrine**, a Shinto memorial to the war dead.

Along the western edge of the Imperial Palace runs the broad ditch with a massive wall on its inside edge. Near the south-western corner is the modern theatre and the **Parliament Building** to the south.

Many of the government buildings are on the southern perimeter of the palace grounds; close by is **Hibiya Park**, just a few steps east of the **Ginza** district, reached by following the northern side of Hibiya Park by the road leading south-east and under the railway line. Window-shopping in Ginza, Tokyo's main shopping quarter, is quite an experience, especially at week-ends when the shops are open but the streets are free of traffic. This is particularly impressive in the evening as it gets dark and the flashing neon adverts light up the sky. About 1500m/1640yds south of Ginza you come to **Harmarikyu Park**, the garden of the imperial Villa Hama.

Chuo-dori, Ginza's main street, runs north through Kyobashi to Nihombashi, formerly the business centre of Tokyo. Turning west you get to the vast Tokyo Station (see Rail Travel), departing point for the Shinkansen bullet trains and many of the commuter trains to the suburbs. Further west you get to **Marunouchi**, another main business centre and beyond it the area of the Imperial Palace again.

All the rest of Tokyo's sights lie outside this area and are therefore best reached by taxi or train. These include the **Tokyo Tower**, with its magnificent panoramic views, the **Meiji Shrine** in the inner garden in Shibuya-ku, the **Sengakuji Temple** in the Minato-ku district, with the tombs of the 47 Ronin, and the **Shinjuku** shopping and entertainment district with its skyscrapers and new **Town Hall**.

Anyone with more time to spare should spend a second day visiting the lovely **Ueno Park**, containing Tokyo's greatest museums, the Tokyo **National Museum**, the **National Science Museum** and the **National**

Second Day

Museum of Western Art, plus the Zoo. East of Ueno Park is Asakusa's entertainment quarter around the imposing **Asakura Kannon Temple**. Also worth visiting are the **Sword Museum** in Shibuya-ku and the **Paper Museum** in Kita-ku.

You need to plan another day of visits for **Tokyo Disneyland** and **Tsukuba Science City**.

Excursions

For longer visits it is worth taking trips out to some of the places around Tokyo, especially since the excellent rail connections make it relatively easy to get to even some of the more distant destinations.

Kamakura, 50km/31 miles south-west of Tokyo, with its Great Buddha and many interesting temples, is a popular destination for excursions and holidays.

If you plan to climb **Fuji-san**, Mount Fuji, 80km/49 miles south-west of Tokyo, you need to allow at least two days.

Nikko, 150km/93 miles north of Tokyo, is well worth a visit for its shrines and magnificent landscape.

The old imperial city of **Kyoto**, 600km/373 miles south-west of Tokyo, is only three hours away by Shinkansen, and **Nara**, the cradle of Japanese culture, is only about 40km/25 miles further south.

Sport

Aikido	International Aikido Federation Station: Shinjuku. Information: tel. 3203–92 36 Open: to spectators daily 6.30–7.30, 8–9am, 5.30–6.30, 7–8pm
Horse-racing	Tokyo Racecourse Fuchu, about 35km/22 miles west of the city centre
Judo and Kendo	Kodokan Judo Hall Station: Korakuen (Marunouchi line). Open: Mon.–Sat. 3.30–8pm Nippon Budokan Hall Station: Kudanshita. Open: Mon.–Sat. 6–7pm
Karate	Nippon Karate Kyokai (Japan Karate Association) Station: Ebisu. Information: tel. 3462–14 15 Open: to spectators Mon.–Sat. 10.30–11.30am, 4–5pm, 6–8pm
Kyudo	All Japan Kyudo Federation Kishi Memorial Hall, 1–1–1 Jinnan, Shibuya-ku; tel. 3467–31 11
Summer skiing	Sayama summer ski-piste World's largest indoor artificial indoor ski-run, 400m/438yds long, 2 ski-lifts
Sumo wrestling	Sumo Hall (with Sumo Museum) 1–3–28 Yokoami, Sumida-ku 8 Station: Ryoguko. Open: Mon.–Fri. 9.3am–4.30pm
Swimming	See Baths See also Facts and Figures: Customs

Taxis

Tokyo has plenty of taxis. Relatively cheap, they are to be found in front of stations and hotels, and can also be hailed on the street. Since most of the drivers do not understand English it is important to give them a sketch-map of where to go as well as the address. They do not expect a tip.

Taxi doors open and close automatically. Public transport finishes at mid-night and it can be difficult to get a taxi after that, with long queues at the taxi-ranks in Ginza and elsewhere. Trying to hail one on the street then becomes a pointless exercise.

The red light behind the taxi windscreen means it is free and the green light mean it is taken. If they fail to stop try hailing them with two fingers indicating that you are willing to pay twice the fare. Fares are also higher at night.

Tea Ceremony

The tea ceremony is taught in a number of schools and these are also open to visitors. Visits can be arranged in advance either through the hotel or with one of the following locations:

Imperial Hotel Tokoan; tel. 3503–11 11
Station: Hibiya. Daily apart from Sun. and holidays 10am–noon and 1–4pm

Hotel Okura Shoshoan; tel. 3582–01 11
Station: Toranomon. Daily 11am–noon and 1–4.30pm

Hotel New Otani Seiseian; tel. 3265–11 11
Stations: Akasaka-Mitsuke, Yotsuya. Thu., Fri., Sat. 11am–noon and 1–4pm

Tea Room of Suntory Museum of Art; tel. 3470–10 73
Station: Kayabacho. Tue.–Sun. 11am–5pm

See also Facts and Figures: Customs

Telecommunications

Most Japanese cities have direct dialling. There are five kinds of public telephones, in various colours.

Red telephones:	local and long-distance calls. Ten yen coins only
Yellow telephones:	mainly long-distance calls. Ten and 100 yen coins.
Green telephones:	local and long-distance or international calls. Some take ten or 100 yen coins, others are phonecard only.
Blue telephones:	credit cards
Grey/blue telephones	international phones with digital display, with instructions for use in English or Japanese, for both internal and international calls, and which usually take coins and phonecards.

Unused 10 yen coins – but not 100 yen coins – will be returned after the call has ended.

Phonecards are gaining in use in Japan as elsewhere. They are sold at Nippon Telegraph and Telephone (NTT) offices and from vending machines and are mostly for 500 and 1000 yen.

Phonecards

Telecommunications

Directory enquiries

For directory enquiries in English call 3201–10 10.

Telegrams

Telegrams can be sent from NTT offices plus some post offices and hotels. The NTT office at 1–8–1 Otemachi, Chiyoda-ku (tel. 3211–55 88) is open round the clock.

International calls

There is keen competition between the private telephone companies for international calls. The access numbers for the different companies for international dialling are:

KDD (Kokusai Denshin Denwa)	001
ITJ (International Telecom Japan)	0041
IDC (International Digital Communications)	0061

For International Direct Dialling (IDD) call the company access number followed by the national code (Australia 61, Canada 1, Eire 359, New Zealand 64, South Africa 27, United Kingdom 44, United States 1), the area code and the subscriber's number.

To direct dial an operator in your home country call 0039–611 for Australia, 0039–111 for Canada and the USA, and 0039–441 for the United Kingdom.

For the international operator in Tokyo call 9951.

To call Tokyo from abroad dial your own international code followed by 81 for Japan and 3 for Tokyo then the subscriber's number.

Theatres

Noh

Ginza Noh Theatre (Ginza Nogakudo Hall)
5–15 Ginza 6–chome, Chuo-ku; tel. 3571–01 97

Kanze Noh Theatre (Kanze Nohgakudo Hall)
16–4 Shoto 1–chome, Shibuya-ku; tel. 3469–52 41

Kita Noh Theatre (Kita Nogakudo Hall)
6–9 Kami-Osaki 4–chome, Shinagawa-ku; tel. 3491–77 73

Bunraku

National Theatre
4–1 Hayabusacho, Chiyoda-ku; tel. 3265–74 11. Underground: Nagatacho

Kabuki

National Theatre (see above)

Kabukiza Theatre
4–12–15 Ginza-Higashi, Chuo-ku; tel. 3541–31 31. Underground: Higashi-Ginza

See also Facts and Figures: Theatre

Ticket Agencies

Ticket agencies for concerts, etc. include:

Playguide Service
Isetan Department Store (6th floor) 14–1 Shinjuku-ku; tel. 3352–40 80

Sukiyabashi Ticket Guide
5–1–7 Ginza, Chuo-ku; tel. 3571–40 60

Akagiya Playguide
2–7–1 Nihombashi, Chuo-ku; tel. 3273–54 81

Kyukokyudo Ticket Service
5–7–4 Ginza, Chuo-ku; tel. 3571–04 01

Time

Japan is 9 hours ahead of Greenwich Mean Time, and does not have Summer Time.

Tipping

In Japan rapid calculation of percentages is unnecessary since tipping is not expected – the customer has after all already paid for the service, whether it be in a restaurant or some other business. The few exceptions are Western hotels, where about 200 yen will be expected for taking luggage up to the room, and taxis when they have to carry a lot of luggage. Also, in a ryokan it is usual to tip the maid at the start or end of your stay. However, tipping should always be done discreetly since it is deemed tactless to hand over money in public.

Toilets

Here it is often a question of doing as the locals do and squatting, rather than sitting comfortably, to use the type of sunken toilet which is common in Asia and parts of Southern Europe.

In some cases special toilet slippers will be provided.

You will look in vain for public toilets on the street so go to the nearest hotel or café and ask for the otearai, toiret or, if all else fails, benjo.

Travel Agencies

The larger travel agencies have special foreign tourist departments with English-speaking personnel.

Japan Gray Line
Pelican Building
3–3–3 Nishi Shimbashi, Minato-ku; tel. 3436–68 81

Japan Travel Bureau
1–13–1 Nihombashi, Chuo-ku; tel. 3276–78 03

Some Tokyo
travel agencies

Kinki Nippon Tourist
Tokyo Kintetsu Building
19–2 Kanda, Matsunaga-cho, Chiyoda-ku; tel. 3255–61 31

Travel Documents

A valid passport is all that is required for most English-speaking tourists visiting Japan. Provided they do not engage in any remunerative activity citizens from Ireland and the United Kingdom are then entitled to stay up to six months, while those from Canada and the United States can stay up to 90 days. It is always wise to carry a separate photocopy of your passport in case it gets lost or stolen and needs to be replaced through your embassy or consulate.

Vaccinations

Vaccination or innoculation certificates are only required if someone is coming from an affected area.
Information about such areas can be obtained from the Japanese Tourist Information Centres (see Information), travel agencies, and if necessary Japanese diplomatic representations abroad (see also Health Care).

Currency

See entry

Customs
Regulations

See entry

Visiting Cards

Visiting cards (meishi) are a necessity in Japan, and are the first things to be exchanged at any meeting.
Consequently anyone in Japan on business should have an ample supply of cards, as should any other visitor who intends meeting the Japanese. This makes introductions and dealing with foreign names much easier.

There are firms in Tokyo who can print visiting cards in English and Japanese in a few hours. Japan Air Lines also offer a similar service for anyone travelling on business.

When to Go

Climate

See Facts and Figures

Seasons

Tokyo, on the same latitude as Teheran and Crete, has four distinct seasons.
Winter (December, January, February) is a season of frosts (and very occasionally snow) accompanied often by sunshine and clear blue skies.
Spring, from March until May, is a good time to visit Tokyo since the weather can already be warm and mild.
Summer (June, July, August) is absolutely the wrong time to go since it gets oppressively humid and very hot, and is the season of thunderstorms and torrential monsoon rains.
The autumn months of September to November are the best time of year to visit Tokyo. The weather is pleasantly warm and mild, although unfortunately this also coincides with the season when typhoons sweep up from the south.

Clothing

See entry

Young People's Accommodation

Central Plaza Building, 21–1 Kaguragashi, Iidabashi, Shinjuku-ku; tel. 3235–11 07. 138 b.

Tokyo International Youth Hostel

3–1 Kamizono-cho, Yoyogi-kamizono, Shibuya-ku; tel. 3467–91 63. 150 b.

Yoyogi Youth Hostel

7 Kanda Mitoshiro-cho, Chiyoda-ku; tel. 3293–19 11. Men only.

Tokyo YMCA Hostel

1–8 Kanda Surugadai, Chiyoda-ku; tel. 3293–54 21. Women only.

Tokyo YWCA Hostel

3–46–2 Minamidai, Nakano-ku; tel. 3360–47 81

English House

11–32–1 Hyakunin-cho, Shinjuku-ku; tel. 3361–23 48

Okubo House

1–19–14 Toyo-cho, Koto-ku; tel. 649–95 44

Yoshida House

3–19–3 Nishi-Ikebukuro, Toshima-ku; tel. 3971–37 66

Kimi Hotel, Kimi Ryokan

See entries

Hotels, Ryokan

Index

Imprint

83 illustrations, 5 town plans, 3 maps, 7 drawings, 1 general map, 1 subway map, 1 large map at end of book

Original German text: Hans Kirchman
Revision and additional text: Baedeker-Redaktion (Peter M. Nahm)
General direction: Dr Peter Baumgarten, Baedeker Stuttgart

Cartography: Gert Oberländer, Munich, Mairs Geographischer Verlag GmbH & Co., Ostfildern-Kemnat.

Source of Illustrations: The majority of photographs supplied by the Japan National Tourist Organisation (JNTO), Frankfurt am Main. Others by: dpa 2, Hackenberg 26, Kirchmann 3, Messerschmidt 1, Schmid 3, Travelpot/Attinger 3

Original English Translation: Babel Translations, Norwich

Revised text: David Cocking, Brenda Ferris, Crispin Warren

Editorial work: Margaret Court

2nd English edition 1995

© Baedeker Stuttgart
Original German edition 1994

© 1995 Jarrold and Sons Ltd
English language edition worldwide

© 1995 The Automobile Association: United Kingdom and Ireland

Published in the United States by:
Macmillan Travel
A Simon & Schuster Macmillan Company
15 Columbus Circle
New York, NY 10023

Macmillan is a registered trademark of Macmillan, Inc.

Distributed in the United Kingdom by the Publishing Division of the Automobile Association, Fanum House, Basingstoke, Hampshire RG21 2EA

Licensed user: Mairs Geographischer Verlag GmbH & Co., Ostfildern-Kemnat bei Stuttgart

The name *Baedeker* is a registered trademark

A CIP catalogue record of this book is available from the British Library

Printed in Italy by G. Canale & C.S.p.A – Borgaro T.se –Turin

ISBN 0–02–860490–3 US and Canada